BANG

in the

MIDDLE

Robert Shore

BANG
in the
MIDDLE

A Journey Through the Midlands
– The Most Underrated Place on Earth

The Friday Project
An imprint of HarperCollins
77–85 Fulham Palace Road
Hammersmith, London W6 8JB

www.harpercollins.co.uk

First published in Great Britain by The Friday Project in 2014

ISBN: 978-0-00-752442-6

Printed and bound in England by
Clays Ltd, St Ives plc

Conditions of Sale

MIX
Paper from
responsible sources
FSC® C007454

For Hector

Froth at the top, dregs at bottom, but the middle excellent.

Voltaire

Contents

TO MANSFIELD

Queen Victoria's blinds, John Gielgud's private parts, and the great Robin Hood feud

So there we were, sprawled across the floor of our living room in South London, happily building a Lego Pharaoh's Quest Flying Mummy Attack, when Hector dropped The Big Question.

'Dad?'

'Hmm?'

'Where are you from?'

Hector had been asking a lot of questions lately – partly because, at five years of age, he was in the middle of the classic 'why/where/when' stage of child development, and partly because his school topic for the term was 'About Ourselves'.

'I'm from England,' I said confidently. 'Your mother is from France and I am from England.'

'I think he needs a little more detail than that,' my wife said, entering the room to deliver her line and then immediately

1

exiting again, like an actor with a walk-on part in a French farce.

'Okay, if it's more detail you want,' I steadied myself, 'I'm from Mansfield.'

'Oh,' mused Hector. 'Where's that?'

'You know, where Grandma and Grandad live. It's in the Midlands.'

'Oh,' he mused again. 'What's the Miglands?'

'Don't you want to finish the biplane so we can start launching our flying attacks on the mummy?' I said, trying to change the subject. A father likes to be able to answer his son's questions with authority, and I wasn't sure that I had anything very definite to tell him on the subject of my origins.

'Miss Kate says she wants parents to come in and tell us about where they're from,' Hector persisted. 'Do you want to come to school and tell us about the Miglands?'

I could just imagine the scene: a parade of parents from Bosnia, Bologna and Baghdad, all with amazing tales to tell to boggle the imaginations of a class of wide-eyed five-year-olds, and then me, bringing up the rear of this exotic, multi-lingual procession, turning bright red with embarrassment as I desperately tried to think of something interesting to say on the subject of Mansfield and the Midlands.

My wife is a Parisian, so on his mother's side Hector's heritage is rich: berets and *haute couture*, baguettes and *haute cuisine*, moody philosophers in black polo necks, and a general all-round *je ne sais quoi*. As cultural legacies go, you can't ask for better. My contribution is thinner. Mansfield was named the sixth and ninth worst place to live in Britain, respectively, in the 2005 and 2007 editions of Channel 4's popular *The Best and Worst Places to Live in the UK* show.

2

As for the Midlands – well, as a badge of identity, it's not like coming from the North, is it? Few people would know where to draw the boundary lines that separate the coastline-free Midlands from the North and South of England, those two monolithic and self-mythologising geographical constructs that sit above and below it on the national map. Just as importantly, whereas most people could attempt at least rudimentary definitions of the North and South as cultural entities – flat caps versus posh accents, or, in the terms of Guy Ritchie's *Lock, Stock and Two Smoking Barrels*, 'Southern fairies' versus 'Northern monkeys' – very few would find much to say about the Midlands' 'identity'. And that includes Midlanders.

I grew up in the Midlands, but I can't remember anyone ever referring to themselves or me as a Midlander – there was a distinct lack of what you might call 'Midland consciousness'. When I then went south to university, I was perceived as a Northerner, principally because I pronounced the word 'class' with a short 'a'. 'You're quite well-spoken,' I was assured by one of my Home Counties-scented, RP-channelling peers, 'but you've got funny vowels. Might you be from the North, old boy?' Since I didn't much fancy spending the next three years propping up the bar with the college's real Northerners, mithering on about dinner being the meal you eat in t'middle of t'day, lad, and how Southerners couldn't take their drink, I grew self-conscious about my pronunciation and avoided making any unnecessary references to grass, glass or taking a bath in my conversation.

Even in this great Age of Identity Politics, coming from the Midlands is tantamount to coming from nowhere in particular. You can be a Professional Northerner (it's a crowded field, but there always seems to be room for fresh recruits), but a Professional Midlander? The very word 'Midlands' is rarely employed outside

3

specialised or technical contexts. It occurs most frequently in weather and travel reports (there are a lot of roads in the Midlands). Beyond that, it pops up in the camp idiom of a certain vintage: in his letters, the (London-born) classical actor John Gielgud refers to the zone between his legs and midriff as 'the Midlands'. We all come from there at a biological level, of course, but in a geographical context there's little social cachet in announcing yourself as hailing from the nation's meat-and-two-veg.

* * *

I decided to do what I have done so many times before at moments of crisis in my life. I called my mother.

(Sound of a phone ringing out. The receiver is eventually lifted and a small intense woman, audibly gurning, speaks.)

'Hello?'

'Hi, Mum. It's your second-born.'

'Ey up mi duck.' My mother is hardly a strong dialect-speaker, but she does enjoy slipping into the local argot from time to time. 'Can I call you back later? I don't really have time to talk at the moment.'

'Then why did you pick up the phone?'

'In case it was something important.'

I went into my hurt-silence routine, honed over decades.

'Come on,' she chivvied me. 'What can I do you for? Spit it out.'

'Mum, there's a question I need to ask you.'

'I love you and your brother both equally. I've told you before.'

'Not that.'

'Oh good, I was getting a bit tired of it.'

'Mum, what does it mean to be a Midlander?'

Now it was her turn to go silent.

'Mum?'

'I don't know,' she said, noisily chewing her lip. 'I've never thought of it before.'

'Well, would you think about it now, please?'

'All right, keep your hair on ... Well, I suppose it means we're neither one thing nor the other – not Northern, not Southern. We're just a bit middling.'

And that was all she could think of to say. In one respect – the stoical acceptance of one's own inconsequentiality – it was a thoroughly Midland sort of response. On the other, it was baffling, since my mother is anything but middle-of-the-road. Quite the opposite, in fact: she's one of the most extreme characters I've ever known. That's a Midland paradox.

At that moment I realised that something important – life-changing, even – was happening to me: I was reconnecting with my Inner Midlander. This sort of thing happens to Northerners all the time, of course. It's easy for them because there are so many clichés about Northern identity that they can tap into. But if you're a Midlander? Instinctively, as well as in point of strict bio-geographical fact, I had always known I was one, of course, but I had no idea what that might signify in a wider sense. What *is* a Midlander?

'Right,' I said, putting the phone down and turning to my son with unwonted firmness of purpose. 'You wanted to know where I am from, Hector. I say to you now that I don't really know. Not geographically, obviously – show me a map and I will unerringly pin the tail of a donkey to the precise point on it where Mansfield lies. It's just above Nottingham and a bit up and to the right from Derby. But in a broader sense – culturally, philosophically – I've no idea what it means to be a Midlander. So I must find out. *We* must find out. You have asked me the question and together we will discover the answer. Son, let us get into the car immediately and set off in search of my – I mean, *our* – identity.'

I thought my speech stirring, but Hector just looked a bit confused and upset. After all, he'd been planning to watch *Megamind* on DVD.

Putting her head round the door precisely on cue, his French mother came to his rescue again. 'Hector's got a birthday party this afternoon and we're having lunch with the Downings tomorrow, so there's no question of us going anywhere this weekend.'

'Oh,' I quivered, momentarily thwarted. 'All right then, we'll go next weekend instead.'

* * *

In truth, I was glad to have an opportunity to do a little research before setting off in search of my Midland heritage, and that is what I spent every spare moment of the following week doing. What I discovered by leafing through classic accounts of tours around England was very illuminating. Pretty depressing too, if truth be told.

If you want to know about attitudes to the Midlands, you could do worse than start with Bill Bryson's *Notes from a Small Island* (1995). Bryson is an American who settled in the UK – in North Yorkshire, to be precise, a choice that may be significant in itself – and made a reputation for himself as a travel writer. In *Notes from a Small Island* he set himself the task of explaining the British to themselves by undertaking a tour of this 'small island' – not so small, however, that he felt the need to engage in any detail with its sizeable middle swathe. No major Midland towns are marked on the map at the front of Bryson's book. We find London, Oxford, Leeds, even Bournemouth and Halkirk ('Where?' I hear you cry), but no Nottingham or Birmingham – the latter being the largest city in the UK after London.

Flicking through its pages, there's a sense that for the most part Midland locations are beneath Bryson's notice. When he does write about them, he adopts a tone of gentle condescension. Retford, for instance, he declares 'a delightful and charming place'; 'the shops seemed prosperous and well ordered. I can't say that I felt like spending my holidays here.' Worksop is 'agreeable enough in a low-key sort of way'. After he quits the South, the people he encounters only really come to life again and begin to talk with vivid local accents when he reaches the great city-states of the North, Manchester and Liverpool, where 'bus' suddenly vowel-shifts into 'boose'. If you tried to arrive at a working definition of the Midlands from *Notes from a Small Island*, you might be tempted to characterise it as the lowland bit between the national peaks, however defined – geographically, socially or culturally.

Bryson's book is part of a much wider tradition. The great surveys of the country tend to bypass the Midlands or emphasise its anonymity by other means. In his classic interwar study *In Search of England*, for instance, H.V. Morton names Rutland in the Midlands as 'the smallest and happiest county in England', but then adds: 'I am the only person I have ever known who has been [there]. I admit that I have known men who have passed through Rutland in search of a fox, but I have never met a man who has deliberately set out to go to Rutland; and I do not suppose you have.' Morton pays Rutland a great compliment, but in such a way as to stress its invisibility at a national level. As he says, 'most people think [it] is in Wales' – which, let's face it, isn't meant as a compliment.

Another mid-century guidebook pays tribute to the beauties of the Midland landscape, suggesting that the 'Peak District in

Derbyshire – with Buxton spa as a Convenient Centre – is worth a visit'. It turns out to be a qualified recommendation, however: 'Whoever cannot go to Cumberland, Northumberland or Yorkshire will find compensation in the moorlands and hills of the Peak District, and in its deep valleys and rugged cuttings.' In other words: for *real* English scenery, you'd be better off in the real North. The Midlands can be delightful, the author allows, but it's never more than a 'compensation', a second-best option, a silver medallist at best in the race for national gold.

When an opinion is expressed about the region as a whole, it's usually thoroughly damning. In 2003, the East Midlands found itself listed in a *Spectator* magazine travel special under the heading 'Best Avoided: Places That Suck'. Recent research confirms how widespread this perception is. 'Industrial, built-up, heavily popu-lated, busy, no countryside; Uninteresting, nothing there, not tour-isty, unromantic; Dark, dirty and grey; Cold and windy' were the words used to summarise the views of foreign respondents in a tourist-board survey of perceptions of the region. Booked your summer holiday yet? Well, now you know where you should be going.

The West Midlands fares little better in the popular imagina-tion. Researchers at King's College London recently announced that, for most people, Birmingham accents were inextricably linked with low intelligence. Most non-natives remain blind to the region's charms, a tradition that stretches back at least as far as the Industrial Revolution. When Queen Victoria travelled through the Black Country – so named owing to the soot and grime that coated this highly industrialised area in the nineteenth century – she insisted on having the blinds pulled down in the royal train. Figuratively at least, it's with the shutters firmly closed that most people still prefer to experience the Midlands. Americans call their Midwest – that big bit between the exciting, trendy coastal states – the 'flyover states'. We're a much smaller country and less given to taking domestic flights, but by analogy we could call the Midlands the 'drive-through counties' – the boring bit you drive through to get to where you really want to be.

In her spiky survey *Class*, Jilly Cooper – she of the saucy horsey romps – complains about 'the terrible flat "a"s and dreary, characterless Midlands accent … which conjure up a picture of some folkweave goon', before declaring, in the chapter on 'Geography', that for the upper classes and, by extension, anyone from the smart set: 'The Midlands are beyond the pale.' Dispiritingly, many Midlanders wouldn't disagree. There's a thread on the Amazon website that's very revealing of what might be called Midlander status anxiety. One contributor says: 'Strictly speaking, coming from Derbyshire, I suppose I live in the Midlands but I feel like a Northerner. It has to do with accent, values and the time of day you eat your dinner.' Another from Stoke-on-Trent agrees: 'Though perhaps geographically we are in the North Midlands, we are very much a Northern city in spirit, outlook and feeling.' Contributors regularly refer to the Midlands as a kind of 'no-man's-land' or 'minor melting pot' that is 'caught between stereotypes' of North and South and that consequently lacks a distinct character of its own.

Soap operas have been prime conveyors of ideas about the major varieties of English identity for decades. Unsurprisingly the North and South dominate: London has *EastEnders*, Yorkshire *Emmerdale*, Manchester *Coronation Street*. It's perhaps just as well that the Midlands no longer has a major evening TV soap to its name – let's face it, the woolly-hat-wearing simpleton Benny in *Crossroads* wasn't doing the region's image any good. These days, of course, reality shows are as integral to our sense of identity as soaps and, in so far as they are geographically defined, the North and South again rule the roost: *Desperate Scousewives*, *The Only Way Is Essex*, *Educating Essex*, *Educating Yorkshire*, *Made in Chelsea*, *Geordie Finishing School for Girls*, *Geordie Shore* ... Industry myth has it that a novice producer from the Black Country suggested *The Only Way Is Wolverhampton* but before the ITV2 commissioners could green-light the project their sides split *and they literally died laughing*. The Midlands, it would seem, just doesn't have the necessary clout to carry a reality show.

When, against massive odds, one of the Midlands' many beauty spots does make it onto TV, its actual location is often obscured. For instance, a recent episode of BBC2's *Town with Nicholas Crane* was devoted to Ludlow, the Shropshire idyll celebrated by John Betjeman as 'probably the loveliest town in England'. It was described in the opening moments as 'landlocked' – the key attribute of the Midlands, after all – but the term 'Midlands' was never actually deployed in the programme: the BBC probably thought that kind of dirty language inappropriate for the show's genteel target audience. Instead Ludlow was described as being 'on the Welsh border', which is true, although if a similar programme about Sheffield failed to mention that it was in the North but stated instead that it was 'on the border of the Midlands' it would cause uproar among the locals. Viewers might have come away thinking Ludlow lovely but the association wouldn't readily have been made with the broader idea of the Midlands. And that's a real problem for the area.

A friend of mine with a deep knowledge of the broadcasting industry thinks the BBC's neglect of the Midlands is structural. 'The Beeb is set up in a way that is institutionally biased against the Midlands!' he laughs. 'It's spent a lot of money in recent years to get more regional television in, so it now has all these designated regions: there's London, the West and Wales (centred on Bristol),

Manchester and the North, Scotland and Northern Ireland. And all of these blocs have pots of money earmarked for them, but the Midlands doesn't fall into any of the remits. Hence it's almost impossible to get anything commissioned there.'

Perhaps it would be a kindness simply to abolish the Midlands. That's precisely what one academic map did recently. Tellingly, that map was created in Sheffield and displayed in Manchester, cities that are both – as if you didn't already know it; and how could you not, given that region's genius for self-promotion? – in the North of England.

Ah, the North, where they eat dinner at midday as God (and Geoffrey Boycott) intended, say 'bath' not 'baarth', speak their minds freely and plainly without recourse to any circumlocutory Southern waffle, where lager is a girls' drink, blah-di-blah. You certainly know where you are with the characterful North. It's not much of a place to live – ask all those BBC types who have been dragging their feet over their recent enforced relocation to Salford, the MediaCity development being one of the most flagrant bits of social engineering in recent English history – but you have to admit that, as a piece of branding, 'The North' has real genius, starting with the fearsome granite firmness of the name itself. The words 'I'm a Northerner' pack so much punch and communicate a ton of attitude. No wonder people from cities as radically different as Manchester and Newcastle are happy to share an overarching, aggregated 'Northern' identity. The Midlands, by contrast, has never really gone in for that sort of branding. Around Birmingham, the tourist-board people like to talk about the region as 'The Heart of England'. But try saying 'I'm a Heart of Englander' and it just sounds naff. It might work as a piece of signposting for tourists but it'll never catch on where it really counts, among Midlanders. As a clever acquaintance suggests: 'The Midlands is less a discrete geographical category and more a state of mind. Roundabouts. Retail parks.' If that's the case, that's hardly going to pull in the tourists, or provide the locals with a proud sense of belonging. The linguistic associations of the word 'Midlands' itself are no better: fair-to-middling, caught in the middle, middle management, midlife crisis. An alliteration-loving friend recently relocated to Northants. 'I'm growing fond of the Midlands,' he texted me. 'Must be middle age setting in.' See? Midlands/middle age. The connections made at the verbal level are nothing short of lethal.

* * *

The following Saturday we get in the car to head for Mansfield and the Northern propaganda begins even before we're out of London. The motorway signpost at Archway roundabout immediately announces 'THE NORTH' in block capitals – if you take the M1, you must be going to the North, it tells you. Note that it doesn't just say 'North' – a direction – but *The* North, a destination. The message is repeated, in the same bold typography, all the way up the motorway, next to each and every place name. Watford? 'The NORTH.' Luton? 'The NORTH.' Only when you get to the edge of Milton Keynes – where the region actually begins: there's no advance warning – does 'The MIDLANDS' finally get a mention. And then, as suddenly as it appeared, the word vanishes again, so that the names of all the major towns and cities of the East Midlands – Northampton, Leicester, Nottingham – are unerringly accompanied by the words 'The NORTH'. No wonder a lot of Southerners think the North begins as soon as you leave London: that's what the road signs tell you.

I'm not put off, though. We've come to discover what it means to be a Midlander and we're darn well going to find out, good or bad.

Neil Young's 'Everyone Knows This Is Nowhere' is playing on the car stereo as we finally cross the border into Northamptonshire. I give a loud cheer.

'Is Dad all right?' Hector asks his mother, who raises a quizzical eyebrow in my direction.

'I was cheering,' I explain, 'to indicate that we are home. Well, *I* am home. We are in the Midlands, my ancient homeland. We are now surrounded' – I wave an arm airily to left and right, trying not to lose control of the car as I do so – 'by my tribespeople.'

That quizzical Parisian eyebrow stays raised. 'I didn't realise you had such a sense of cultural belonging. We've been married thirteen years and you've never mentioned your tribespeople before,' my wife says.

'Let's just say I'm rediscovering who I really am,' I sniff.

* * *

'What is civilisation?' asked the great art historian Kenneth Clark (not to be confused with the great Midland politician Ken Clarke) in the opening moments of his famous 1960s BBC arts series *Civilisation*. 'I don't know … But I think I can recognise it when I see it; and I am looking at it now.' Clark, standing with Notre Dame Cathedral in Paris peering over his left shoulder, wasn't taking much of a chance when he made this statement. But would he have been able to say the same if he'd been plonked in the middle of Mansfield market square one Saturday afternoon in autumn?

Probably not. Mansfield has recently been subjected to a gruelling bout of 'regeneration', with results that are largely indistinguishable from ruination. Most of the big commercial operations have relocated to the retail parks dotted around the ring road, leaving much of the town centre boarded up. Pubs ('Gerrem in!' is

13

an essential item of local dialect), pawnbrokers and betting shops dominate the historic market square, which is so run-down that even the Poundshop has closed down, or so it appears. (There's a Pound World that's still open around the corner, mind, not to mention Savers, another budget store.) The most characterful shop here is Eden Mobility: mobility scooters are enormously popular in Mansfield. If you don't watch where you're going, you're likely to get mown down by one in the market square.

Not that Mansfield is without history: it actually received its royal charter as far back as 1227. As its moniker might lead you to expect, Mansfield is full of men, *real* men at that, but its name is actually derived from 'Maun', the name of the river on which it stands. It used to be a mining town and – perhaps the two go hand in hand – it also used to be home to the largest independent brewery in the UK, Mansfield Bitter, until the latter was sold off in 1999. The skyline-dominating brewery building has now been demolished and the local bitter's glory days – encapsulated in the quaintly provincial Eighties ad campaign featuring a picture of Ronald Reagan and the tag line 'He may be president of the most powerful nation on Earth but he's never had a pint of Mansfield' – are now little more than a folk memory.

Mansfield may mark the spot where the North meets the Midlands. In fact, some people question whether there's any difference between the North Midlands and the 'real' North at all. As I mentioned before, some anxious Derbyshire- and Potteries-based posters on that Amazon thread don't seem to think there is. Others see subtle differences. 'Midlanders are a bit more sophisticated, like – we can string a few sentences together. Northerners swear more,' one eccentric friend told me. 'On the other hand, we're both from Viking stock. We both like to plunder and pillage,' he added wolfishly. There's a takeaway called Viking's in Mansfield, and it's certainly the Nordic-invader legacy rather than what is normally considered the more socially cohesive Anglo-Saxon heritage that permeates the atmosphere around here. In the good old days, when pubs used to close in the afternoon, you could see gangs of men (and the occasional woman) marauding across the streets at three in the afternoon, stopping the traffic while they pissed all over the traffic bollards. Part of the recent 'regeneration' of the town centre included the installation of a showpiece fountain, prompting fears that local merrymakers would use it as an open-air urinal.

Football is very important in Mansfield, as is violence. The two have often combined to striking effect at Field Mill (or the One Call Stadium, as it's currently known), the home of Mansfield Town Football Club. A noteworthy outburst of aggro came when the Stags (nicknamed in homage to the regal fauna of that nearby long-vanished Edenic idyll, Sherwood Forest, where Norman and Plantagenet monarchs disported themselves and Robin Hood and his Merry Men evaded the attentions of the wicked Sheriff of Nottingham) were relegated from Division 2 and consigned to non-league status in April 2008: fans showed their displeasure by physically attacking club owner Keith Haslam. The resulting head wounds were severe enough to necessitate a visit to the big local hospital, King's Mill – it has to be big to accommodate Mansfield's legions of unhealthy inhabitants: the town's poor health record is one of the principal reasons for its appearance in that chart of the top ten worst places to live in the UK, and for the ubiquity of those mobility scooters.

Field Mill, King's Mill … As you may be beginning to surmise, mills and millers play a major role in Mansfield folklore. The naming craze can probably be traced to a tale involving Henry II and the 'Miller of Mansfield' found in an eighteenth-century collection of ballads and songs known as *Percy's Reliques*. The story goes that King Henry lost his way while hunting in Sherwood Forest and met a miller, who, failing to recognise his regal interlocutor, kindly offered him hospitality for the night. When the monarch's retinue turned up at the miller's humble cottage the following morning, the host was astonished to discover the true identity of his guest. The king, of course, thought it all very amusing and bestowed a knighthood on the miller, who henceforth gloried in the name of Sir John Cockle (there's still a local pub of that designation). *Percy's Reliques* wraps the story up:

> *Then Sir John Cockle the King call'd unto him,*
> *And of merry Sherwood made him o'er-seer;*
> *And gave him out of hand three hundred pound yearlye;*
> *'Now take heed you steale no more of my deer;*
> *And once a quarter let's here have your view;*
> *And now, Sir John Cockle, I bid you adieu.'*

The tale's slightly patronising tone sums up the classic relationship between the Southern Establishment and Midlanders. The latter, usually presented in a slightly yokelish light – the men-in-tights vibe is inescapable – are tolerated or occasionally even encouraged in a mildly condescending manner, but are never treated as equals.

Olympic and Commonwealth swimming champ Rebecca Adlington aside, few famous people have come from Mansfield. There's Richard Bacon, a *Blue Peter* presenter unceremoniously sacked after the *News of the World* suggested he took cocaine, who's clawed his way back to respectability and a huge following on Radio 5 Live. Bernard William Jewry made his stage debut here at age four, but coo-coo-ca-choo'd his way out of town long before metamorphosing into Alvin Stardust, glam rock icon. The incestuous, club-footed Romantic poet Lord Byron inherited an ancestral pile just down the road, Newstead Abbey, which is now a highly atmospheric ruin – not unlike Mansfield town centre, come to think of it. And twenty minutes up the dual carriageway, 'where the Peak District meets Robin Hood Country', you can find the historic market town of Chesterfield, home to the Crooked Spire, the 228-foot-high thirteenth-century church steeple that twists some nine and a half feet from true centre and is to the Midlands what Pisa's Leaning Tower is to Tuscany.

Unimpressed? Good. That's the way Midlanders like it. Unlike Northerners, we don't believe in blowing our own trumpets all the time. All the same – let's call it the Midland Catch-22 – some of us would still like to know what it means to be a Midlander, especially when, for our son's sake, we need a cultural identity to rival that of Parisians. That kind of thing usually involves locating a foundation myth for your tribe, discovering your rootedness in history.

So what are the deeds that tell Midlanders who they are? The South has King Alfred repelling the Vikings, the North has the Venerable Bede – and, perhaps more influentially these days, Oasis's first album. But what about the Midlands?

Foundation myths are usually just that: more acts of creative imagination than actual heroic deeds – our idea of 'The North' is largely the result of a very successful branding exercise. To define and unite a culture, what you need above all else is the chutzpah to make up something grandiose-sounding. All that stuff about Alfred being the first king to unite England has been overstated and, let's be honest, *Definitely Maybe* is mediocre at best. But, as cultural gathering points, they've proved extremely successful.

Hungry for possible leads on this unseasonably warm autumn afternoon, I scout feverishly through the magazine racks at Mansfield town library and the local WH Smith. Eventually I alight on an issue of *Nottinghamshire Life and Countryside* that looks promising: the cover announces a piece about 'The Pyramids of Nottinghamshire'. I can't remember any mention of a 'Sutton Sphinx' when I was a boy or of Mansfield's role in the development of ancient Egyptian civilisation, but that doesn't put me off. Anticipation growing, I turn rapidly to the article and discover that the 'pyramids' in question are actually dovecotes, and fairly recent ones at that, but I'm nonetheless full of admiration for the magazine's feverish overstatement and it persuades me to think big. If the Midlands was the source of my family, why shouldn't it have been the source of everything else too? Why shouldn't civilisation itself have begun here?

Well, for one reason – which is that the Midlands is usually said to have no 'deep' history. (As a Midlander you sometimes get the impression that the principal aim of history in general is to let you know that you and your kind have played no part in it.) The immemorial mists of time are typically thought to have dispersed to reveal that nothing actually happened here until around 1842. To quote one twentieth-century source on the subject: 'England's prehistoric antiquities are mostly to be found south of a line drawn from Worcester to Ipswich; and north of a line drawn from Blackpool to Hull' – lines that seem almost deliberately conceived to exclude the Midlands.

But history is a remarkable thing. Although by definition it's all in the past, it keeps turning up again and transforming itself – and everything else with it – in the present. What if evidence suddenly emerged that Nottinghamshire genuinely did have pyramids, and a corresponding Pharaonic era? Unlikely, I know, since everyone seems to agree that the middle band of the country has no prehistory, but a development of the sort isn't *entirely* out of the question. After all, think of the evolution of our own species.

18

Even on a matter as fundamental as that, the question isn't entirely settled. We know that *Homo sapiens* first appeared on the African continent about 200,000 years ago, before gradually migrating north, through the Middle East, to Europe and Asia. But, around the time of my writing this, fresh archaeological finds in Israel, Spain and China emerged to throw into question some of the finer details of the development of modern man. Even prehistory is in the process of rewriting itself. And if Israel, Spain and China can get in on the evolutionary act, why not the Midlands?

* * *

After Hector has gone to bed, I explain the challenge I've set myself to my parents.

'Don't you think you're taking it all a bit seriously?' says my mother, the queen of taking-things-too-seriously: most nights she can't sleep for thinking about all the things that worry her but over which she has zero control. 'Just tell Hector's school mates it's a good place for a punch-up and have done with it.'

'Hey!' interjects my father. 'We're worth a bit more than that. Tell them about Cloughie and Forest.'

'Fighting and football' I scribble down on my notepad.

'There's Robin Hood, of course,' I say. 'I thought we could go and look at the Major Oak tomorrow. Hector will like that.'

'Well, there you go then,' says my mother encouragingly. 'Robin Hood'll do, won't he? What more do you need?'

'I don't know,' I reply earnestly. 'He might be a start. I want to know what makes us Midlanders: where we came from, who we are, where we're going, to borrow a phrase from Gauguin.'

'Go what?' mugs my mother. 'Well, I'll tell you this for nothing: I don't think people from Blidworth [where my mother was born]

19

are much like people from Sutton [a couple of miles away, where my father was born]. For one thing, we used to make fun of people in Sutton because they said "*bwaan bwead*".'

'I'm not really interested in the microscopic differences between Blidworth and Sutton, Mum. I'm looking for the bigger picture.'

'Well, if I'm not allowed to make fun of your father, I don't want to play. Shift yersen, Denis, I need to walk around a bit. My leg's killing me,' she huffs as she pulls herself to her feet.

'Shift yersen' provides the cue for a brief discussion of local dialect terms. With the help of one of those mysterious photo-copied documents that seem to circulate among old people keen to relive the linguistic glories of their youth, we laugh over 'Ayer masht?' (Have you made a cup of tea?), 'Arkattit' (Listen to the rain), 'Ittle norrocha' (You won't feel any pain) and 'Mekitt goo bakuds' (Put the car into reverse gear): all classic Notts locutions. My personal favourite is 'Ittim weeya poss', or 'Hit him with your purse'. It perfectly captures the delicacy of the local female popula-tion – by which I mean my mother really: no offence to anyone else.

I'm not sure these phrases are getting me any closer to my grail of a foundation myth, however.

'This used to be the centre of the hosiery trade, didn't it, Dad?' I say airily to move the conversation along a little.

A bit of an obvious question, really, since that was my father's line of work and, across a forty-odd-year career, it carried him from one end of the Midlands to the other.

'Yes, I've got a couple of books about it upstairs,' he responds. 'They'll tell you more about it than I can.'

'But it's *your* impressions I want. You worked in the industry for five decades. I want to tap into your experiences.'

He shifts uneasily in his seat. This kind of waffle doesn't really appeal to him. He's not the sort of man who likes the idea of being 'tapped into', thank you very much. To escape further questioning he gets up to put TalkSport on the radio, ostensibly because former England manager Steve McLaren, aka 'the Wally with the Brolly', has just quit as boss of Nottingham Forest – my dad's team for the past seventy years – and he thinks they might be discussing it.

I turn my attention back to my mother.

'All right, Mum. Answer me this: is Mansfield civilised?'

'Not totally, no,' she begins after reflection. 'For instance, we've got two supermarkets: Sainsbury's and Tesco. Now if you ask me about the people who go into Sainsbury's, I'd say maybe. If you ask me about those who go into Tesco, I'd say maybe not. And then there's the way they stack the shelves ...'

(For the record, I should say that my mother happily shops in both Tesco and Sainsbury's, which by her own reckoning makes her simultaneously both maybe civilised and maybe not civilised. Which sounds about right – maybe.)

'All right,' I stop her. 'Let me ask you this: Do you think that people from Mansfield and Nottinghamshire and the Midlands generally have contributed much to world civilisation?'

'Oh yes,' she replies with surprising certainty.

'In what way?'

'We've turned a lot of good people out. This region invented the hosiery industry. That was worldwide. Then there was Raleigh bikes in Nottingham. And Metal Box in Mansfield: that was good for trays. It was worldwide too. Cars of course were Birmingham. Birmingham's the Midlands too, of course, although Brummies are very different from us. And our coalmines were very profitable. So yes, we've contributed quite a bit really.'

'Okay. Now I'd like to take it one step further, perhaps going further back in history.' I'm beginning to sound like Melvyn Bragg on *In Our Time* on Radio 4. 'If I said to you, human civilisation first developed in North Nottinghamshire, what would you say? Does that sound likely, Mum?'

'Erm …'

'If I told you that the wheel was invented in Mansfield, for instance.'

'Yes, I could believe that. A lot of damn good engineers have come from Mansfield. There was a lot of talent in Blidworth – not much in Sutton, of course … *Was* the wheel invented in Mansfield, Robbie?'

'It hasn't been disproved.'

'Well, we've got Robin Hood anyway,' concludes my mother, growing weary. 'I'm going to put the kettle on.'

* * *

Actually, how much longer Nottinghamshire and the Midlands will have Robin Hood is open to question. Ever since someone noticed that the early ballads mention a few locations across the border in Yorkshire – principally Barnsdale – there's been a campaign to turn the original Nottinghamshire Man in Tights into a Salt-of-the-Earth Northerner™. Not so long ago, a Yorkshire MP could be heard demanding that roadside signs proclaiming Nottinghamshire 'Robin Hood Country' be taken down. 'We believe very strongly that Robin Hood was a Yorkshireman and we are aggrieved to read that we are now entering Robin Hood country [when we drive south into Nottinghamshire],' David Hinchliffe, the absurdist ex-Member for Wakefield, was quoted as saying in the *New York Times* in 2004. 'It's a very, very serious business. The way things are going, the signs are going to get torn down by angry Yorkshiremen.' Perhaps it was the report in the *NYT* that gave Russell Crowe the idea of basing his accent on Michael Parkinson's dour growl when he played the lead in the most recent Hollywood *Robin Hood* movie, or perhaps it was the fact that Doncaster in Yorkshire suddenly developed a 'Robin Hood Airport' in 2005. If Yorkshire nationalists get their way, one day in the not too distant future 'Oodie is likely to find himself transformed into a plain-talking Yorkshireman, with a whippet instead of a bow under one arm and a flat cap instead of a green feathered hat on his head. There's a small conceptual problem that might need to be addressed before that can happen, though. It's hard to see how Robin Hood's reputation for stealing from the rich to give to the poor can be reconciled with the stereotype of Yorkshire folk as tight-fisted – an image that's been actively embraced and promulgated by many of the natives of 'God's own county' (such modesty!). As the 'Yorkshireman's Creed' has it: 'If ever tha does owt for nowt / Do it for tha sen.' In that sense, Robin of Sherwood is the antithesis of the classic Northerner.

On Sunday morning we all pile into the car and drive out through Clipstone, past the overgrown pit heads and towards the little village of Edwinstowe and the Sherwood Forest National Nature Reserve, which contains the Major Oak, the mystical thousand-year-old tree that – legend has it – served as the Merry Men's meeting place.

What does Robin Hood stand for exactly? What values does he represent? Social justice (stealing from the rich to give to the poor), obviously; but more resonantly he's also a symbol of 'Merrie England'. 'Merrie England' is the way that nostalgic Victorians, dismayed by the effects of the growing urbanism of their own age, liked to idealise their country's pre-industrial past. Indeed, it was with a reference to Robin and his crew that the nineteenth-century essayist William Hazlitt popularised the concept of England's idyllic, liberty-loving medieval past: 'The beams of the morning sun shining on the lonely glades, or through the idle branches of the tangled forest, the leisure, the freedom … were sufficient to justify the appellation of "Merry Sherwood", and in like manner, we may apply the phrase to *Merry England*.' It's interesting that the most romantic representative of this pastoral paradise of ancient freedoms should have hailed from the East Midlands, the area characterised as 'Industrial, built-up, heavily populated, busy, no countryside' in that recent tourist-board survey. That's obviously not how an earlier age thought of the region. John Hamilton Reynolds elaborated on the idea of Robin as the symbol of this Edenic utopia in a sonnet to his friend John Keats:

Robin the outlaw! Is there not a mass
Of freedom in the name? …
It tells a tale of forest days – of times
That would have been most precious unto thee:
Days of undying pastoral liberty:
Sweeter than music old of abbey chimes –
Sweet as the virtue of Shakespearian rhymes –
Days, shadowy with the magic greenwood tree!

'Now, Hector, what we're about to go and look at,' I explain enthusiastically as we set off along a winding path from the car park, 'is Robin Hood's special tree. It's absolutely enormous. Robin and Alan-a-Dale and Friar Tuck and Little John and all the rest of the merry band used to climb up inside it to hide from the nasty Sheriff of Nottingham.'

I can see I'm losing his attention.

'I'm a little bit bored, Dad,' he says, pulling his beloved Ben 10 figurine from my bag.

'Smile and I'll get you an ice cream.'

He gives me a pained grin so I buy him a 99. A deal's a deal.

My mother begins to recount a favourite family story as we near our destination. 'Your Auntie Madge brought the Americans here when they came over for Jeff and Karrie's wedding,' she begins. 'She told them she was going to show them the biggest tree they'd ever seen. So they drove over and Madge gave them the spiel as they were walking over from the car park – I think she even called it the biggest tree in the world – and then when they got into the clearing she said: "Well, isn't it amazing?" And Karrie's parents were really nice about it but Madge could see they were a bit underwhelmed. Anyway a few years later she went over to California to visit Jeff and Karrie, and while she was there they took her to Yosemite. That made her feel a bit embarrassed. "And you know, Kath, you couldn't even see the tops of the trees there. That's how tall they were," Madge said to me. Well over 200 feet, Californian sequoias are. The Major Oak seemed a bit diddy by comparison. That put her in her place.'

At this point we emerge into a clearing and there it stands – history, mystery, majesty, all rolled together in the eye-filling spectacle of the glorious Major Oak …

'Ooh, look at it!' my mother exclaims mockingly. 'It's only just a bit taller than your dad.'

'It stands 52 feet,' I correct her. I don't want Hector going back to school and telling his friends that the Major Oak is barely the size of a domestic Christmas tree.

'Well, your dad's a good size,' my mother replies. 'That's one of the main reasons I married him, so that I'd produce decent-sized children.'

She scrutinises me briefly. She's never quite forgiven me for not being as tall as my father.

It's true that the Major Oak isn't much to look at. Gnarled and bloated, as fat as it is high, these days it has to be held upright with an elaborate system of ropes and poles. Hector is decidedly underwhelmed. Crestfallen, I decide to abandon any further attempts at tour-guide propaganda with my little boy.

Afterwards we wander back for lunch at the visitor centre, where my mother declares herself astonished by the freshness of the rolls. ('Who'd have thought you'd get such fresh rolls in Edwinstowe?' she says with genuine wonderment, holding the admirable sandwich up for us all to coo over. She doesn't then go so far as to actually eat it – she doesn't really like food – but she's still eulogising its memory a couple of days later.)

Like the Major Oak itself, the centre isn't particularly spectacular – but that's no surprise since Midlanders don't go in much for 'look at me'-style self-congratulatory display. They hold a festival here every August in 'celebration of the life and times of the world's most famous outlaw', with jousting, falconry displays and court jesters by the dozen, so that's probably the best time to come if you want the medieval scenery to be painted in for you. You hardly need it, though. There's an ancient atmosphere here that you can still tap into if you give it a chance; you'll soon find your imagination responding to its promptings. That friend of Keats wrote another sonnet, in 1818, on just this theme:

The trees in Sherwood Forest are old and good,
The grass beneath them now is dimly green;
Are they deserted all? Is no young mien,
With loose slung bugle met within the wood?
No arrow found – foil'd of its antler'd food –
Struck in the oak's rude side? Is there nought seen,
To mark the revelries which there have been,
In the sweet days of merry Robin Hood?

Go there with summer, and with evening, go
In the soft shadows, like some wandering man,
And thou shalt far amid the Forest know
The archer-men in green, with belt and bow,
Feasting on pheasant, river-fowl, and swan,
With Robin at their head, and Marian.

As I begin reciting the lines to Hector, a little boy dances past in a Robin Hood outfit, armed with a bow and arrow, and the portly, balding man whose hand he's holding metamorphoses into Friar Tuck; the woman behind them with the twelfth-century face and courtly air might be a royal lady-in-waiting come in disguise to pass vital secret information to Maid Marian. The trees begin to rustle in the rising wind and suddenly you can hear weary travellers clip-clopping their way through the fairytale wood, full of mystery and danger; as darkness begins to encroach, the eyes of the Sheriff of Nottingham's men blink into life in the undergrowth. Hazlitt was right when he said, invoking Keats, that Robin Hood 'still, in imagination, haunts Sherwood Forest'. There's still magic in this salvaged tuft of the ancient Forest of Sherwood all right.

'Dad?'

Hector, who has momentarily laid his Ben 10 figurine aside, can obviously feel it too.

'Yes?' I say expectantly. He is wearing his most angelic smile.

'Dad … Can we please never come here again? It's *really* boring.'

Oh well. No quest worth the trouble is ever that easy. The Midlands wasn't built in a day, you know, and its reputation won't be restored in a day either. Later that evening as I prepare to wave Hector and his mother off at the railway station – Hector has school the following day and his mother has better things to

27

do than to go scouting for foundation myths in Mansfield – my wife asks when they can expect me home again.

'Why, when I have staggering tales of Midland glory to tell, of course!'

'Oh. I hadn't realised this was *adieu* rather than *au revoir*,' she laughs.

I do my best 'hurt' face. The train is about to leave.

'Only kidding,' she smiles. 'I'm sure you'll discover lots of interesting things.'

Hmm. I'll show her – or, rather, the Midlands will show her! By the time I've finished, coach parties of French tourists will be jamming the approach roads to Warsop. You'll see.

The importance of Goose Fair, a prawn sandwich with a Midlands-denier, and proud to be a scab

'Who wants to barf?' A couple of dozen thrill-seekers, encased behind an ominous-looking grille, gamely raise their hands in response to the MC's taunting question, and the ride – one of those terrifying lurching contraptions designed to toss you around like an old pair of jeans in a tumble dryer – suddenly comes to life, whipping its human cargo screaming into the air.

You can hear the low rumble of Goose Fair as you walk towards it from Nottingham city centre and cross Forest Road, home to my *alma mater*, Nottingham High School, and the city's red-light district. (My mother told me a joke when I first came to school here: *One day Thor is walking along Forest Road when he bumps into a young woman in torn stockings with a big smile on her face. 'I am Thor, god of thunder!' the Norse deity booms. 'Well, I'm thor too but I'm thatithfied,' lisps back the young woman.* Eleven years

29

of age and not exactly worldly, I had no idea at the time why it was supposed to be funny. Mother, what were you thinking?) The fair's current home, the Forest Recreation Ground, lies about fifteen miles south of Edwinstowe and the Major Oak, but it too used to be part of Sherwood Forest. In the nineteenth century, as urbanisation gripped, this particular stretch was known as the 'Wastes', and there was a grandstand to accommodate spectators who gathered to watch horse racing and the other entertainments held here. Today, for the fifty-one and a half weeks a year when the fair isn't in town, the Rec is used for sports and as a car park for Park-and-Riders.

The origins of Goose Fair's name are lost in the mists of time. The annual gathering, for a long period the largest in Europe, was first held around 1284. Geese obviously played a part – it's been suggested that they were brought over from Lincolnshire and even Norfolk in their thousands, their feet coated with tar and sand to help them survive the journey, to be sold in Nottingham at the onset of autumn. The fair may have begun with fowl – it's always been held at the beginning of October around Michaelmas, when geese are a traditional treat – but by the eighteenth century it was most renowned for its cheese. There was even a cheese riot in Nottingham in the 1760s, with discontented locals bowling the overpriced produce, conveniently supplied in wheel-like units, down the hills leading out of the Market Place, where the fair was held until 1928. The mayor, protesting against the rioters, is said to have been knocked off his feet by one of the cheesy missiles and to have landed, with severe consequences for his dignity, in the mud of Wheeler Gate.

There's not much in the way of cheese or geese on view nowadays – apart, that is, from the large plastic goose that sits proudly on the Gregory Boulevard roundabout for the fair's duration every year. The character of the gathering definitively changed with the advent of the railways. Improved transportation made the year-round supply of food more dependable and reduced the need to stock up on provisions before the coming of winter. As such, Goose Fair began to be viewed simply as an opportunity to have a good time – not that all that cheese rolling hadn't been entertainment of a sort – and there was a sudden invasion of five-footed sheep and men on stilts, not to mention a big hand-turned roundabout, Twigdon's Riding Machine. Madame Tussaud was so impressed by the fair's drawing power that she was twice tempted to bring her collection of life-size wax figures, in 1819 and 1829.

Since then, of course, it's all got a big more high-tech. Some of the food – hog roast, hot peas, candyfloss – has its roots in tradition, but flashing lights, blaring music ('We will – we will – ROCK YOU!') and sulphurous smoke bathe proceedings in a deep sensory smog of modernity. A rodent-themed rollercoaster shakes punters up and down, then, for good measure, whirls them round and round as well, to make doubly sure they achieve that freshly eviscerated/post-sickbag look just in time for their free souvenir exit portrait. Over at another ride two lone teenage girls are being strapped into their seats, ready for lift-off. A crowd of onlookers has gathered to watch the torture as a voice on the seemingly never-ending warm-up tape intones, in exaggeratedly precise Euro-English: 'Are you ready? Are you R-R-READY?!?' A safety cage descends over the youngsters, one of whom is busy flicking her middle finger at a laughing woman – her mother? Her sister? – who stands filming them on her phone; her mate meanwhile is making hot eyes at the ride attendant. 'In the interests of safety,' the voice on the tape continues, growing shriller for the killer punchline, '… HOLD ON TO YOUR PANTS!' And then the music starts – the inevitable 'O Fortuna' from Nazi favourite *Carmina*

31

Burana, heard everywhere these days from Old Spice ads to *The X Factor* pre-title sequence – and the girls are whipped up into the stratosphere. The crowd cheers as a garland of vomit loops its way back down to earth and the cage continues its vertiginous ascent.

* * *

Goose Fair is the setting for one of the most iconic scenes in Alan Sillitoe's great Angry Young Man novel *Saturday Night and Sunday Morning* (1958), where anti-hero Arthur Seaton gets his comeuppance for messing around with another man's wife and is beaten up by a group of squaddies. Ironically, given that it's set in Nottingham, aka the Queen of the Midlands, Sillitoe's classic novel – along with Czech director Karel Reisz's no-less-classic film adaptation (1960) – helped to launch the phrase 'It's grim up North'.

Lots of people get the story's setting wrong, some unwittingly – for instance, in his *Hope and Glory: Britain 1900–1990* (2004), the distinguished Cambridge historian Peter Clarke describes the novel as a 'class-conscious account of the industrial north'. Others, however, do it quite deliberately. A notable representative of the latter tendency is Stuart Maconie in his popular paean to the North, *Pies and Prejudice*, where he discusses the late Fifties/early Sixties British cinematic New Wave, describing it as that 'glorious swathe of films about the experience of love, sex, work and struggle among the working classes of the industrial north'. In this category he includes the film of *Saturday Night and Sunday Morning* starring Albert Finney. 'I know Sillitoe's book … is set in Nottingham,' opines Maconie, a Northern exile who actually admits to living in the Midlands, for god's sake, 'but Finney and his film are indisputably northern.' Given that all the key scenes in both book and film take place at Nottingham landmarks, this is a distinctly odd thing to say. Maconie apparently feels he has the right to claim Seaton for the North merely because, as he argues, he has 'provided me [i.e. Maconie] with some of my favourite catch-phrases … That's the truth, as Albert Finney as Arthur Seaton would say. The rest is propaganda.' The problem is, to anyone with ears attuned to the speech patterns of Nottingham and its environs, anti-Establishment rebel Seaton sounds exactly like what he is: a Midlander, not a Northerner. Now *that's* the truth, and what Maconie writes is classic cocky Northern propaganda. (The Arctic Monkeys, those musical darlings of the North, adopted another of Seaton's most resonant phrases for the title of their debut album: *Whatever People Say I Am, That's What I'm Not.*)

We shouldn't be too surprised by Maconie's act of cultural appropriation: after all, Northerners have been nicking bits of Midland heritage and claiming them as their own for centuries – since the Northumbrian monk the Venerable Bede, the so-called 'father of English history', set the pattern with his *Ecclesiastical History of the English People* in about AD 731, in fact. And as the instance cited above suggests, it's more than just a matter of poor geography – Maconie knows Nottingham isn't in the North; he actually says as much. It's actually part of a conspiracy to strip the Midlands of its identity and claim the most distinctive elements for the North instead. As Maconie says, he likes the way Seaton talks and feels a kinship with him, which means – in the wonderful logic of Northern appropriationism – that Seaton must therefore be a Northerner like him.

Midlanders have traditionally been slow to react to such acts of daylight robbery. I once asked Alan Sillitoe about the wavering accents in the film version of *Saturday Night and Sunday Morning*, for which he wrote the screenplay, and he explained that the problem was that they simply hadn't been able to find 'a clutch of actors who all came from Nottingham'. As a result, it ended up 'a kind of mish-mash of South Yorkshire and Scouse and this, that and the other'. Didn't it worry Sillitoe – the late twentieth-century Bard of Nottingham – that his works could so easily be claimed for the North? 'That's other people's problem. Who cares about the North, or indeed about the South?' he told me. For him, the Midlands was a place of 'illimitable frontiers'. Then, after a pause, he added, 'Bugger the North!' and excused himself as his tea was waiting for him in the other room. Where uppity Northerners rage and bluster for attention, stoical Midlanders just shrug and concentrate on more important matters – buttered toast, for instance.

The cinema has never been particularly helpful where Midland identity is concerned. Take the more recent example of Shane Meadows's *Once Upon a Time in the Midlands* (2002). With a title like that, you'd think that Meadows's starrily cast modern spaghetti western would deliver a firmer, more differentiating picture of life as it is lived between North and South. Indeed, with a title like that, you might even think that that was one of its principal *raisons d'être* – especially as Meadows is himself a Midlander. So it's curious that there's no attempt to make the setting of the film identifiably Midland – the locations are all anonymous, unromanticised suburbs of the kind that can be found anywhere in the UK – or even to make the characters *sound* like Midlanders. Rhys Ifans speaks with a Welsh accent, Ricky Tomlinson – who plays 'the Midlands cowboy' – is audibly Scouse, while Kathy Burke, though she does use the very North Notts term of endearment 'mi duck' when talking to her brother (a very Scottish-sounding Robert Carlyle), is her usual salt-of-the-earth, Norf Lunnon self. So there you have it: a drama that announces boldly that it's about the Midlands, but that then goes on to look and sound anything and everything but. Go figure.

* * *

The day after my visit to Goose Fair I've arranged to meet a friend for lunch. Elizabeth spent her childhood just up the road from me in Chesterfield, home of the not-much-vaunted Crooked Spire. Like me, she now lives in London but makes regular jaunts to Nottingham to visit family. We're due to meet outside the Victoria Centre, one of the two big shopping malls that sandwich the city centre. So long as I pay for lunch, she's agreed to answer my questions about her impressions of the region.

When she arrives, she looks quite flustered. Apparently she's just had a nasty experience in the Nottingham Poundland (what she was doing there I can't imagine as she's only really comfortable antiquing in Notting Hill). I'd been hoping to lure her for a boutique burger around the corner at groovy 'eatery and funhouse' Spanky Van Dyke's, which captures Nottingham's youthful spirit so well (this is a big student city). But after her budget-store trauma she insists on a cup of Earl Grey and a prawn sandwich in the more reassuring surroundings of John Lewis, which just happens to occupy a large portion of the Vicky Centre.

Elizabeth looks like a classic Twenties flapper and holds down a very serious job. Given her general profile, you might expect her to speak with an RP accent. And for the most part she does – middling aristocracy, I'd say she sounds – until she pronounces one of those great North/South divide words, like 'laugh' or 'bath', when her vowels suddenly become as flat as those of any no-nonsense muck-and-brass Northern industrialist. This peculiarity in her pronunciation reflects the influence of her father, who grew up in

35

Barnsley and, in the best Yorkshire tradition, 'is very clear what he thinks about things and very blunt when he speaks about them' (Elizabeth's own description).

Duly settled in a corner of JL's 'Place to Eat', I press the button on my recording device and begin my interrogation.

'Right, Elizabeth. Question one: What's the best thing ever to come out of the Midlands?'

She raises a hand to stop me.

'Can I ask a question? Are you counting Staffordshire as being in the Midlands?'

'Obviously. Because it is.'

'Good … And how about Birmingham? I hope Lincolnshire isn't on your list, because I know that isn't the Midlands …'

I think I've already mentioned that a lot of people don't know where the Midlands begins and ends, including Midlanders. Well, Elizabeth falls into that category.

'Anyway,' she goes on, 'if Staffordshire's in, lots of brilliant things like trains and bridges were invented there. But I don't know much about them.'

Oh well, I comfort myself, I can deal with the genius of Staffordshire folk later on in my tour.

'I'll tell you one of the *worst* things to come out of the Midlands,' she announces with sudden and excessive passion, 'and that's a little tea shop I went to last time I was here. What was its name? Anyway it's over near the Lace Market. I ordered a scone with jam and some special blend of tea they were promoting. And do you know how they served it?'

She stops and looks at me, as if I am actually going to attempt to answer her plainly rhetorical question.

'No, Elizabeth, I don't,' I say after a pause. 'How *did* they serve it?'

'They brought the tea leaves separately, exposed on a saucer!

When I asked why they did it that way the girl said: "Customers like to be able to see them." Apparently in Nottingham people go into tea shops just to stare at the leaves.'

Interesting as this phenomenon is (although I hasten to add that I've been unable to find any other references to it – to the best of my knowledge, Elizabeth is the only person to have experienced it), I decide to change the subject by mentioning Jilly Cooper's injurious declaration that, for the grander sort of people, 'The Midlands are beyond the pale'. 'What do you think she meant by that, Elizabeth?' I ask.

'Perhaps she'd just been to that tea shop. It *is* beyond the pale.'

'No, seriously,' I encourage her.

After a pause, she shakes her head. 'I can't comment on that because, you see, I don't actually come from the Midlands. Chesterfield is really the North. I think you'd class the Peak District as the North, because there's an association of the word "Midlands" with the idea of industry, and particularly deprived Victorian-style industry. And although Chesterfield has a bit of that, it's mostly a Northern market town on the edge of a hilly area.'

I've known Elizabeth a long time and have heard her say many extraordinary things over the years (don't get her started on the Moon landings – faked, obviously), but I'm genuinely taken aback by this. Elizabeth, it turns out, is a Midlands-denier.

'Okay, your father's a Yorkshireman, but you were born and bred in Chesterfield. Elizabeth, are you seriously telling me that you're not a Midlander?' I fix her with a searching look.

'That's right,' she says, holding my gaze and flattening her vowels with classic Northern vehemence. 'I'm sorry, Robert, but Chesterfield is in the hills, and hills are Northern.'

'All of them? Exclusively?'

'All the proper ones, yes. I'm not including those *slopes* you go up and down when you're coming into Nottingham, obviously. Sherwood *Rise*, ha!'

'I'm sure if you asked anyone on Derbyshire County Council they'd tell you Chesterfield was part of the East Midlands.'

'Oh what do they know, silly people!' she says, agitatedly putting down her teacup and rooting fruitlessly through her handbag. When she looks up again, her cheeks have turned quite red.

'I know, for instance,' I go on, wanting to press my point home and show off a little of my research at the same time, 'that Derbyshire County Council are dependent on the East Midlands Development Agency here in Nottingham for various kinds of funding. Which would appear to confirm that Derbyshire is in the East Midlands.'

Elizabeth looks briefly crestfallen.

'Well, that's very interesting,' she says with a mildly hysterical laugh. 'I accept, then, if I must, that I am by some definition a Midlander and that Derbyshire is, again by some definition, in the Midlands. But I would say that it is a border area, in the same way that Belarus and the Ukraine are ... Is Warwickshire in the Midlands? It's an interesting thing but I think the general perception is that rural counties aren't in the Midlands.'

'I'm getting the impression that you wouldn't want to live in Nottingham, then?'

'I wouldn't want to live in a city anywhere, if I'm honest, although I have to say I'd rather live in Leeds than Nottingham.'

'Why's that?'

'Because Leeds has got a fresh Northern feel, whereas Nottingham just feels a bit depressed. It does! It's like that everywhere in the Midlands. I took a train from Birmingham to Nottingham a few weeks ago and it nearly undermined my will to live. Go to Wilkos here and I challenge you not to be depressed!'

Poundland, Wilkinsons – it sounds an improbable itinerary for a woman like Elizabeth. But it's telling that she seems to think her misadventures uniquely expressive of life as it is lived in the Midlands.

* * *

Can you locate Nottingham on a map of the UK? Probably not, at least if *Private Eye* is to be believed. The London-based satirical magazine marked the recent, much-trumpeted opening of a major new art gallery in the city with a *Young British Artists* comic strip by illustrator Birch.

'It all sounds very exciting!' says one metropolitan YBA enthusiastically of the inaugural exhibition, which was designed to put Nottingham on the art map.

'I wouldn't go that far,' replies his pal.

'No, nor would I. Near Liverpool, isn't it?' rejoins the first YBA, returning to his senses and moving from the figurative to the straightforwardly geographical.

'Even further, I think,' concludes his sceptical mate. (Just in case you're unsure: Nottingham is 120 miles from London, Liverpool is 200.)

The message being: Nottingham, like the Midlands generally, is even more alien to the Southern media than the North, and nothing the city does – not even the brilliant Nottingham Contemporary art gallery – is going to tempt the Establishment to reconsider its attitude.

When they do manage to locate it, outsiders often find it hard to take Nottingham seriously; respect can be hard to come by when you used to be known by the name of 'Snottingham'. That was in the Middle Ages, when it was settled by Saxons led by or descended from a chap named Snot. In more recent times, Nottingham has been no less unglamorously known to millions as 'Dottingham', the go-to railway destination for all cold-sufferers, thanks to that bloody ad for Tunes cough sweets. Condescension is thus the preferred mode when metropolitans deign to notice the Queen of the East Midlands. For instance, when another London-based publication, briefly warming to the charms of its chic Lace Market district (once the centre of the nation's fashion industry – while we're on the subject, Sir Paul Smith, the classic-with-a-twist design guru, is Nottingham born-and-bred and still has a flagship store in a beautiful Grade II-listed town house in the centre of town), recommended the city as a weekend getaway destination, it couldn't help adding patronisingly: 'Sales of tights can't be high in Nottingham. Or coats, for that matter. This is the kind of town where outfits start low and end high, and the fine art of going out has been honed to perfection. Don't knock it, they have a style of their own – it's just not style as we know it.' How we laughed.

Still, at least the magazine's assessors claim to have enjoyed themselves in Nottingham. One of the great heroes of the Golden Age of British detective fiction, Inspector Alan Grant of Scotland Yard, hailed from the Midlands. But when, in the 1929 mystery *The Man in the Queue*, an investigation carries him from the metropolis to Nottingham, his heart sinks: 'Grant came out of the station into the drone and clamour of trams. If he had been asked what represented the Midlands in his mind, he would unhesitatingly have said trams … Grant never heard the far-away peculiar sing of an approaching tramcar without finding himself back in the dead, airless atmosphere of the Midland town where he had been born.' 'Dead', 'airless': sounds irresistible, doesn't it? You'll be glad to know that, after doing without one for several decades,

Nottingham has recently reinstituted a tram service – you can catch it from the Forest Recreation Ground when Goose Fair isn't on. Inspector Grant *would* be pleased.

Anyway, if, despite the best efforts of journalists and that Tunes ad, you *are* planning a visit – and until the arrival of the gangs and guns and the Channel 4 programme *The Best and Worst Places to Live in the UK*, Nottingham was regularly cited as one of the nicest, most welcoming places in Britain – here are a few local highlights to look out for:

1. The vast Market Square is the largest (about 22,000 m²) in the country. It's also rather dull.
2. The tallest freestanding work of art in the UK, Ken Shuttleworth's *Aspire*, is here. You almost certainly won't have heard of it before, although you will *definitely* have heard of the much-photographed, much-publicised – and much smaller – *Angel of the North* by Antony Gormley. Gormless's Gateshead icon gets written about and photographed a lot more because it's self-advertisingly *Northern*. By contrast, Shuttleworth's much more ambitious structure has a lame pun for a title (it's like *a spire*, see, and it's on a university campus, where the students presumably *aspire* to reach new intellectual heights). It should have been called *Midland Thrust* or something like that instead, but, as we've already seen, the Midlands doesn't go in for that kind of self-promotion.
3. The castle. William the Conqueror was responsible for the original building, which quickly became the chief royal fortress in the Midlands. Crusading King Richard had to lay siege to it to reclaim it from his wicked, Robin Hood-bothering brother, John, in 1194. Most of the original

structure has been destroyed; the Italianate building that has replaced it is rather anaemic.

4. There's a statue of Robin Hood – did I mention that he was a local? – at the foot of the castle. The most important 'Oodie-related site, however, is the Major Oak out in Edwinstowe. Robin's paramour has her principal incarnation in the form of a ring road that encircles Nottingham city centre, Maid Marian Way. Romantic, like.

5. The pubs. Like Mansfield, Nottingham takes its drinking seriously. You can tell because a lot of the local hostelries claim the distinction of age. The Bell Inn on Angel Row, running along the bottom side of the Market Square, says it's the oldest in Nottingham, although its purported foundation date (c. 1437) pales besides that of Ye Olde Salutation Inn, which traces its origins to around 1240. Nestling in a half-timbered building beneath the castle, Ye Olde Trip to Jerusalem goes one better and claims to be the oldest inn *in the whole of England*. It's said to date from 1189, the year Nottingham-loving monarch Richard the Lionheart ascended the throne. Legend has it that when old Dickie *Coeur de Lion* announced his intention to lead a crusade against the Saracens, the king's followers had a swift one at the inn before setting off on their journey to Jerusalem – hence the name. So if you find Nottingham a bit characterless and try-hard, you can at least rest assured that it's a great place to get smashed.

After lunch with Elizabeth, I wander away from the city's busy commercial centre, up past the curved Newton and Arkwright Building of Nottingham University – named for two Midlanders who helped shape the modern world, I note in passing – and plunge into the manicured calm of the Arboretum, the first public park to be opened in the city, back in 1852, when industrialisation had begun to impact on the environment and the authorities judged it politic to provide locals with a little green breathing space. Today leaves carpet the ground in a rich tapestry of autumnal colours, while the foliage overhead offers a rich mix – a symphony, no less – of russets and greens. I can see that lots of different types of tree are involved in creating this eye-catching effect – it's obviously all been planned with loving care by the landscapers – but I'm a city boy and so am completely incapable of telling you what they are, for which I apologise. What I can tell you is that, in the heart of this green oasis, there's a little bridge that lovers usually find romantic and under which they pause to kiss. Personally, as a schoolboy I always found it rather sinister and fully expected to be knifed to death whenever I had to pass through it after dusk. My fantasies of murder aside, this is a nice place. 'Thank you for visiting the Arboretum,' says a notice as you exit, extending various options to those who might like to leave feedback on their park experience. Yes, it's a very polite place these days, is Nottingham.

Not bland, though. Nottingham stands on the river Trent, which is often taken as the line separating North from South. Certainly, it's often served as a national dividing line: this is where Charles I raised his standard on 22 August 1642 to signal the beginning of the Civil War. The award-winning Galleries of Justice Museum characterise Nottingham as a 'rebel city', and it's a title the city well deserves. The spirit of Arthur Seaton – that emblematic Nottingham Man, *pace* Stuart Maconie – runs deep in the city's history.

Nottingham sport has had its fair share of nonconformist Seatons. The county's cricketing history is full of rebels, eccentric individualists for whom conformity was never an option. 'Clown prince' Derek Randall is a classic example. When Dennis Lillee tossed a bouncer down at the Nottinghamshire and England batsman's head in an Ashes Test in 1977, Randall whipped off his cap and reputedly called out: 'No good hitting me there, mate. There's nothing to damage.' When he was finally out – for 174; Randall may have been a bit of a joker but he was no clown with the bat – he exited the playing area by the wrong gate and found himself climbing the steps towards the royal enclosure. '[The Queen] was very nice about it,' Randall reported. 'She smiled. Someone else quickly put me right.' The spirit of Sir John Cockle lives on, it would appear.

Randall is part of a fine tradition of local cricketing unorthodoxy. In May 1930 the whole of the Nottinghamshire side famously took to the field in lounge suits on the final day of their match against Hampshire in Southampton. The previous day's play had ended with the home side requiring just a single run for victory. The Notts captain, Arthur Carr, didn't think it was worth the trouble of putting on whites the following morning: opening bowler Bill Voce actually wore an overcoat. His second ball yielded the necessary run.

A couple of years later Voce was back in the headlines, albeit in a less whimsical context. It was the Nottinghamshire pacemen Voce and 'bloody frighteningly fast' Harold Larwood who led the England attack on the infamous Bodyline tour of Australia in 1932–33, when the visitors caused uproar by their use of so-called 'fast-leg theory'. The latter – which involved bowling at the batsman's leg stump and getting the ball to rise into his ribs – had been devised by the respective captains of Notts and England, Arthur Carr and Douglas Jardine, to neutralise the threat posed by the great Australian player Don Bradman, who at the time boasted a surreal batting average of around 100. The strategy worked so well that it nearly caused a riot in the Third Test at Adelaide, when deliveries by Larwood hit Australian captain Bill Woodfull above the heart and fractured Bert Oldfield's skull – police had to intervene to stop angry Australian spectators from attacking the England team. We tend to think of Aussies as tough, but Nottingham Man is an altogether steelier proposition. When the Australian cricketing board accused the tourists of using 'unsportsmanlike' tactics, the English team threatened to withdraw from the remaining matches.

In the event the series went ahead, and England claimed the Ashes by a 4–1 margin. The row reignited the following summer, though, when the governing body of English cricket, the Board of the Marylebone Cricket Club (MCC), which had dismissed the Aussies as 'squealers' the previous winter, had a chance to witness 'fast-leg theory' in action at home, this time against the West Indies. Suddenly the powers-that-be decided that Bodyline was indeed a mite unsporting, and so demanded that Larwood make a personal apology to the Australians. If he refused, the MCC said, he would forfeit his England place. The furious Nottingham man, feeling that he was being scapegoated, pointed out that the tactic had actually been the idea of his Oxford-educated captain – the plot having notoriously been hatched in the sumptuous surroundings of the Piccadilly Club in London. Why should he, a working-class pro who had previously been employed down t'pit, shoulder the blame for the supremely well-connected 'gentleman amateur' Jardine?

Larwood refused to back down and as a result never played for England again. Ironically, having been vilified in his own country, he decided to emigrate to Australia. A sad fate, but Midlanders are natural outsiders: like Larwood, they generally accept their lot graciously. The great working-class fast bowler's refusal to accept the blame for his officer-class captain's tactics has since come to be seen as a key event in breaking down class distinctions in English cricket. All that stuff about working-class rebellion being a distinctively Northern phenomenon just isn't true, you know.

Sport is one of the major reasons why the Midlands lacks much in the way of national profile: the perennial footballing giants Manchester United and Liverpool are two of the biggest reasons why everyone knows where the North is. By contrast, no one outside Nottinghamshire takes the sport played here very seriously. Trent Bridge, the home of the County Cricket team, regularly hosts Tests, but its international matches rarely generate the excitement of the equivalent games played at Lord's (the home of Southern cricket) or Headingley (the home of cricket in the North).

Just around the corner from Trent Bridge is Meadow Lane, which hosts the oldest – and one of the least celebrated – of all professional football teams in the country, Notts County. They're not very good at the game, of course, but that's not the point – they've been not very good at it for longer than anyone else, and that's what really matters. County scored major back-page headlines a few years ago when former England coach Sven-Göran Eriksson was appointed as their new director of football as a result of the club securing fresh financial backing from a Middle Eastern consortium called Munto Finance. Amidst feverish talk of an ambitious 'project' to get the Division 2 stragglers into the Premiership, the super-Swede was treated to a typically eccentric welcome on his arrival at Meadow Lane. 'I had a wheelbarrow, the wheel fell off,' a hundred or so supporters serenaded Svennis, much to the bafflement of national sports writers and presumably the Magpies' new director of football himself. Shortly afterwards Munto pulled out and Eriksson resigned after the club was sold for a pound to former Lincoln chairman Ray Trew. Though obscure in utterance, the County fans' prophecy proved correct: the wheel did well and truly fall off the barrow.

Which brings us to County's local rivals, Nottingham Forest, and another great Midland eccentric: Brian Clough. Strictly speaking, Ol' Big 'Ead, as Clough was affectionately known, was raised in the North-East but as local sports writer Al Needham has put it: 'Cloughie … was pure Nottingham. Chelpy as you like, stubborn as anything, gobby enough to have a go at Muhammad Ali on *Parkinson*, and he chinned Roy Keane. He was Nottingham's surrogate Dad, and we were his lairy, sometimes bemused but always fiercely loyal kids.' That loyalty was displayed after Clough's death in 2004, when thousands of fans turned out in the Market Square to mourn his passing.

It's interesting that Clough, one of the most successful football managers of all time, should only ever have triumphed at unfashionable Midland clubs: before their world-beating reign at Forest, he and his long-term managerial partner, Peter Taylor, led the no less unheralded Derby County to the league title in 1972. But when Clough then took over an already successful, bona-fide Northern club, Leeds United, he was an abject failure, and his gobby, stubborn, chelpy (it's not just the North that has dialect, tha knows) managerial style so displeased the Yorkshire club's spoiled superstars that he lasted just forty-four days in office. When Clough went south to Brighton there was a similar cultural misunderstanding. Only Midland clubs were equal to Ol' Big 'Ead's idiosyncratic and abrasive style of management.

Forest were a terminally unglamorous outfit when Clough and Taylor took over in 1976. The duo gained the club promotion to the top table in 1977, then won the championship at the first attempt in 1978. The European Cup was secured for the Midlands the following year, and again in 1980. (Every year, when the last club from the metropolis was knocked out of the Champions League, Forest fans held a special 'Nottingham 2 London 0 Day' to mark the fact that Clough's team secured the top European prize twice while no London outfit had ever won it. What a pity Chelsea triumphed in 2012 – although the score remains Nottingham 2 London 1. Actually, make that 9–1, since a homesick Nottingham lacemaker named Herbert Kilpin was responsible for creating Italian footballing giants AC Milan, who have won the biggest European prize seven times.) And then there was the little matter of the League Cup in 1978, 1979, 1989 and 1990 – an astonishing record when you consider that it was achieved without major financial backing. Clough wasn't generally interested in making star signings (Trevor Francis being the exception that proves the rule): in fact, that's probably why he was cold-shouldered by the North and South big-money boys. Only in the Midlands was success possible on Clough's terms.

It wasn't only in his ability to pick up key players for peanuts that Clough's managerial style was unique. There's also the matter of his celebrated *bons mots*. 'At last England have appointed a manager who speaks English better than the players,' he noted sardonically on the appointment of Sven-Göran Eriksson as national manager. Which Liverpool or Manchester United manager has ever matched Clough for wit? And it wasn't only Clough's words that were memorable. After Forest supporters mounted a pitch invasion at the conclusion of a League Cup victory over Queen's Park Rangers in 1989, an appalled Clough took to the field himself and punched a number of errant Forest fans; he was fined £5,000 for his trouble, and banned from the touchline for the rest of the season. The attacked supporters refused to press charges, however, and when they realised who their aggressor was begged his forgiveness. What a strange incident that was. But life under Clough was full of such curious, heart-gladdening spectacles. He was famous for reprimanding his players – telling star striker Trevor Francis to take his hands out of his pockets as he was presenting him with an award on one occasion – and he had a similar authority when it came to handling crowds. As a boy, I remember watching as a sign was hauled out and placed in front of the Trent End terrace. It read: 'Gentlemen, No Swearing Please – Brian.' The famously foul-mouthed Trent Enders got the point – and the joke. Afterwards away supporters were routinely greeted with chants of 'You're gonna get your flipping head kicked in', while on-field officials who made decisions that disappointed the Forest faithful were treated to a chorus of 'The referee's a naughty'. Only in the Midlands.

As Brian Glanville observed in an obituary of the Forest manager: 'Clough's methods were unique. He was essentially a dictator, and not always a benevolent one.' Given his much-quoted pronouncements on his dealings with his players, Clough could hardly have disagreed with this assessment. 'We talk about it for twenty minutes and then we decide I was right' was how he once explained his manner of dealing with team members who questioned his tactics. He rarely indulged in self-doubt: 'I wouldn't say I was the best manager in the business. But I was in the top one,' he famously opined. Yet despite (or perhaps even because of) that, when the end came for him professionally – Forest relegated, Clough battling alcoholism – he cut a peculiarly pathetic figure. And, of course, he never made English football's top job – manager of the national team – a failure he deeply regretted. 'I'm sure the England selectors thought if they took me on and gave me the job, I'd want to run the show. They were shrewd, because that's exactly what I would have done,' he commented. For all his successes, Clough remains the archetypal Midland tragic hero.

There's also a more serious, socially engaged side to this eccentric, rebellious Nottingham spirit. It's a tradition that begins with the *Gest of Robin Hood*, written in about 1500 – 'For he was a good outlaw, / And did poor men much good' – and finds particularly strong expression in the region's line of Nonconformist (i.e. dissenting from the Church of England) religious radicals. It strikes me that there's more than enough matter here for a Midland foundation myth or two.

If you head south-east from Nottingham city centre, you find yourself climbing out of the Trent valley and up Sneinton Hill. Here, outside 12 Notintone Place, stands a weathered statue of a preacher with arm upraised in full oratorical flow. This is William Booth, founder of the Salvation Army, and the building he guards is the William Booth Birthplace Museum.

Like his fellow Midlander Margaret Thatcher, Booth (1829–1912) was a Methodist with an extraordinary zeal for his chosen line of work. 'His spirit was like a white flame ... There was nothing of the gentle saint about him,' a journalist named Philip Gibbs reported in 1902.

> On the day I went to see him, on behalf of the *Daily Mail*, he started by being angry, and then softened. Presently he seized me by the wrist and dragged me down to my knees beside him. 'Let us pray for Alfred Harmsworth [the great press baron and owner of the *Mail*],' he said. He prayed long and earnestly for Harmsworth, and Fleet Street, and the newspaper Press that it might be inspired by the love of truth and charity and the Spirit of the Lord.

Amen to that – but did Booth intend this little performance to be at least semi-humorous? Certainly Gibbs paints the scene comically, and there is evidence elsewhere that, for all his spiritual dedication and blood-and-thunder rhetoric, Booth had a splendid sense of the absurd. For instance, the early Salvation Army was a notable equal-opportunities employer, a progressive idea to which Booth gave memorable verbal form when he exclaimed: 'My best men are women!'

Indeed, Booth's heady strain of Midland eccentricity was his greatest spiritual weapon, and it was only when he began to give full vent to it, in 1878, that he really found his feet as a preacher. It was at this time that Booth literalised the notion of Christian soldiers fighting sin by reorganising his Christian Mission along quasi-military lines and renaming it the Salvation *Army*. Booth himself took the title of 'General', with his ministers also being accorded military ranks, and all now began to 'put on the armour' (the Salvation Army's own uniform) for their ministry work. It was a daring, potentially silly idea – but it captured the public imagination: within four years, one London survey estimated that on a particular weeknight the Salvation Army attracted 17,000 worshippers while the Church of England got only 11,000 through its doors.

Booth's influence as a reformer extended well beyond purely spiritual matters. His bestselling book *In Darkest England and the Way Out* (1890) in many respects served as the blueprint for the British welfare state in 1948. Booth compared industrialised England with 'Darkest Africa' and found the former wanting. In 'The Cab-Horse Charter' he wrote: 'when a horse is down he is helped up, and while he lives he has food, shelter and work'; the same basic level of social assistance, he suggested, should be extended to humans too. The rest of the book is concerned with various schemes to improve the living standards of millions of poor and homeless people in Britain.

Booth was no Northern socialist, though. Rather, it's the Midland spirit of self-sufficiency, or the yeoman ideal, as it's sometimes called, that underpins his thinking. Where the state would not or could not act, the individual must step into the breach, Booth believed. Thus when the General and his wife, the redoubtable Catherine, discovered the national shame that was 'Phossy Jaw' (a condition caused by the toxic fumes given off by yellow phosphorus which caused the premature deaths of innumerable female match-factory workers by destroying their faces), the Booths' response was simple: they opened their own factory, using only harmless red phosphorus in their manufacturing process and paying their workforce twice as much as traditional employers such as Bryant & May. Booth was justly proud of his achievement and organised tours of his 'model' factory for MPs and journalists.

Despite his extraordinary influence, Booth struggled to find favour with the Establishment. Actually, that's not quite true – like all true Midlanders, he never even *tried* to curry favour with the Establishment. If Lord Shaftesbury chose to brand him the 'Anti-Christ', so be it. If others were outraged by his 'elevation of women to men's status', let them complain: time would prove him right. And indeed, as the tide of opinion shifted, Booth found himself granted audiences with kings, emperors and presidents. When he died – or was 'promoted to Glory', as the organisation's own terminology has it – in 1912, the Salvation Army was at work in fifty-eight countries; 150,000 mourners attended his funeral. As even the archbishop of York came to acknowledge, the distinctively unconventional flavour of the Army's meetings and services – characterised by joyous singing and a Midland informality – allowed Booth and his followers to get their message across to people whom the Anglican Church had traditionally been powerless to reach.

* * *

It's getting late so I drive north out of Nottingham, through the suburban sprawl of Sherwood Rise and Arnold, into the rolling farmland around Papplewick, on through leafy, wealthy Ravenshead with its Byronic ruins, and back to the 'once-romantic, now utterly disheartening colliery town', as local literary celeb D.H. Lawrence characterised Mansfield in his infamous dirty book *Lady Chatterley's Lover*. Lawrence made this pronouncement eighty-odd years ago and, though it's still a disheartening place, Mansfield is no longer a colliery town. Thereby hangs a tale, and perhaps a key to unlocking the character of Mansfield folk, and of Midlanders more generally.

In common with the rest of the country, most of the collieries in the Mansfield area closed in the wake of the miners' strike of 1984–85. The fabled industrial dispute has often been portrayed as a good-versus-evil struggle pitting ordinary working people, mostly in the North, against an uncomprehending and vengeful government, entirely in the South. Thus, when Channel 4 commissioned an artist (from London) to create a work commemorating the strike, it was an event in South Yorkshire – 'The Battle of Orgreave', a confrontation between police and picketing miners at a British Steel coking plant – that the artist in question, Jeremy Deller, chose to focus on. 'On 18 June 1984 I was watching the evening news and saw footage of a picket at the Orgreave coking plant in South Yorkshire in which thousands of men were chased up a field by mounted police,' Deller has written. 'It seemed a civil war between the North and the South of the country was taking place in all but name.' That last sentence is quite wrong – the strike affected the whole of the UK – but it fits nicely with the mythology of the North/South divide so it's unlikely to raise many eyebrows. But were events in Yorkshire and the North, and the stand-off between police and striking miners, the only or even the main 'story' of the strike? If they were, it's hard to understand

Mansfield's role in it, or why chants of 'scab' – meaning someone who refuses to join a strike – ring out from the terraces whenever Mansfield Town Football Club plays against its South Yorkshire soccer rivals.

The strike was a very emotive business: lives were destroyed and even lost as attitudes grew increasingly polarised. As I said just now, it's been mythologised as a struggle between the right-wing government (and its puppet police force) and the traditional working classes. But though it's certainly true that Margaret Thatcher had unfinished business with the unions when she came to power, the strike was more complicated than that. For one thing, it was also a matter of miners against miners.

The catalyst for the initial walkout was the announcement on 6 March 1984 by the National Coal Board (NCB) that it intended to close twenty pits with the loss of 20,000 jobs. Six days later Arthur Scargill, the Barnsley-born former Young Communist president of the National Union of Mineworkers (NUM), called a national strike. Colliers in Scargill's own county, Yorkshire, and Kent were the first to heed their master's voice, followed by pit employees in Scotland, South Wales and Durham. Others, meanwhile, refused to strike. These 'scabs' – you might alternatively call them courageous independents: given the physical threats and actual violence offered in the subsequent struggle, continuing to work was certainly not a coward's option – were led by the Nottinghamshire miners, with Mansfield men in the vanguard.

In fact, you could say that the strike's great fault line ran straight through Mansfield: one of the great mass marches was held here in May 1984, when dockers and railways workers made common cause with colliery workers; and it was here that the breakaway union, the Union of Democratic Mineworkers (UDM), was eventually set up. Note the name: democracy was at the heart of the

Nottinghamshire miners' resistance to the NUM's strike declaration. Looking back years later, Roy Lynk, the founder of the UDM, insisted that it was Scargill's refusal to hold a national ballot of his members – rendering the strike technically illegal – that led to the bitter division among miners and the break-up of the NUM.

When an area ballot was held during the early part of the strike, Nottinghamshire miners voted to carry on working. They were far from alone in rejecting strike action, but the NUM's use of flying pickets intimidated most of the initial refuseniks into joining the strike willy-nilly. The Nottinghamshire men showed particular resolve, then, in standing firm against the bullying of Yorkshireman Scargill and his militant cohorts. 'In a sense sending pickets was a self-defeating exercise. The more they picketed the more people would keep going [to work]. No one wanted to back down from what they were doing,' Lynk told the *Chad*, the local Mansfield newspaper, two decades later. 'A lot of people resent being told what to do and go against it if it's being forced down their throats.'

I come from a mining family. My maternal grandfather spent his whole life 'wokkin' in wattah fah two tiddlahs', as the local dialect has it. (Roughly translated, that means he laboured hard in extremely damp conditions in return for a bit of extra money, or overtime.) He died in 1980 – he had long suffered problems with his breathing; that's what a lifetime on the coalface does for you – but my Uncle Jimmy was still employed as a pit engineer at the time of the strike and vividly remembers the hail of bricks that greeted him and his fellow workers on their path into work or the sound of battering at the door as wild-cat strikers tried to smash their way into the pit workshop. The fact that he disobeyed Comrade Arthur and continued working meant there was little tension between him and my Auntie Hilda's husband, Alf, who was a policeman and consequently very unpopular with

NUM loyalists. Of course, some local miners did go on strike and there were plenty of striking non-locals who were in the habit of hanging around town at the time too, which put an extra crackle of electricity in the air – not to mention long scratches down the sides of parked cars whenever there was a show of militant unionist strength locally.

Alf is dead now, but my father used to go down the pub with him on a Friday night. 'When the strike was on, you'd get all the NUM supporters on one side of the pub, and all the UDM people on the other,' he recounts. 'There would always be friction across the bar, and at some point during the evening a member of the NUM lot would approach Alf looking for a fight, and there'd often be a bit of nonsense between the NUM and UDM factions outside. Every Friday without fail someone wanted to take Alf on.'

A friend recently reminded me of an incident that reflected the general atmosphere at the time. 'We'd thrown a party at my parents' house and some kids we hadn't invited had turned up and were wrecking things. It was really getting out of hand,' he says. 'The neighbours noticed and called the police, and because of all the aggro in the area from the miners' strike the riot squad turned up! That sorted them out, I can tell you.' There were moments when you were grateful for all that added police presence. As Jimmy remembers, without it, 'There'd have been a piggin' bloodbath.'

Naturally, the harsh realities of Midlanders' experience of the strike are ignored or dismissed in the film of Deller's 'The Battle of Orgreave'. Instead, we get references to wealthy Notts colliers airily driving around in Range Rovers, Mercedes and BMWs. 'They're just a bunch of scabbing bastards' is the documentary's verdict on their role in the affair. And that's just not true.

The Notts men knew that the strike was futile, if not positively damaging to the industry's chances of survival. As another ex-miner tells me: 'The government wanted a fracas like that so they'd got a damn good excuse to shut the mines.' Modernisation was inevitable, as was restructuring. 'Without a strike they wouldn't have shut all the pits, but they'd certainly have thinned them out. There were too many around here. Blidworth, Rufford, Sherwood, they were all about two miles apart. With the new equipment that had been introduced since the pits were first sunk, you could go underground and travel six, eight, ten miles on the trains to your work real quick, like. You didn't need all this "one pit here, one pit there" business.'

It's too easy to caricature the non-strikers as cash-grabbing 'scabs'. The decision to go on working wasn't just about money. It was about democracy; it was also about realism. Pragmatism is less sexy than heroism, but sometimes it's more progressive. It's time we rethought that idea of the miners' strike as a civil war between North and South.

The nation's great individualists, Midlanders are above kneejerk class-based political loyalties. The Mansfield-led Nottinghamshire miners were accused of being Thatcherite stooges, but name calling, and actual violence, made no difference to their resistance to Scargillite coercion. Truculent independence of mind is a very Midland attitude: we're used to our outsider status. Perhaps it's because of this – and because we're excluded from the lazy black-and-white cultural distinctions inherent in the idea of the North/South divide – that Midlanders are able to take a more nuanced view of life's little complexities. It is, if you like, a mark of our civilisation. And that means I'm proud to come from a scab – or, if you wanted to make it sound more romantic, you might instead say an outlaw – town.

TO MELTON MOWBRAY

*A bit of crust and jelly, Thomas Cook and crook-back Dick,
and the call of the Shires*

'Shut yer clack, Denis!'

Mum's in a grump. Dad and I are waiting for her in the car but she's resisting all our attempts to hurry her along. In fact, she's now decided that she doesn't want to come to Leicestershire with us at all as she'd rather go into Mansfield with her friend Joan, or 'Scooter Girl' as my father calls her. (Joan is a seasoned member of the Mansfield mobility scooter club.)

After much persuasion the Joan project is dropped – her friend threads her scooter in and out of pedestrian traffic with such dizzying virtuosity that she leaves her shopping companions in a spin, so it's a relief not to have to go with her, my mother eventually decides – and we are able to set off. In the car, my parents are up front bickering merrily, while I'm strapped in behind them feeling vaguely nauseous in the back: it's just like being a boy again.

We had been tempted to begin our tour of Leicestershire by heading south-west to the extravagantly named Ashby-de-la-Zouch, with its castle ruins and celebrated four-storey Hastings Tower. Afterwards we might have gone on to nearby Breedon-on-the-Hill, with its remarkable views and church, St Mary and St Hardulph. The latter is built on the site of an Iron Age hillfort and contains some splendid (and historically highly enigmatic) Anglo-Saxon carvings. The fact that the friezes look Byzantine in character has given rise to all sorts of academic speculation: did the Emperor Justinian really go on a mini-break to the East Midlands in the year 535 to avoid having potentially fractious talks with the Ostrogoth king Theodahad? I was looking forward to giving that question a bit more consideration but my mother insists that we head south-east to Melton Mowbray instead as she'd like to bring one of the famous local pork pies back for her brother Jimmy.

In addition to Mum, I've brought along another sceptical travelling companion, the *Rough Guide*. Now I know that quality is more important than quantity, but you can tell something about this particular publication's general perspective on England's cultural highlights by the fact that it devotes 368 pages to the South, 231 pages to the North and just 108 to the whole of the Midlands. Leicestershire it dismisses as an 'apparently haphazard mix of the industrial and rural', which I find rather puzzling. After all, what part of the developed world isn't a bit haphazard in appearance? And why 'apparently'? Do the authors think there's some secret power at work in the Leicestershire hierarchy conspiring to make it *look* haphazard, while the effect is actually quite deliberate? If so, we need to be told.

Fortunately Leicestershire itself betrays no such doubts about its purpose or make-up. As you drive out of Nottinghamshire along the A606, the landscape begins to roll sumptuously and a sign at the county border confidently announces that you are entering 'The Heart of Rural England'. Seeing this puts me in mind of my friend Jerry, who grew up in nearby West Bridgford (which is on the Notts side of the border) and who's always talked enthusiastically about the natural beauty of this part of the Midlands, which he calls 'the Shires', a term you rarely hear these days. A glance is enough to confirm that the local landscape has little in common with the 'Industrial, built-up, heavily populated, busy, no country-side' East Midland stereotype reported in that tourist-board survey.

I ask my parents about 'the Shires', but they laugh so hard at the mere mention of Jerry and West Bridgford, whose affluent inhabitants were apparently a source of much mirth (and envy) when they were growing up, that they forget to answer.

'Bread-and-Lard Island, we used to call West Bridgford,' my dad says. 'A place of unimaginable, mythic luxury to a simple Sutton lad like me.'

'The houses there all had net curtains and a phone in the window,' says my mother, ever the suspicious Blidworth girl. 'The phones weren't actually connected, mind. It was all for show.'

Our route skirts the Vale of Belvoir, which fully merits its name (*Belvoir* means 'beautiful view'), before finally leading us into Melton Mowbray, the self-styled 'Rural Capital of Food', home to both the classic English pork pie and Stilton cheese. The latter may take its name from a village in Cambridgeshire, eighty miles north of London, where it was marketed as a local speciality to travellers on the Great North Road, but it has never actually been produced there: Stilton is a strictly Midland phenomenon, and there's a Certification Trade Mark to prove it, so don't you try making your own at home and passing it off as authentic Stilton. It's just a shame that the name doesn't underline its geographical rootedness: Yorkshire pudding says so much about the values of the

North; a rebranded Stilton could do the same for the Midlands. As for pork pie, the distinctive Melton Mowbray variety was accorded Protected Geographical Indication status by the European Union in 2008. It turns out the EU is good for something after all.

* * *

I don't know which is more terrifying: my mother in her default nothing-impresses-me mode, or (much less common) in her making-an-effort, now-isn't-that-fascinating? guise. After we park up in Melton, she suddenly switches to the latter (is it the sight of a startlingly large portrait of grinning, perma-tanned Tory MP Alan Duncan in the window of the Rutland and Melton Conservative Association that's effected this change of mood?) and stops short as we round a corner into the pedestrianised market area.

'What's this?' she asks, looking up and preparing to be dazzled.

'It's a Lloyds TSB, Mum.'

'Well, it looks really *nice*, I must say.'

'Put your specs on, Kath, for god's sake,' my father says, before adding darkly: 'Remember what happened last time.'

You don't have to pretend to be impressed by Melton Mowbray – it *is* impressive. In the first place, it's handsome. There's a lovely 1930s polychrome Art Deco cinema, the Regal, and a magnificent parish church, St Mary's, whose scrubbed limestone tower dominates the surrounding landscape. And though the streets are largely peopled by senior citizens on the day I visit – I've brought two of my own along just in case more are needed to make up the numbers – this is a town with a strong pulse. Melton appears to be defying the high-street meltdown that's affecting the rest of the country. Its markets are legion: beyond the gleefully spreading street market that dominates the town centre, there are cattle, farmers', antique, and fur and feather markets too. And that's just Tuesdays.

'Ye Olde Pork Pie Shoppe' is obviously a major attraction – signposts insistently direct you towards it – but there's a lot more to the culinary charms of Melton than a bit of pig wrapped in crust and jelly. Why, there's such an abundance of butchers, cheese shops and fishmongers, all seemingly thriving in the deep shadow of the huge Morrisons that lurks at the bottom of Sherrard Street, this could almost be France. Though the tempo of life is unhurried and there's a definite accent on the more traditional aspects of life, there are signs of contemporaneity too: a speciality Polish food store suggests that immigration is making its mark, while boutiques offering beauty treatments and spray tans (much frequented by Alan Duncan, judging by his skin tone in that huge portrait) point to a more youthful town presence.

We wander out towards the edge of town, past the British Legion and Conservative Club to the Melton Carnegie Museum. This contains tidy, informative displays about various aspects of local life, not least Melton's status as the 'Rural Capital of Food': heritage and food and 'country living' events draw over a million tourists to the area annually. But the most revealing display relates to the long history of fox hunting in the region. It turns out it's no coincidence that those 'Heart of Rural England' signs that greet you at the county border bear images of foxes. The earliest known fox hunt using hounds may have taken place in Norfolk, and Wikipedia might tell you that the oldest formal hunt is probably the Bilsdale – which is in Yorkshire, *naturally* – but fox hunting in the form we know it today really developed in fashionable Leicestershire in the eighteenth century. Hugo Meynell, the father of the modern sport, lived locally. As master of the Quorn, he developed the idea of 'hunting to a system' and helped to breed a new species of hound, which could chase harder and smell more keenly, encouraging the use of thoroughbred stallions that could charge faster and jump the hedges of the newly enclosed fields more reliably. As a result of these revolutionary innovations, hunts began to gather later in the day – previously they had been obliged to go out early, when foxes would still be digesting their food, to have half a chance of actually catching one – and so started to develop much greater social allure.

Melton was the new leisure activity's most fashionable centre. As John Otho Paget wrote in his *Memories of the Shires* at the beginning of the last century: 'Melton is the fox-hunter's Mecca, and he should make his pilgrimage there before he dies. Other parts of England have their bits of good country, but nowhere else is there a centre surrounded by glorious hunting ground.' Writing at about the same time, T.F. Dale noted: 'A man who has money and some well-mannered horses can, even if he is not an enthusiast about hunting, have a capital time at Melton. He ought never to be bored; he ought to eat well and sleep well and to be sufficiently amused … [Mr Cecil Forester helped make it] the chief hunting centre of England; and from that day to this there has been a steady flow of fashion and wealth to it.' By the early 1800s, the town had stabling for five hundred horses and was the meeting point for several of the biggest hunts, including the Quorn, Belvoir and Cottesmore. Even the fox-hunter's distinctive scarlet evening coat was popularised here. Like me, you don't have to have a love of fox hunting and its lore to appreciate the implications of this snippet of history. Like the signs say, this – Leicestershire and the Midland Shires, not the Home Counties, not the North Country – really is the Heart of Rural England. Creeping industrialisation may have obscured its centrality in the twentieth century ('It has been said that the day of Melton is passing, that the town has been invaded by manufactories,' Dale warned in 1903) but in the post-industrial age the glory of the East Midland landscape is beginning to reassert itself. You don't have to ride a horse or want to hunt foxes to appreciate it. Come and see for yourself.

While I'm looking at the museum displays, my mother does her usual thing of befriending loitering teens. She wanders over to the internet access points, where a couple of adolescents – one male, one female – are merrily Facebooking. The girl is happy to chat to her and boasts that she has 343 online Friends, but the furtive-looking boy stays schtum and hastily closes a window on his computer screen. While this scene unfolds, I approach the lady at reception – whom my mother has proudly told that her son is writing a book about the Midlands – to ask her about the origins of the phrase 'painting the town red'. It's regularly ascribed to an incident that took place in Melton on 6 April 1837, when the Marquess of Waterford and his hunting pals – no doubt high on pork pie, a favourite foodstuff with the horse-and-hound fraternity – went on a 'spree', daubing the buildings on the high street with red paint. The 'Mad Marquess' was a former Oxford undergrad; it sounds as though he may have been a Bullingdon man too. On this occasion he got comeuppance of a sort: he and his fellow rioters were all fined £100 at Derby Assizes.

Not that such demonstrations of animal spirits were unusual in Melton at the time, a fact that Paget puts down to the absence of women:

At the beginning of the [nineteenth] century Melton was rapidly becoming a fashionable hunting centre, and the men who assembled there were the cream of hard riders from other counties, but for several years previous to that date a few sportsmen had made the town their headquarters. In these early days, and for some years

later, only bachelors visited Melton, and the married man left his
wife at home. This will account for the mad pranks which history
tells us were frequently played after dinner by the hunting men,
such as painting signs, wrenching knockers and other wild freaks.

I ask the lady in the museum whether any of Waterford's daubs
are still visible and she says that red traces were allegedly found
when the sign on the White Swan was taken down for cleaning in
the 1980s. They've all gone now unfortunately. Still, the Marquess's
paint job appears to have survived for a century and a half before
finally being scrubbed away – not bad for an *ad hoc* afternoon's
work.

The Carnegie Melton is an evocative little museum with
the ability to do that splendid thing – transform the way you
perceive your surroundings. After spending a happy half-hour or
so under its roof, rather than pensioners sniffing out a bargain,
you re-emerge to be met with the spectacle of Napoleonic War-era
dukes, financiers and industrialists cantering through the Melton
streets on their mounts, and the sound of Waterford and his pals
carousing at a local pub and planning another spree. I do anyhow,
but perhaps I'm just funny that way.

We head back into town via St Mary's, an architectural gem
whose splendid tower, described by one early hunt commentator
as 'a grateful sight to a returning sportsman on a beaten horse',
probably served as a finishing post in the early steeplechases that
'thrusters' attracted by the local hunting rode in here. (The name
'steeplechase' is derived from the fact that a church steeple or tower
usually served as the finishing line.) One of the great heroes of
English classical music, Sir Malcolm Sargent, began his career at
St Mary's as choirmaster and organist in the period around World
War I. His celebrated productions of Gilbert and Sullivan operas

regularly attracted the Prince of Wales as a spectator during the latter's hunting trips to the county. In keeping with its location in the 'Rural Capital of Food', the church now hosts the annual British Pie Festival – it's not just pork pies that are accepted for consideration either, but any pie answering to the broader defini- tion of 'a filling totally encased in pastry' – as well as a Christmas Tree Festival, when the nave suddenly becomes a dense forest of trees, creatively decorated to reflect themes from recycling (made of carrier bags) to cleaning supplies (hung with hygiene hair nets rather than tinsel and baubles).

We finally surrender to the inevitable and pay a visit to Dickinson & Morris's Ye Olde Pork Pie Shoppe on Nottingham Street. After all the fanfare and build-up, I'm slightly disappointed by what we find. Not because I'm one of the 'many' who, according to my truculent friend the *Rough Guide*, 'find the pie's appeal unac- countable'. Quite the opposite. But I had begun to imagine the pork-pie equivalent of London toy emporium Hamleys – five floors rammed with every possible variety of pie: flying ones, Playmobil and Scalextric ones, online multiplayer video-gaming ones – when in fact YOPPS only offers a modest selection, sanely counterbal- anced by a range of sausages, breads and Hunt Cake (a rich cake spiced with Jamaican rum, also favoured by hunters). Perhaps my hopes were unreasonable: even Meltonians can't be expected to live by pork pie alone. And enthusiasts will find some compensation in the fact that you can book a Pork Pie Demonstration or arrange to attend a Make & Bake Experience, and there's a sign on the wall revealing the secrets behind a great pork pie: the meat should be fresh and not cured, and chopped rather than minced or pureed; preservatives are strictly *verboten*, only natural bone stock jelly will do and seasoning with salt and white pepper is highly recom- mended; and the baking should be carried out without the use of a supporting hoop or tin so as to produce the classic rounded, gently bow-sided Melton Mowbray pie shape. So now you know.

* * *

I'm sitting in the front of the car now. Mum much prefers the angle of attack offered by the back seat and has positioned herself behind my father, ready for her next assault.

'I think your hair's returning on the top of your head, Robbie,' she says, still unable to accept the fact that her little boy has gone bald.

We take the A607 and proceed pleasantly through Frisby-on-the-Wreake and Queniborough but the landscape is gradually turning more suburban. 'Anybody who can do anything in Leicester but make a jumper has got to be a genius,' Brian Clough once said by way of tribute to former Forest player Martin O'Neill, who as a manager brought unwonted success to Leicester City FC in the late Nineties. Well, my father's pretty smart but basically what he used to do in Leicester was make jumpers. The purpose of our trip to the city today is to revisit some of the sites where he worked.

Finding them isn't proving easy, however. We pick up signs for the National Space Centre, a brilliant, heavily interactive museum which happens to contain the only Soyuz spacecraft in Western Europe, and then for the Golden Mile, one of the most vibrant Indian shopping districts in the country, which offers a dynamic mixture of restaurants, jewellers and clothing stores. Some say, rather prosaically, that this stretch of the Belgrave Road got its nickname because it used to have more than its fair share of amber traffic lights, but the spectacular annual Diwali, or Hindu Festival of Light, celebrations probably offer a more satisfactory explanation. (Over 25 per cent of the city's population is Indian in origin.)

'I don't recognise a bloody thing,' Dad says encouragingly.

'They used to call Leicester the wealthiest city in Europe,' says Mum, ignoring Dad.

'The wealthiest in *Britain*,' corrects Dad, simultaneously executing an obviously wrong turn away from the city centre.

Mum's having none of it. '*Europe*. We always said Nottingham was a big town whereas Leicester was a city. In Nottingham we'd got the Lace Market and a good red-light district,' my mother chuckles (I think for a moment that she's going to roll out her favourite 'Thor but thatithfied' joke – but no, we're spared this time), 'but Leicester had the De Montfort Hall. It was better for entertainment. It had bigger factories and bigger concert halls.'

We drive past a huge John Lewis, and my father briefly thinks he knows where we are. 'There used to be the most fantastic factories around here. A lot of these were knitting units. They all look like they've been converted into flats now.'

He's right. As recently as the mid-1990s, when my father retired, proud, red-brick Leicester was still dominated by the hosiery and textile industries. As J.B. Priestley wrote in the early 1930s in his bestselling travelogue *An English Journey*: 'Leicester has been a hosiery town these last three hundred years. Since the Industrial Revolution, it has specialised in worsted hosiery, for which the Leicestershire long wools are very suitable.' In order to capture the spirit of the city, the most appropriate thing Priestley could think of doing was to visit three Wolsey knitwear factories – after all, Wolsey 'has factories all over the town'. No longer. After two centuries' dominance of the global market (including supplying underwear to Scott of the Antarctic), Wolsey has recently been relaunched as a much-scaled-down 'luxury British heritage brand', while the historic Wolsey Building – bearing a mosaic of the English cardinal who gave his name to the company – has just been turned into care flats. Other former Wolsey production units lie in a state of mournful dereliction.

If the pipe-sucking Priestley, a proud Yorkshireman who is – surprise, surprise – generally briskly dismissive of the Midlands in his book,[1] were to return to the city today, what he'd surely notice first is the student presence. Instead of three Wolsey factories, he might now spend an afternoon casting his Northern-patrician eye over three world-renowned institutes of higher education: the University of Leicester, the De Montfort University and (a dozen miles down the road) the University of Loughborough. There's a high density of hard-working grey matter in this part of Leicestershire; the student presence also ensures that there's a lively nightlife too.

'I haven't got a bloody clue where we are again,' Dad sighs. Ring roads, pedestrianisation and one-way systems have contrived to render a driver's basic directional sense almost useless; a disadvantage almost. You may know for sure that what you're looking for is off to your left – you can actually see it! – but these days you probably need to steer a hard right to get there.

'I never liked Leicester people,' my mother pipes up gaily from the back of the car. 'They were avaricious to an extraordinary degree. The hosiery industry made them rich and horrible. When we lived in Godalming in Surrey briefly in the 1960s, there was a young man there who had worked in Leicester but he'd come home

---

[1] For instance, Priestley dismisses the way people speak in Nottingham as having 'the harsh quality of the Northern accent without the leavening and salt of rich dialect'. They were insufficiently Northern to count, in other words. By the by, it's astonishing that he could have declared Nottinghamshire lacking in local patois in the immediate aftermath of the publication of D.H. Lawrence's *Lady Chatterley's Lover*, which contains some of the richest dialect in the English language. And how about 'Arkattit'?

because he found the people so unfriendly. He said he could earn three times as much in Leicester as he could in the South, but it wasn't worth it. You had to belong to get on in Leicester.'

My father concurs: 'They were cliquey.' (He pronounces it 'clicky'.)

'Yes,' agrees my mother, 'very cliquey.' (She pronounces it 'clicky' too.)

At this moment of unwonted harmony between my parents, I notice that we are driving past Leicester train station.

'Stop!' I shout, and my father executes an impressive emergency stop, endangering the lives of literally dozens of other drivers and pedestrians in the process.

'What is it? What's the matter?' he half-screams.

'Oh, I just wanted to take a look at the statue of Thomas Cook,' I say. 'It's outside the station here.'

'You …' he begins, wagging a fatherly finger in my direction, but I've jumped out of the car before he can complete his phrase.

Cook is one of Leicester's most famous sons. Midlanders have always been great innovators in matters of travel – perhaps it's because people always seem to want to pass through the region as quickly as possible that we've specialised in developing new, ever faster methods of locomotion to help them achieve their goal. Cook's career as a pioneer of modern tourism began at the railway station here, though it wasn't exactly leisure that was on the then-cabinetmaker's mind when he arranged for some 540 temperance activists to be carried by train to a rally in nearby Loughborough. Raised a Baptist, Cook was a fervent campaigner against the evils of alcohol and, as he walked by the newly opened station in the summer of 1841, 'the thought suddenly flashed across my mind as to the practicability of employing the great powers of railways and locomotion for the furtherance of this social

71

reform'. The canny Cook was quick to see the wider commercial opportunities offered by the newfangled train network, however, and struck a deal with the Midland Counties Railways, which had just come into existence to carry coal and other necessaries to the rapidly industrialising region. As he later noted, 'thus was struck the keynote of my excursions, and the social idea grew upon me'. By the 1850s Cook's travel agency was transporting visitors in their thousands across the Channel to gawp at the wonders on display in the Paris Exhibition. Shortly afterwards it had expanded its activities as far as the Holy Land, and by the 1880s it had its own fleet of steamers on the Nile.

The statue of Thomas Cook was unveiled in 1991, to mark the 150th anniversary of that first historic Leicester-to-Loughborough anti-booze cruise, and shows the great pioneer of modern tourism appropriately laden with luggage. The sculptor, James Butler, is responsible for several other statues of iconic Leicester figures. First, there's *The Seamstress*, located outside the City Rooms, which pays tribute to the historic centrality of the hosiery industry to Leicester life. Then, in Castle Gardens, there's a bronze likeness of Richard III, who spent his last night on earth in the city in 1485 before being killed nearby at the Battle of Bosworth. His body was then brought back to Leicester to be laid to rest – where exactly no one was sure until a skeleton was recently recovered from underneath a city-centre car park. Subsequent DNA tests identifying the remains as those of King Richard sparked a controversy with strong echoes of the kerfuffle over Robin Hood's mythical bones. A group identifying itself as the Richard III Foundation called for the remains of 'Richard, our hero and martyr, to be brought home to the city that he loved [York], and where he is still loved to this day'. 'York was Richard's city,' declared Andy Smith on behalf of the foundation. 'It is where he belongs, and it is only right that this great Lord of the North should return home to Yorkshire after more than five hundred years' enforced absence.' The *Guardian* was quick to report the story 'of the growing enthusiasm for the "vilified Yorkshireman" to return home' – no doubt Richard, as a true son of 'God's own county', insisted on eating his dinner at midday, even if, as one linguistic expert amusingly pointed out, the available evidence suggests that he probably spoke with a Brummie accent.

Actually Leicester is an ideal final resting place for Richard, the great outsider king of English history. Under pressure from his Southern Tudor paymasters, Shakespeare portrayed the last Plantagenet as a physically deformed monster with a hunchback, an out-and-out villain who had his princely nephews done in and generally rejoiced in the misfortune of others. But other historical sources suggest that Richard wasn't like that at all. Butler's statue in Leicester attempts to set the record straight by picturing Richard as a youthful, attractive, reforming king who was keen to do the ordinary folk a bit of good – very Robin Hood, in fact, far removed in spirit from the 'Yorkshireman's Creed'. Rest assured: Richard's bones are perfectly at home in the Midlands.

* * *

Once I'm back in the car, we drive around for another frustrating half-hour until my father suddenly lets out a cry of delight: 'There it is! That's Corah's!' He points to a vast, imposing red-brick building that looks equal parts castle (my father's word) and prison (mine). The signage on the front announces that it's now occupied by H.M. Hosiery, manufacturers of 'high-performance socks', although it looks as though they're only using the bottom floor.

'I started working here in 1959,' my father coos delightedly, home at last. 'I was in quality control. This was at a time when pretty much all the clothes that people in this country had access to were made in Britain. There were, I don't know, five, six, maybe even eight thousand employees, mostly women, and it was arranged in units of two lines of about forty machines each, with a conveyor down the middle. The work would come down in bags and the girls would take it off the conveyor to do their bit.

'A lot of the work we did was for Marks and Spencer. At that time almost everything M&S sold bore their own label: St Michael. Corah's were the only manufacturers who were allowed to use their own label on garments for M&S – we were St Margaret,' he says with obvious pride.

We drive on. We want to find the factory where my father worked when he returned to Leicester in the late 1970s but we quickly lose our way again. At last, the sight of St Margaret's Bus Station throws us a lifeline. A few minutes later we're parking up in Langton Street.

'This was the most magnificent knitting factory you've ever seen in your life,' Dad declares euphorically. We get out to investigate but the building is no longer occupied by manufacturing units. In fact, it appears to have been converted for use as a police station. None of us has ever done anything particularly criminal, but the discovery causes us to slink away guiltily.

Back in the car, we look for signs for the motorway to head north back to Mansfield. 'I think this will take us out across what we used to call Frog Island,' my father says in another sudden access of enthusiasm. 'God knows why it was called that. It used to be all textile dyeing and finishing works. The canal runs behind it, and the river's there, and they used to use water from both in the dye baths. Most of the hosiery companies have gone, so presumably most of the dye works have too.'

They have indeed, we soon discover, to be replaced by what looks like a fairly lively music and arts scene.

'I'll tell you what, Denis,' my mother says, rousing herself to perform one of her famous volte-faces. 'From what I've seen this afternoon Leicester has improved a lot. It's actually quite nice now.'

A silence falls in the car as two ideas battle for dominance: my father's nostalgia for a vanished industrial world and my mother's sense that the demise of mass-manufacturing might, on a spiritual level at any rate, have been good for Leicester.

'The textile industry remained reasonably buoyant into the Eighties,' my father picks up again. 'But the Mansfield Hosiery Mills execs had started searching for new sites in Indonesia, the Philippines, Sri Lanka. They were looking for "busy fingers" – that was the expression they used – people who would do more, faster, for less money. The first factory we had was in Morocco, I think. Most of the work on the garments was done there, then they were brought over to England for the final examination and labelling and boxing. The idea was that using these Third World sites would garner a bigger profit for us as a company, but of course it made a lot of our workers redundant, and anyway M&S were wise to what we were doing and found their own "busy fingers" in the same countries. And that was the beginning of the end for the company.

'It seemed very shocking at the time. But now you can see it was part of a much broader shift – the start of globalisation really. It had become so easy to ship goods around the world. It was that moment of transition, when Britain went from being a place where we mass-manufactured things to one where we mostly manufactured money – the rise of the City. We'd seen the signs a few years before when venture capitalists began buying up reasonably successful manufacturing groups, stripping out the most valuable bits and then selling off the premises. "But what is it you actually *make*?" journalists would ask this new breed of asset strippers, and they'd reply, "Why, money of course!" No one bats an eye at that sort of thing now but it felt outrageous back then.' And so it was that the industrial Leicester my father knew – and the industrial Leicester J.B. Priestley had known before him – began to recede into history.

We're approaching the motorway now, and my mother interrupts my father's flow to tell him to stop talking so much and concentrate on the road instead. He responds sharply that he's perfectly capable of having a conversation and steering a car at the same time, thank you very much, and promptly takes a wrong turn onto the southbound carriage of the M1. Mum sighs, Dad curses and we speed off away from Mansfield, in the direction of London.

* * *

While Mum is preparing dinner – a dish involving Melton Mowbray pork pie, naturally, though Stilton is excluded since the very sight of blue cheese causes her to gag – I make a couple of phone calls.

First I speak to Jerry, my friend from 'Bread-and-Lard Island', to tell him about our visit to his beloved Shires.

'You didn't drive through Flawford, did you?' he inquires, his tone immediately wistful.

We didn't, I tell him truthfully. He sighs. In the graveyard by the deconsecrated Saxon church at Flawford is where Jerry – who is still in his forties and in excellent health – would like to be buried. Since he lives in London at the moment, he rarely gets to see his desired final resting place.

I ask him about the term 'the Shires'.

'It's a vague term, although a very ancient one,' he explains.

'For me, they're South Derbyshire, most of Leicestershire, South Nottinghamshire and Northamptonshire, stretching over into Lincolnshire. As a boy, I had a very strong sense of the Shires. In West Bridgford you're right on the edge of the Nottinghamshire wolds, which roll into the Vale of Belvoir. I spent a lot of time out and about on my bike, and that was a stronger ambient culture or defining feature of the Midlands for me than north of the Trent, where everything got sucked into the North. The countryside around there still felt quite feudal. You had lots of grand houses around you. There's also a certain homogeneity about the topography of the Shires. A lot of them are wolds – open, rolling countryside – and they're rich, settled agricultural land. Hunting is still part of the identity around there.'

I've known Jerry for a long time but, despite his deep love and knowledge of the East Midland landscape, I've never heard him proselytising on the subject. You wouldn't be able to spend an hour in the company of a Yorkshireman with a similar feel for his *terroir* without hearing all about the magic of the moors, but Jerry has to be positively goaded into singing the praises of the Shires. Why is that?

'I don't know. Put it down to my natural East Midland reserve if you like,' he laughs. 'It's true of everything, though, isn't it? Take the example of something I'm particularly interested in: monastic settlements. Everyone now thinks of Rievaulx and Jervaulx in Yorkshire – the propaganda tells you that's where the real action was – but actually the densest area of Benedictine monasteries is where I lived as a boy. Ancient churches and sites of monastic settlements are peppered across the Midlands, and much of monastic and ecclesiastical history revolves around the Midlands. But because the landscape's more vivid and the population's frankly just more gobby, Northumbria and Yorkshire have nicked the limelight.

'I've always been a walker and when I was a young man I was attracted to the most dramatic landscapes, so anywhere but the Midlands basically. But as I've got older that's changed. There's a subtlety and a richness about the Midlands that few stop to notice. There's a lyricism about the rolling farmland in what some people – sneeringly or otherwise – call the Heart of England that is quintessentially English. It isn't twee and it's not that well known, and because it's not been designated a "beauty spot" it's retained a certain amount of naturalness. You don't feel you're going to be joining a queue at the stile to get over the next fence. There's a kind of privacy and an intimacy about it that I like. Why would I want to spoil that by talking it up so that everyone else starts taking their holidays there? I don't want to have to queue!'

Good old Jerry. His nonchalance sometimes reminds me of the great Midland politician Stanley Baldwin, who declared shortly before becoming prime minister for the first time – he went on to serve in that post under three different monarchs, the only British PM to have done so – that his dearest wish was to retire to his native Worcestershire 'to read the books I want to read, to live a decent life and keep pigs'. It's the sort of attitude that shows a real *savoir vivre*, but I can't afford to be infected by the characteristic regional spirit of languid contentment if I'm going to demonstrate the fundamental drive and dynamism of the Midlands, the 'Bang in the Middle' of English life. Unyielding clarity of vision and a firm persuasive purposefulness are what are required to put this material over properly.

I call my wife to practise the aforesaid unyielding clarity of vision and firm persuasive purposefulness as I tell her about the staggering things I've discovered today. I babble on enthusiastically for half an hour or so before pausing for breath.

'Impressive, eh?' I ask.

'Pullovers, pork pies and a so-called "sport" that's now illegal,' she summarises with mildly ungenerous (but not entirely unreasonable) Gallic precision. 'Didn't you say your discoveries were going to be staggering?'

Oh.

I'm obviously not selling this stuff very well. But you wait, reader. What's coming *is* going to be staggering. That's a promise.

TO GRANTHAM

*The North/South divide, cultural backwaters and distant
seawaters, and the MT Question*

I once proposed a Midland-centric programme idea to the BBC.
Thanks but no thanks, came the response: as a subject, I was
told, the Midlands was simply too 'regional' to merit coverage
on a national network. Interestingly, at the same time BBC4 was
screening a season of programmes entitled 'Planet North'. The
Midlands is a mere region, but the North is a whole other planet!

Actually, according to Professor Danny Dorling, who created an
influential map separating England strictly into North and South,
the Midlands isn't *even* a region. 'The country is best typified as
being divided regionally between the north and the south. Ideas
of a midlands region add more confusion than light,' the professor's SASI (not to be confused with the Stasi) group opines on its
website. You won't be surprised to hear that the Midlands-denying
SASI (the acronym stands for Social and Spatial Inequalities) is

based at the University of Sheffield (in the North), or that Dorling's map was created for an exhibition at the Lowry in Salford (also in the North). According to Wikipedia, the professor was born in Oxford (the South) and went to university in Newcastle (the North). All in all, it's no surprise he finds the Midlands dispensable.

The BBC – in common with pretty much every national newspaper and media outlet – can't resist the idea of the North/South divide: it likes it so much, in fact, it forcibly moved a sizeable portion of its programming to Salford to turn itself into a classic North/South operation. The Corporation was obviously very taken with Dorling's map – it commissioned writer Ian Marchant to make a two-part radio programme about it. In *North and South: Across the Great Divide*, the presenter travels along the prof's dividing line – plotted using statistical data relating to health, unemployment, house prices, voting patterns etc – to canvass local opinion. The usual clichés are aired: the North represents 'warmth' and 'friendliness' whereas the South is synonymous with 'cold-hearted high-handedness'; the North is about 'sharing', the South 'money, privilege', etc. In Louth, Marchant asks random punters whether they think they are in the North or the South. When someone has the temerity to propose that they might actually be in the Midlands, the suggestion is ignored – the 'M' word clearly isn't considered appropriate language. Necessarily: as soon as you allow mention of the existence of the Midlands, the idea of the North/South divide begins to lose its power – as does the idea of the North, come to think of it, the great English 'Other', radical outrider to the normative South.

How radical or 'Other' is the North these days, in fact? To judge by Paul Morley's *The North (and Almost Everything in It)* (2013), very. The book begins in fuzzily impressionistic, poetic vein ('Here is the north, up here, where all things start … the north, at the top of the page, black marks on a white void, distant and remote, not quite sure what will happen next') – a good way to conceal a lack of genuine substance, you might feel – and includes a litany of resonant quotes from the usual Northern-trademark cultural idols (Morrissey: 'You're southern – you wouldn't understand. When you're northern, you're northern for ever'; Ian Brown: 'The north is not where you are, it's where you're at'). If you like fine-sounding pieces of nothing, you won't be disappointed.

But there's a problem when Morley tries to insist on the North's outsider status, its 'difference', its 'myriad forms of otherness'. It's a classic, oft-repeated trope, of course, but when you stop to think about it, hasn't that last word – 'otherness' – become rather nonsensical in relation to the North? The 'other' (or 'Other') is the label that mainstream society tends to apply to those qualities or characteristics that don't fit in with its favoured self-definition or that it wants to exclude from its idea of itself. Now, if it was once true that the North played fractious, rebellious Other to the English South's more staid, normative Self, that's surely no longer the case now. English popular culture – soap operas, football, music – is dominated by the North. Nothing better defines mainstream English attitudes than the BBC, and a large part of the BBC's output is now being produced in the North. Almost all of the presenters on 6 Music are distinctively Northern, as are quite a lot of the voices on Radio 3 if you tune in for the live broadcasts in the evening. As if to underline quite how Establishment the North has become, before it had even been published, Morley's celebration of the North was given the Book of the Week slot on Radio 4. Seriously, how much more *mainstream* can you get? The pretence of its Otherness is the myth by which the North lives, but you can't be a rebellious outsider when you're simultaneously so unquestioningly celebrated by the Establishment. Isn't the latter the definition of an *Insider*, in fact?

However illusory they may be, binary oppositions of the North/South kind dominate geopolitical thinking, and not just in England. The US is usually configured in terms of a culture clash between either North and South (Yankees versus Confederates) or East and West (New York versus California): the vast Midwest and the no-man's-land beyond, patronisingly portrayed as full of provincial bumpkins with straw between their teeth, are usually treated with mistrust and/or disdain. When the London magazine *Time Out* – which regularly publishes a North versus South London issue – ran a travel piece about Germany, it was headlined 'Nord und Sud'. 'There are still two Germanys,' announced the introduction. While the Iron Curtain divided Europe, those two Germanys were East and West; now, the article said, Germany was divided between North and South (a division with deep historical roots). But what about the centre? Isn't that just as German? Why is the middle so rarely granted an independent existence?

Structuralists – an influential group of theorists who included among their ranks the great twentieth-century French anthropologist Claude Lévi-Strauss – draw attention to the ubiquity of binary oppositions in human thinking generally: male and female, young and old, war and peace, love and hate, optimism and pessimism, fish and chips. (Did you spot that that last pairing doesn't really belong in this list?) Lévi-Strauss and company don't take such black-and-white divisions lightly: for them, they are the very stuff of life, part of the 'deep' structure of human existence. Without such paired opposites, or antonyms, we apparently struggle to organise our ideas about the world satisfactorily. But what's the opposite of the Midlands? There's the rub: it has no obvious binary opposite. Binary thinking, you could say, has reduced the Midlands to the status of a mere slash sign by so insistently imaging the country in terms of a North/South divide. Hence the ease with which the likes of Professor Dorling can wipe the Midlands from the map altogether. And hence the unthinking way in which pivotal historical events such as the 1980s miners' strike can be misunderstood as expressions of the North/South divide.

There is an upside to this, however. The thing about paired opposites is that they can't do without one another: they're co-dependent. What would the word 'big' signify if we didn't also have the word 'little'? Would we value peace without knowing about war? What good would fish be without chips? And where would firebrand Northerners be without cosy, establishmentarian Southerners? Identity-less, that's where. We Midlanders by contrast stand proudly alone, our identity untainted by contamination with the values of an Other. Now all we need to do is work out what that identity is and we'll be home free.

* * *

Standing beside a huge Crimean War cannon in Retford in Nottinghamshire, I suddenly have the feeling I'm not in the Midlands any more, or the twenty-first century for that matter. The sensation of space-time travel doesn't last long: the church outside which the big gun stands, St Swithun's, is very English Perpendicular in appearance, and the air is thick with contemporary car-exhaust fumes. But the cannon, captured by British troops at the siege of Sevastopol in 1854–55, isn't the only detail that speaks of more far-flung climes. A few miles down the road there's a small, modern, seemingly featureless settlement called Spion Kop – or 'Spy Hill' – that was named for a battle in the Second Boer War. Even in the middle of the Midlands, in the heart of nowhere, you're not insulated from the outside world. If you want to do a global tour of important nineteenth-century battle sites but can't afford the time or airfare, spend a day or two in Retford and its environs instead. It's the next-best thing.

The renowned architectural historian Nikolaus Pevsner didn't much care for Retford, dubbing it 'a singularly unattractive town'. Bill Bryson enjoyed his visit a little more but still felt the need to declare that he didn't want to spend his holidays here – as if anyone had asked him to! Retford doesn't exactly pretend to holiday-destination status. It's dotted with handsome Georgian town houses, and there's still an air of gentility – or at least of remembered gentility – about the place. The Drawing Room and Opera Tea Rooms on the market square tap into this vibe. But it's all very English-provincial, with the exception of that sudden burst of Crimean War exoticism in Cannon Square.

So why am I here? For no better reason than it's on my itinerary of places to visit on the Great North Road, the vantage point from which most travellers would have experienced the great Midland plain as they made their way up and down the country in bygone centuries. The Great North Road took shape in the early-modern period as increasing numbers of coaches laden with letters and parcels sped on their way between London and York and then on to Edinburgh. The coaches' cargo wasn't just postal, of course, but extended to humans too. As a result of this growing number of travellers, a network of high-quality inns developed at the principal staging posts along the route. (The Bell Inn in Stilton, Cambridgeshire was one such. It was from here that blue-veined Melton Mowbray cheese was launched to national fame.)

The Great North Road was – comparatively – fast. In the 'Golden Age of Coaching', just prior to the arrival of the railways in the 1840s, the journey from London to York (and vice versa) could be made in under twenty hours. A century earlier, everyone's favourite murdering highwayman, Dick Turpin, is said to have made the journey in just fifteen hours astride Black Bess – the road surface was probably rather better then than it is today. The journey along the Great North Road is rich in romantic associations. It was at the foot of the road, just as he was about to head home to Gloucester, that Midland pauper Dick Whittington heard Bow Bells ringing and decided to turn again, so destining himself to become Lord Mayor of London.

As coach and horse were replaced by the motorcar and mechanical horse power, the Great North Road became the A1, which remained the main artery for traffic travelling up and down the country until the opening of the M1 in the 1950s. For the sake of speed and directness, many of the towns and great coaching inns associated with the old road were bypassed by this new incarnation, so draining much of the commercial and cultural life out of previously thriving towns such as Retford.

Unsurprisingly, the Great North Road also provided prime locations for Eng. lit.'s greatest picaresque novel, Charles Dickens's *The Pickwick Papers* (1836), not to mention J.B. Priestley's lesser picaresque epic *The Good Companions*, which was nonetheless a huge success when it was first published in 1929. The Priestley novel relates the adventures of Northern working man Jess Oakroyd after he is laid off in his native Bruddersford (Bradford) and hits 't'road' in search of exotic adventures 'down South'. Priestley manages to squeeze almost every North/South divide cliché known to man into his account of his hero's dealings. Try the following, which rehearses the classic Northern manliness versus Southern effeminacy trope: 'Mr Oakroyd himself had always regarded with suspicion any person – not counting affected southrons and the like – who showed a readiness to say "Please" and "Thank you", and was genuinely troubled afterwards by the thought that perhaps his travels were already sapping his manly independence.' Big Jessie is a bluff, plain-speaking Northerner; people who aren't like him and who come from further down the country are 'southrons' and that's all there is to it. As Priestley's novel confirms, the Great North Road is a binarist's delight. Its very name tells you that if you're not in the South, you must be in, or on your way to, the North; there's no room for any interloping Midlands here. And yet most of the Great North Road actually lies in the Midlands.

The Great North Road also crops up in a famous passage from George Orwell's *The Lion and the Unicorn* (1941). As one of the most influential commentators on twentieth-century British culture, Orwell did much to give currency to the myths of the industrial North in his *The Road to Wigan Pier* (1937), written on the model of Priestley's *An English Journey* of a few years before. In *The Lion and the Unicorn*, he evokes the diversity of the nation as follows: 'The clatter of clogs in the Lancashire mill towns, the to-and-fro of the lorries on the Great North Road, the queues outside the Labour Exchanges, the rattle of pin-tables in the Soho pubs … all these are not only fragments, but *characteristic* fragments, of the English scene.' From Lancashire, Orwell implies, it's straight down the Great North Road to London. The Midlands is not allowed to offer any '*characteristic* fragments' of 'the English scene' on the way. There's just a bloody big road there; that's all you need to know about the Midlands.

* * *

In fairness, it's not only the idea of the North/South divide and Messrs Priestley and Orwell (although they are key recent figures) that have displaced the Midlands from its place in national history and, consequently, in the national self-image. There is also the small matter of that briny bath in which our island floats. In John

Buchan's much-quoted phrase: 'The sea has formed the English character and the essential England is to be found in those who follow it.' This is a sentiment to be taken with a pinch of (sea) salt, but the fact remains that much of England's history has been determined by its inhabitants' relationship to the ocean. In the early sixteenth century, Henry VIII saw England's future as being on the Seven Seas, at the centre of a great trading empire: Drake's piratical activities in Lima harbour in 1579 offered a foretaste of the imperial adventures that dominate English history across the next centuries. The Midlands, on the other hand, is by definition landlocked – it is literally mid-land – and hence has been largely alienated from this experience: Nottingham, the principal city in the East Midlands, is about as far as you can get in the UK from any coastline. No wonder I was thirty-five years old, and long resident in London, before I learned to swim.

One of the practical consequences of this distance from the sea, at least in centuries gone by, was a lack of cod. 'As for fish, we are an inland town, and indifferently provided for it,' an innkeeper confesses to his London guests in George Farquhar's 1707 Midlands-set stage comedy *The Beaux' Stratagem*. Another – and perhaps more important – cultural consequence is that the Midlands has tended to be viewed as an intellectual backwater. Academic tradition not unreasonably locates the engine for human development at the point where the ocean meets the land. To take one recent expression of this idea: Barry Cunliffe, in his *longue durée* survey of human development *Europe between the Oceans* (2008), writes that it is 'no accident that Europe's first civilization – the culture named by archaeologists as Minoan – began in the Aegean, where the ratio of coast to land was at its greatest… the seashore is a liminal place where unexpected things can happen'. Cultural exchange, voyages of discovery, invasion and migration

– in short, the great motors of change in human history – are all strongly linked to the shoreline. Early human populations favoured coastal lands owing to the increased accessibility of resources there. By contrast, inland regions can give the impression of a kind of eternal unchangingness – a very unfashionable quality these days. Of course, it's never actually been true of the Midlands, which has been at the heart of English innovation throughout history: lacking natural ports, Midlanders with a hunger to create and trade simply invented canals instead.

Still, the Midlands' image would be enhanced greatly in the popular imagination if the area had at least one coastline. (Yes, I do realise that at that point it would no longer be called the 'Midlands' – this is a thought experiment only.) In the first place, the region would no longer be excluded by definition from popular national surveys such as the BBC television series *Coast* and *Britain and the Sea*. It would become more of a holiday destination too. But perhaps it would make Midlanders too blasé about espying the ocean. As the Northants writer H.E. Bates said: 'When you live absolutely in the centre of a country … the sight of the sea on a shining summer's day can only be likened to the sudden sight of the Promised Land.' And we wouldn't want to lose that sense of wonder, would we?

* * *

My next stopping-off point is Newark, another key staging post on the Great North Road which even the churlish *Rough Guide* allows to be an 'amiable' sort of place.

And so it proves. In feel Newark isn't unlike Melton Mowbray – a gentle-paced but still vibrant market town where you sense people are still living the good life: even if it is the good life circa 1958. But if modern Melton has been shaped by pork pies and its horsey heritage, the two factors that have moulded Newark are quite different. The first is its proximity to the River Trent: the town was constructed on the lowest fording point of the Trent and grew up around the river trade, making its citizens wealthy in the pre-railway age. Warehouse and brewery buildings still crowd the river bank, as does a large Waitrose, which provides some sort of socioeconomic barometer for the area's fortunes.

The second is the Civil War, an essentially Midland happening that redefined the national politics and ushered in the modern age. Newark was fiercely royalist in the 1640s, its population swelling to many times its prewar size after it was occupied by troops loyal to King Charles. Three times it was besieged and three times it repelled its Cromwellian foes. Only after the king himself surrendered did the good burghers of Newark finally capitulate. The scars of the fighting in that long campaign are still in evidence, so a nice way to see the town today is to take the 'Civil War Trail', which leads you past the Old White Hart, the lovely timber-framed Civil War Governor's House, now somewhat incongruously a Greggs (what historic building on England's high streets isn't these days?) and out of town to the Queen's Sconce, an earthwork fortification built to defend the town against parliamentary incursions from the north and south. Then there are the picturesque ruins of the medieval castle which stand guard over the river. Today the Victorian landscaped gardens and bandstand are bathed in peaceful autumnal sunshine. All that remains of the original royalist redoubt are the north curtain wall and gatehouse, bombarded by the parliamentarian besiegers and then stripped of facing stone by looters in later centuries, but the location still offers an evocative vantage point over the Trent.

The town's vibrant market square is dominated by the imposing spire of St Mary Magdalene's. Like so many fine English churches,

St Mary Magdalene's is a bastardised blend of successive waves of construction, from Norman through to Tudor, which was given its current internal configuration in the 1850s by Sir George Gilbert Scott, who designed not only the Albert Memorial but also the hotel building at St Pancras Station in London, a Gothic Revival masterpiece. (In a brilliant piece of nineteenth-century branding, when the region was rampant, it was originally named the Midland Grand; after many years' desuetude, it has recently reopened under the new moniker of the Renaissance, which tells you something about the current standing of the Midlands.) St Mary Magdalene's also has its own bit of Civil War heritage. If you circumambulate the exterior with your head raised to the heavens, you'll spot a big hole in the church spire. It was made by a parliamentarian cannonball during the extended sieges of the town.

It's all about cannons today, for some reason.

* * *

I'm just getting back into the car when Elizabeth calls me on my mobile.

'Look,' she begins, attempting to sound as businesslike as possible. 'About that conversation we had in John Lewis. I've been talking to someone from work who's also from Chesterfield and he says you're wrong about it being in the Midlands. The Peak District is in the North. So if you have to put me in your silly book, please make sure you quote me on that.'

'Elizabeth, a *part* of the Peak District is technically ...'

'I'm sorry, Robert, I have to put the phone down now.'

And with that she's gone.

This reclamation of the Midlands business certainly touches a nerve with some people.

Unperturbed, I continue my odyssey down the Great North Road. It should come as no surprise that the signalling of the SOUTH, in aggressive block capitals, is just as insistent on the A1 as the repeated annunciations of the NORTH are coming in the opposite direction up the M1. I don't think I've seen a single mention of the MIDLANDS yet today. Yep, where road signage is concerned, the binary opposites of North and South have certainly got the country sewn up.

A dozen or so miles later I arrive in Grantham, where a sign at the traffic island offers drivers a stark choice: 'Superstore', 'A&E' or 'Through Traffic'. In other words: A) Go to Tesco, B) seek immediate medical assistance or C) drive straight on by, nothing to see here. You could say there's a distinct lack of fizz about the approach to Grantham.

I park up by the crematorium – that's where the long-stay car park is, appropriately – and head for the main shopping area. As I turn the corner onto St Peter's Hill, I find myself at the foot of an imposing statue of an allegedly great Grantham politician – no, not Her: there's no statue of Margaret Thatcher in the town. Rather, it's of Sir Frederick Tollemache. The most interesting fact I've been able to glean about the latter is that his surname is a corruption of an ancient word meaning 'tolling of the bell'. Sir Fred For-Whom-the-Bell-Tolls. Ominous, huh?

I always say if you want to find out about a place's heritage, go to the local museum. I always say it; I don't always do it, of course. But today I'm genuinely in need of information and Grantham Museum happens to be handily sailing into view on my right, so I stride over and tug expectantly at the doors. Locked. There's nothing to indicate when they're going to open again either. Is the museum closed on Tuesdays? Or just at lunchtimes? Or has it closed down completely?

Oh well. There's very visibly a bit of half-timbered Grantham heritage straight up ahead, on the corner of Swinegate and Vine Street, so I go to investigate that. It turns out to be ye olde hostelry the Blue Pig. As a handwritten notice by the door explains, the Pig is one of only four remaining Tudor buildings in Grantham and part of the group of 'Blue' pubs owned by the Manners family, the grandest of whom was also the Duke of Rutland, with his seat at nearby Belvoir Castle. The Manners were committed Whigs, and the 'Blue' part of the pubs' names – back in the glory days there was also a Blue Lion, a Blue Horse, a Blue Dog – signified their allegiance to their aristocratic landlords' political cause. So it was in the 'Blue' pubs that Whig supporters gathered to drink loyal 'Blue' ale. (Freddie Tollemache, the MP commemorated in that statue, was a member of the Manners clan but was said to be a moderate Tory in his politics.) The notice by the door concludes with a hearty imprecation for the hostelry's long continuation: 'Be that as it may, long may the Blue Pig remain what it is today, a friendly, interesting and historic pub in Grantham.' Hear-hear! Thinking it richly deserving of my patronage, I try the door. It's locked too. I peer in through the window, whereupon it becomes clear that the Blue Pig has gone out of business. First the museum, now the Blue Pig – is Grantham shutting down completely? No wonder *The Sun* once dubbed it the 'most boring town' in England.

Unexciting as it may be as a visitor experience – you can almost imagine the local council employing cohorts of practised jobsworths to parade the streets and discourage any would-be tourists with shouts of 'Move along, move along, people, there's nothing to see here' – Grantham has long been a hotbed of innovation, particularly in relation to transport. Transport, as I mentioned in the last chapter, is something of a Midland speciality. You can understand why: travellers have always been in a desperate hurry to get out of the region, and Midland engineers have accordingly invested a lot of creative energy in rendering their exits faster and more comfortable. Among Granthamites' contributions to this great engineering tradition are the first diesel engine, the first tractor and caterpillar tracks. No matter what the weather or conditions on the road, if you've got a tractor, a diesel engine and caterpillar tracks, you'll always be able to escape.

Grantham has also proved a notable breeding ground for pioneering women. In 1915, the local police force swore Edith Smith into its ranks, making her the first full-fledged female bobby. Today this breakthrough bobbette has a road named in her honour: Edith Smith Way. Grantham also produced the country's first woman prime minister, of course. The town hasn't quite made up its mind to name a street after her yet – but more about that in a moment.

Grantham treats its most celebrated son – Isaac Newton, recently named by the Royal Society as the most influential scientist of all time (Einstein came second) – rather more generously. There's a statue of the man himself, a sculpture of the revelatory tumbling apple and – the least you'd expect for writing the world-shaking *Philosophiae Naturalis Principia Mathematica* – an Isaac Newton Shopping Centre slap-bang in the centre of town.

Few revolutions have reverberated so resoundingly around the world as Newton's, as Alexander Pope noted in his famous couplet:

Nature and nature's laws lay hid in night;
God said 'Let Newton be' and all was light.

Of course, in the popular imagination Newton's genius is encapsulated by the story of him lying stretched out under a tree, yokel-style, and an apple dropping on his head. Iconographically at least, the most influential scientist ever was a bit of a bumpkin. A typical Midlander, then.

(Note to self: Tell Hector about Newton inventing gravity. 'Without the scientific contribution of one great Midlander we'd all still be floating around in space.' He'll like that.)

Quite properly there's a signpost in the centre of Grantham pointing the way to the happy educational institution that nurtured Newton's genius. I'm keen to see it and so follow the arrow. I'm not sure I ever manage to locate it, though. The signage around here is lackadaisical at best, about as useful as when you ask someone for directions and they flail an arm vaguely so as to indicate about 180 degrees of the visible panorama and say: 'It's over there, somewhere.' Still, travelling in hope more than expectation, I head out along Castlegate and discover uniformed children playing in a yard. My deductive powers tell me quick as a flash that this is likely to be a school. It looks quite modern, though. Is this really where the future Sir Isaac disported himself between double maths and Latin?

A huge spire looms just beyond the playground. If in doubt, ask a policeman or a priest, so, since there are no bobbies (or bobbettes) in evidence, I head over to the attached church in search of information about Izzie's early schooling. I'm greeted by a nice lady who appears to be guarding the place. I mumble something about Newton's education – I'm not good in company, can't look people in the eye or speak up in a crowd – and she says, yes, he did go to school next door and probably worshipped in this very church, St Wulfram's. 'I can't tell you where he sat, though,' she smiles. 'I get asked that a lot.'

St Wulfram's is dedicated to a medieval Frenchman who, the historical record suggests, never actually came to England. Still, nominal obscurity hasn't prevented the building and its impressive spire from attracting the admiration of the great and the good down the centuries. An information board quotes the following fascinating fact: 'Father Stanton of St Alban's, Holborn, who frequently travelled through Grantham by train, would make all the gentlemen in his compartment stand up and doff their hats to the spectacle of St Wulfram's Church.' Journalist and architectural historian Simon Jenkins clearly understands where Father Stanton was coming from. In his book *England's Thousand Best Churches*, he declares: 'Here is the finest steeple in England.'

I depart St Wulfram's with a burgeoning admiration for its steeple and confirmed in the knowledge that Newton went to school next door. Only I have a feeling it was next door in the other direction.

No matter. The truth is, the site of historical importance that I'm most interested in today is Mayor Roberts's Grocery Emporium, or, as the local signage has it, 'Margaret Thatcher's Birthplace'. Not that there's much of that signage, which sends you off on a trail that leads to the edge of the town's commercial centre and then promptly peters out. I was expecting a bit of fanfare – ROLL UP! ROLL UP! COME AND SEE WHERE THE IRON LADY WAS BORN! – but I'm soon wandering around lost again. I decide to ask for directions (something I hate doing) and stop a promising-looking middle-aged couple carrying shopping bags. When I approach them with an 'Excuse me …' the woman peels away but the man stops to hear me out. I tell him I've been to see Isaac Newton's school (possibly) and am now in search of Margaret Thatcher's Birthplace. He swings his shopping bags to the ground and gives me a conspiratorial wink.

'Newton invented the cat flap,' he begins unexpectedly.

'Really?'

'That's what they told me in Grantham Museum.'

'So is the museum still open then?' I ask. 'It looked closed when I came past.'

'Oh it's closed right enough,' he assures me. 'This is Grantham. If anything good happens here, you can be sure they'll soon put a stop to it.' Friendly as he is, he isn't exactly spilling over with civic pride. 'I always say the best thing about coming to Grantham is, wherever you go next, it'll be a big improvement. Travel east, west, north or south, you're sure to find yourself somewhere better.' Nothing to see here, folks, move right along – it's becoming a bit of a Grantham motif.

I ask him about local attitudes to Margaret Thatcher. Before venturing an answer, he looks carefully from side to side, as if to make sure that no one is listening in on our conversation. The Thatcher legacy remains a divisive issue in Grantham, he says – even more divisive than it is nationally, if that's possible. A lot of locals would rather forget that the Margaret Thatcher Story began here. On the other hand, there were Mrs T-related artefacts on display in the museum when it was still open. My new friend declines to comment on her political skills but says that he would like to point out instead that, like Newton, she was a scientist. 'Grantham specialises in producing world-changing scientists,' he announces, with what sounds like something bordering on civic pride, before concluding: 'One day they'll put up a statue to her, but it won't be in my lifetime.'[1]

Or perhaps they'll open a club in her honour instead. There's no shortage of slightly louche-sounding nightspots and bars in

---

[1]   Images of the Iron Lady, like her policies, are endlessly controversial. Artist Neil Simmons's eight-foot marble likeness of the former PM, commissioned by the House of Commons, was famously beheaded using a Slazenger V600 cricket bat and metal rope. 'I think it looks better like that,' commented the iconoclastic attacker.

Grantham: Hotshotz, Infernos, The Vibe, Taboo Gentlemen's Club. By day a demure dame, the town seemingly kicks off her knickers at night and turns into a bit of a good-time girl. An Eighties-themed nightclub named Maggie's has recently opened in Chelsea, where revellers are encouraged not only to boogie to the sounds of Wham! and Bananarama but also to listen to the speeches of the former PM as they relieve themselves in the loos. They should open a branch in Grantham.

As his wife comes back into view, the man points me off towards the grand-sounding North Parade and tells me to look out for the Catholic church on the left. Margaret Thatcher, of course, was a Methodist so is unlikely to have set foot inside there as a girl, but her father's shop was across the road from it.

When I finally get there, I discover that Mayor Roberts's grocery store has been converted into a natural health and chiropractic centre. There's a modest plaque acknowledging that this is where the Iron Lady was born, but that's it. No fanfare. Nothing to see here, people, move along, move along …

* * *

Margaret Thatcher has passed away since I visited Grantham. News of her death was marked by tributes from world leaders, special editions of national newspapers and 'Ding Dong! The Witch Is Dead' going straight into the pop charts at number two. When Geri Halliwell tweeted about the passing of the '1st Lady of girl power', she was met with a torrent of abuse and quickly deleted the message. (Perhaps understandably, despite becoming Britain's first female prime minister, Margaret Thatcher has never been adopted as a full-blown feminist icon. All the same, she did a surprisingly good line in subversively post-patriarchal dick jokes, beginning with her famous 'Every prime minister needs a Willie' quip.) The Thatcher legacy remains deeply divisive, even now she's dead.

The taunts began early on, of course, before she became prime minister: she was still only education secretary when she was dubbed 'Mrs Thatcher, the milk snatcher' for putting an end to free school milk for over-sevens (the policy was adopted to save the Open University). The name calling only grew in intensity after she became *prima inter pares*, when a good deal of derision was directed at her roots. 'What else can we expect from an ex-spam hoarder from Grantham?' quipped an exasperated Tony Banks, who, as a conviction Leftist and ex-union man, might have been expected to be above poking fun at someone for the modesty of their origins (as mentioned above, her father was a grocer). The taunts continued unabated after she left office and, if anything, grew in intensity. On the thirtieth anniversary of her elevation to the prime ministership, for instance, the firebrand novelist Hanif Kureishi, writing in the *Guardian*, struck a surprisingly Jilly Cooperesque note when he dismissed the former Tory leader as 'basically vulgar'.

What is it about Baroness Thatcher, *née* Margaret Roberts, that merits such vitriol, even in death? There are policy-related issues that help to explain her continuing divisiveness, of course – the miners' strike, the poll tax, the Eighties 'greed is good' culture of popular satire – but there's something deeply personal about the antipathy to 'that appalling woman', as Neil Kinnock referred to her, that goes well beyond the traditional politics of Left and Right. When you consider her origins – 'state-educated, lower-middle-class, provincial, female', as one commentator put it – and the (democratically mandated) influence she came to wield in recasting British politics, it's extraordinary how little imaginative sympathy she enjoyed. Her official biographer, Charles Moore, observed perceptively that the problem might be that she was 'neither poor enough to attract romantic sympathy, nor grand enough to be entitled to power'. You could translate Moore's rich/poor, disenfranchised/entitled binary into starkly cartographic terms, of course, and say more simply: she was neither a Northerner nor a Southerner. Stuck in the middle geographically, Mrs Thatcher was denied the benefits of belonging to either of the great national clubs: the Lovable Rebels (North) or the Establishment Insiders (South). In his bestselling *Diaries*, the politician Alan Clark noted that it was long rumoured in Tory circles that Margaret Thatcher wasn't the biological daughter of a Grantham grocer at all, but rather the illegitimate daughter of a Northern aristocrat. Even for Clark – who was no Northern propagandist – it was far preferable that his beloved leader should be a Northern toff's bastard than the honest offspring of a middling Midlander. Unquestionably, had she been born in the North and done the things she did, Margaret Thatcher would enjoy a very different – by which I mean infinitely more positive – reputation today.

On the other hand, she *couldn't* have done many of those things had she been anything other than a Midlander. Her political philosophy of self-reliance was avowedly bred in the Midlands. 'I just owe almost everything I believe to my father [i.e., the Grantham spam hoarder and town mayor],' she paused to tell reporters as she entered 10 Downing Street as PM for the first time in 1979. 'He brought me up to believe all the things I do believe … and it is passionately interesting for me that the things I learned in a small town, in a very modest home, are just the things that I believe have won the election.' And so it was that classic Midland self-sufficiency – the yeoman ethic as it is known – became the model for national economic regeneration. 'My background and experience were not those of a traditional Conservative prime minister,' Britain's longest-serving twentieth-century leader wrote with characteristic Midland understatement in her memoirs. 'I was less able to depend on automatic deference, but I was also perhaps less intimidated by the risks of change.' Whether you love her or loathe her (or, like some of Harry Styles's Twitter followers, are too young to have any notion of who she was), the story of Margaret Thatcher's rise and fall is a classic Midlander's tale.

* * *

To end this chapter, I was going to write a brief dissertation setting out the arguments for and against the political policies of the Iron Lady. In it, I was going to quote my *Guardian*-reading, Thatcher-voting mother (I told you she was a paradox): 'She was necessary. She saved us from the unions and she turned the economy round – but there again, with all that North Sea oil money rolling in in the late Eighties, a monkey could have done that.' I was also going to admit that, as a student and armed with a ballot slip for the very first time, I was so deranged by Maggie hatred that in the 1987 general election *I voted for Neil Kinnock*. Quite a confession, I'm sure you'll agree. But in the wake of the fierce outpouring of opinion and emotion that marked her death, it seems a bit point-less to try to say anything meaningful about her political legacy. What I'd like to do instead is point to a handful of the other more general attitudes and character traits that mark Margaret Thatcher out as a Midlander. You may not like them – that's not the point. (Indeed, that's one of the ways you can tell the differ-ence between a Midlander and a Northerner: Northerners, for all their toughness and unruliness, are desperate to be loved, whereas Midlanders, like Millwall fans, know everyone hates them and are quite indifferent to the fact.)

Anyway, here goes with that list:

1. The Lady – notoriously – was not for turning. Margaret Thatcher is a useful corrective to all those clichés about the Midlands being nondescript, bland and thoroughly middling. Though a Midlander through and through – as stated above, her political philosophy was deeply indebted to her Grantham upbringing – she was no fan of the *via media*. So-called 'middle-way' Tories, who favoured consensus and compromise, had dominated the party from the close of World War II to the downfall of Ted Heath, looking on help-lessly as the unions brought down Heath's government in 1974 and then, under Labour, caused the country to grind to a halt in the 'winter of discontent'. The times called for a leader who would not quail in tackling vested interests. That leader – inevitably – was a Midlander. When things got tough, as they did in the early Eighties, and a nearly universal cry for hardline economic policies to be reversed arose, Margaret Thatcher simply kept going (the famous 'Lady's not for turning' moment). Moral: for better or for worse, Midlanders are far from middling.

2. On the other hand, she was quite happy to change her image, displaying a restless appetite for self-refashioning throughout her career. Thus, though the Lady may not have been for turning in the policy arena, she was more than willing to make adjustments, even radical ones, when it came to her appearance, demonstrating an unusual flexibility of spirit in taking up hints, especially from her enemies. Her 'Iron Lady' moniker, for instance, was borrowed from the Red Army newspaper *Jrasbata Zvezda*, which gave her the title after she made a speech criticising the Soviet Union in 1976.

She revelled in the role, addressing one meeting: 'I stand before you tonight in my Red Star chiffon evening gown, my face softly made up and my fair hair gently waved: the Iron Lady of the Western World!' Throughout her time in the political spotlight, her hairstyle and clothing underwent revolutionary changes, as, most famously, did her voice: 'that self-aggrandising, cloying, patronising, agonised and agonising voice oozing out of that vicious, dead-eyed face', as one young commentator wrote many years after she had left office – in the *Guardian* again, of course, which is not only Leftist in tendency but also Mancunian in origin:[2] how could such an overtly *Northern* publication be expected to give an archetypal Midlander a fair hearing? When Margaret Thatcher was advised that she needed to lower her comparatively high-pitched voice to a more commanding contralto in order to convey greater authority, she did not hesitate to hire a vocal coach. Moral: unlike the classic Northerner with his foetal attachment to his 'identity', the Midlander is unafraid to adapt in order to grow – not by coincidence was the theory of evolution born in the Midlands.

3. She rubbished the idea of the North/South divide. Her comments caused outrage, of course – it doesn't take much to shock the Establishments of South or North – but, frankly,

[2] It was first established in May 1821 as the *Manchester Guardian* in the aftermath of the so-called Peterloo 'Massacre', one of the great and most egregiously over-mythologised events in the history of the North, when fifteen people were killed at a pro-parliamentary reform rally in St Peter's Field, Manchester, in 1819. For instance, in *Pies and Prejudice* Stuart Maconie writes: '[Peterloo] had awoken something in the nation as a whole and the north in particular … Red with blood that day, some say Manchester and the north has [*sic*] been red ever since. My theory is that the north has never really trusted Westminster, king or country since.' Calm down, dear!

as I mentioned at the beginning of this chapter, that great national fissure, whether considered geographically, culturally or financially, has never made much sense to those of us who hail from the middle regions. We have a foot in both camps, you see – or rather, we are the Whole, of which the more identity-conscious North and South are mere partial, mutilated abstractions. All the same, Midlanders have good reason to be irked by the continuing obsession with what is regarded as the cut-and-dried national divide. In the space of a couple of weeks when I first began thinking about Margaret Thatcher's Midlandlerishness, the BBC aired at least two programmes about this cultural-geographical will-o'-the-wisp (the first on TV, centred on archetypal Northerner John Prescott, the second on radio, led by archetypal Londoner Ken Livingstone). Continual reinforcement of such a dubious stereotype is important: it is largely owing to the aggressive self-aggrandising strategies of the North, and the concomitant English fondness for the binary stability conferred by the idea of the 'North/South divide', that the Midlands has been peripheralised in the national imagination almost to the point of extinction. Margaret Thatcher's denial of the North/South divide was a strike in favour of the Midlands. Moral: Midlanders are more than mere slash signs!

STDs and HDTV, Lampy – survivor of the great gnome purge, and Bates the true-born Midlander

Now here's a turn-up for the books. I said earlier that you couldn't possibly get a programme idea with a Midland place name in the title past the commissioners who control the British airwaves. And yet, what is this I discover as I frustratedly punch the buttons on my pre-digital-era car radio in a quest for entertainment? A comedy called *North by Northamptonshire*. Okay, it's only on the radio, but at least it's on a national station (Radio 4) and not just a special commission for Northants FM that can't be accessed by anyone beyond the county's borders. It's got a good cast with lots of established names in it too – Sheila Hancock, Penelope Wilton, Mackenzie Crook – so there's even a danger that non-Northamptonshire folk might tune in specially to listen to it. Are things changing? Is the Midlands suddenly becoming *fashionable*?

Judging by the show's opening lines, I'd say not.

'Northamptonshire,' intones Ms Hancock. 'Land of low hills and high-definition televisions. Land of low levels of chlamydia in the under-twenty-fours but high likelihood of nobody being able to point to where you live on a map. Northamptonshire. No excited tourists are ever seen huddled round a "Welcome to Northants" sign thumbs aloft grinning for the camera.' Everything in the imaginary Northants market town of Wadenbrook is so thoroughly *average*, the narrator seems to be saying, that it's almost laughable; the recurrent punchline is how run-of-the-mill everything is here. It's certainly not trying to sell the Northamptonshire Dream. One of the characters has just returned from Australia. 'Nice to be home?' someone asks her. 'Not really,' she responds. Today's episode concerns plans to mount a festival, with the locals frantically racking their brains to come up with the names of 'famous Northamptonshirites'. Nanette Newman? one suggests. 'Apparently Des O'Connor was evacuated to Northampton,' says another. 'Dickens was a regular guest at Rockingham Castle,' remembers someone else. (Rockingham served as the inspiration for Chesney Wold in Dickens's *Bleak House*.) The big joke, it seems, is that these people are from somewhere with no particular character or history or identity; somewhere that's middling and anonymous in every respect and so bland it can't even be caricatured. On the whole, then, it's unlikely to subvert listeners' settled notions about Northamptonshire and the Midlands more generally.

By coincidence, as I listen I'm actually on my way to Northamptonshire, where my Uncle John has pledged to take me on a tour of places of interest *that will literally blow my mind*. If Derbyshire is often thought of as the North, Northants is regularly mistaken for the South. Heck, sometimes the South is even *keen* to claim ownership of the county – it's not only the North that nabs bits of the Midlands when the mood takes it. As the authors of a railway guide wryly observed in the late 1960s: 'In the days when Northamptonshire cricket was at a low ebb, one of our most respectable London newspapers wrote of "that Midland side which has so often helped prop up the County Championship table". It was a different matter when they began to challenge the leaders; then they joined those other "southern" contenders, ie, Surrey and Middlesex!'

Before setting off, I've been canvassing people's opinions about the county, and I think Uncle John might have his work cut out blowing my mind – instead, there appears to be a distinct risk that tedium might make me want to blow my brains out. 'Dead boring,' opines one acquaintance. 'Northants? It's that really long, dreary bit of the M1 when you're driving down to London from Notts, isn't it?' says another. 'You wouldn't catch me stopping there.' 'It's full of shoes,' says a third, at least showing a bit of local knowledge: Northamptonshire is the historic home of the UK's footwear industry. It sounds as though that Radio 4 comedy has got it about right, then: 'Northamptonshire, county of dreams – if a landlocked administrative unit famous for its shoemaking and bordered by Leicestershire features in your dreams.'

* * *

'Do you want to get straight down to work, or would you like to relax first? I thought I could start by telling you a little bit about the county and then we could go for a drive. Care for a biscuit?'

I'm liking this: the briskness, the sense of purpose, the offer of refreshments. My uncle – a distant relation of Elton John, for whom I think he is a dead ringer, although no one else appears to see the resemblance – ushers me through into the sitting room, where it becomes clear that he's been doing his homework. As I take my seat at a table groaning under the weight of a large pile of brochures and guidebooks, he flourishes an exercise book full of neatly ruled, densely written pages divided into columns headed 'Culture', 'History', 'Visits', 'Business', 'Recreation', 'Sport' and the like.

He's retired now but not so long ago John was a top-ranking marketing man. He's clearly using my invitation to him to lay out the beauties of Northamptonshire as an opportunity to flex his professional muscles again. I wouldn't be surprised if he doesn't give me a PowerPoint presentation.

'Those who know the villages around here compare them to the Cotswolds, but not that many people do know them,' he begins. 'The attitude to Northants is a bit like the way people buzz through Somerset on their way to Devon and Cornwall.'

'It sounds like the Midlands in miniature ...' I begin but am interrupted by the appearance of my aunt in the doorway.

'Ah, Denise,' John addresses his wife, 'could you make us some sandwiches so we can eat and get on at the same time?'

Denise is my mother's youngest sister and, like my mum, she's a natural subversive. I don't think I've ever seen her make a gesture or heard her speak a word that wasn't in some degree ironically intended. On this occasion she doesn't trouble to open her mouth but merely makes a mock-curtsey as she retreats to the kitchen.

'There's so much history around here,' John resumes as the door closes behind her. 'When we have visitors over from America or Australia, there's no shortage of places to take them. Most of the major battles in English history were fought around here – this is the place for Civil War re-creations: it was a fascinating founding period for modern Britain, was the Civil War – and there's no shortage of great houses. Leisure-wise, there's a lot to do and see: we're very well served when it comes to sports and the arts. But we'll see a bit more of that when we take our little tour later.'

He runs his finger down the 'Business' column in his exercise book. 'Did you know that your breakfast cereal comes from Northampton?' he smiles, looking up. 'Weetabix has its head office here, and it's Northamptonshire wheat that goes into it. Did you know that?'

'No.' (Actually I don't eat Weetabix, but I do like the idea that Northants is the source of all that traditional breakfast-time goodness for the nation's children. Hurrah for the nurturing richness of Northamptonshire soil! Why didn't they mention that in that episode of *North by Northamptonshire*?)

'Northants is also a source of the highest-quality stone,' John runs on. 'King's College Chapel in Cambridge was largely built using limestone from the quarries at Weldon. You could say we're the building block of Britain.'

He continues to scan his list. 'And did you know that Northampton is the home of Barclaycard?' he asks.

'No.' (Before you ask, I don't have a Barclaycard.)

'Well, it is. It was established here in the mid-1960s. Then there's Avon Cosmetics, Carlsberg, Jeyes Fluid. And obviously all the big shoe manufacturers – Church's, Crockett and Jones, Tricker's, lots more – were all here. Engineering is a big part of the local economy. Silverstone is just down the road, and there's Cosworth Engineering in Northampton. Mercedes performance engines are made just up the road. We also have the headquarters of Travis Perkins.'

'Isn't that Robert De Niro's character in *Taxi Driver*?' I interrupt him. 'I thought that all happened in New York.'

'Travis Perkins are builders' merchants,' he corrects me matter-of-factly, continuing without a pause: 'In terms of communications, Northants has got everything going for it – the canal system, the M1, M45, M6 and A14 take you wherever you want to go. You can go north, south, west, east from here. We're bang in the centre of England. No wonder a lot of the logistics companies have their depots here. Sainsbury's, Argos and lots more have big warehouses in the area. And we have a massive freight terminal at Daventry with acres of land. Transport-wise, there's a huge amount going on.'

I am beginning to believe the hype but when I peer over at John's exercise book I spot the words 'MISSED OPPORTUNITIES' written in large capitals at the top of a page marked 'Downsides'. What's the problem exactly? I ask him.

'Ah.' John looks momentarily pained. 'Well, I'm told that, going back in history, Northampton was picked out to be the principal town of England. Then something went wrong along the way – lack of vision, lack of ambition, I don't know – and it didn't happen.'

To illustrate this, John points to the impressive progress of neighbouring Milton Keynes. The unloved New Town – which is technically in Buckinghamshire, not that the Home Counties are desperate to lay claim to it – has tremendous go-getting energy and is sucking the commercial life out of Northampton. John, a serious rugby fan, is aggrieved that, when his beloved Northampton Saints host big matches, they tend to play them in MK, where the town planners have shown greater vision. 'Last year we got to the final of the Heineken Cup,' he says. 'That's big money which should have been coming in to Northampton, but we had to go to Milton Keynes for the big matches to have a stadium that's big enough. We couldn't hold our quarter- and semi-final matches at our own ground. So all the money goes to Milton Keynes instead!' He doesn't like MK, but he can't help but admire its ambition. 'We've missed so many opportunities in Northampton,' he sighs.

* * *

Here's a brain-teaser for you: what was the third university to be founded on English soil? First there was Oxford, then Cambridge, and then ... Manchester? Leeds? No, neither of those, although Northern nationalists will probably try to persuade you otherwise. Actually (and rather obviously – why else would I be posing the question at this particular point in my narrative?) it was Northampton. Dissident Cambridge students established a university here as long ago as 1261. However, when fighting broke out between King Henry III and his barons a few years later, the student long-hairs foolishly threw their weight behind the uppish aristo Simon de Montfort and, for their pains, found royal backing for the new foundation swiftly removed. The University of Northampton was thus dissolved in 1265, and a historic opportunity for the town to take its place in an evolving triumvirate of academic distinction – Oxbridgeton or, better, Norcamford, as we'd no doubt be calling this Golden Triangle now – was lost. Northampton had to wait 740 years, until 2005, before it was home to an academic institution enjoying university status again.

This part of the country has an unhappy knack of backing political losers. It supported the parliamentary side again in the Civil War – Cromwell's army marched to nearby Naseby in boots that had been lovingly crafted in Northampton – and, as punishment for its disloyalty, had its castle razed by Charles II after the Restoration. This effectively brought to an end a lengthy period during which Northampton Castle had been used as an important royal residence and Northampton town had begun to establish itself as one of the country's main political nodes. Parliament intermittently convened here from 1131 through to the late fourteenth century, when a decision to introduce the first national poll tax sparked the Peasants' Revolt of 1381. Two centuries earlier, Henry II had made the castle one of his

113

regular homes and put Thomas à Becket on trial here, causing the famously 'turbulent priest' to flee to the Continent disguised as a monk. Just as major manufacturers and distribution firms value its centrality today, so England's medieval monarchs found Northampton very convenient as they made their regular peregrinations between London and York. Benefiting from such regal attentions, the settlement flourished. *Robinson Crusoe* author Daniel Defoe later described it as 'the handsomest town in all this part of England'.

Had its university survived Henry III's rage, Northampton would have blossomed even more spectacularly. It's said that the powers-that-be at Oxford University were jealous of their fledgling East Midland academic rival and played a key role in its destruction, applying pressure on the king to have it dissolved. As visitors (and Uncle John) attest, the countryside around here resembles the Oxford-hugging Cotswolds, one of England's most cherished landscapes. So it's hardly the most contentious historical counterfactual you can imagine to propose that Northampton, England's great town of missed opportunities, could have been a contender. It could have been Oxford.

* * *

Denise is back in the room and this time she's armed – albeit only with a tray of sandwiches. Judging by the look on her face, I reckon she's about to say something sarcastic. I decide to try to channel her subversive energies with a question or two.

'How's life in Northampton?' I begin, uncontentiously.

'I hate it! It's vile!' She's laughing as she says it. She's lived here for twenty-odd years so she can't hate it that much. Straight answers are usually in short supply when Denise is around.

'How would you describe the local accent?' I say, essaying a more anthropological tack.

'I don't know. If you go to Corby, it's Scottish,' she quips. 'Apart from that, it's kind of middling.'

(Corby was a sleepy little Northants village until the 1930s, which is when it became known as 'Little Scotland' and the local accent took a marked turn towards the Caledonian as a result of Stewarts and Lloyds opening a huge steelworks there. North Northants's ironstone beds had been known and worked for at least a couple of millennia, but improved ore-extraction techniques made it ripe for industrial development at the beginning of the twentieth century. As a result, the population increased forty- or fifty-fold by the end of the 1960s, with most migrant workers arriving from Scotland and so making Corby one of the best places south of the Scottish border to celebrate Burns Night. It's no longer a particularly good place to find work in the iron and steel industry, unfortunately – not because of the industrial depredations of the Thatcherite Eighties, mark you, but largely owing to a decision on the part of Labour in the previous decade to consolidate steel production elsewhere. One reason for this was Corby's distance from the coast – a defining difficulty for the Midlands throughout history.)

I continue my expert cross-examination of my aunt. I should have been a lawyer.

'But, culturally, do you feel comfortable here? Do you have a sense of belonging?' I ask, subtly.

'I'm from Mansfield. I'm not from here.'

But they're both in the Midlands, I suggest. There's cultural continuity between the two: people from Mansfield and people from Northants share a Midland identity, don't they?

'A Midlander to me is from Birmingham,' says Denise.

'So what are you then?'

Pause.

'I suppose you might call me an East Midlander,' she concedes briefly before returning to the attack: 'But when I'm talking to people, I call myself a Northerner because, as far as I'm concerned, England is the North and the South and the Midlands doesn't exist. So I consider myself a Northerner. And that's all there is to say on the subject.'

Another binarist Midlands-denier! And this one is a member of my own family! I shake my head sadly.

Triumphant, Denise declares her intention to go and ask her neighbour Brian – a Northampton man through and through – whether *he* considers himself a Midlander.

'I have no hang-ups about my identity,' offers John as Denise exits.

No, I say, Southerners rarely do. John grew up in and around London.

'I've lived in Surrey, I've lived in Hertfordshire, I've lived in Nottinghamshire, Somerset and now here,' he says. 'I don't feel I have a strong affinity for any particular part of the country. I like all of it. If I meet someone from the West Country, I can say I used to live down there. I can take my pick.'

'Yes,' I say, smilingly, 'you have that classic Southern sense of entitlement.'

Oh no, I'm beginning to sound like a chippy Northerner!

* * *

By now John has got me into his car. I tell him I quite fancy going to see Kettering railway station, which is where love first blossomed for local author H.E. Bates – 'there should be a plaque on the door of the First Class waiting-room on Platform Number Three at Kettering station, saying *H.E. Bates loved here*,' the old romantic wrote in his memoir *The Vanished World* (1969) – but my uncle is having none of it. Kettering is too urban; he wants to get out into the countryside.

I would never have imagined it but there's a marked Brigadoon effect as you leave industrial Northampton. John lives in a village a few miles north of the town and deer regularly wander past his door, for goodness' sake. There may not be any great mountains of note – most of the county lies on the great 'Midland plain of grass and elm', as that H.E. Bates bloke put it, so the hills rarely reach above 400 feet – but the landscape is pleasingly varied and, yes, quite like the Cotswolds to the west. As the old rhyme has it, Northants is the county of 'mires, squires and spires'.

'Thatchers still get plenty of work around here.' John nods towards some gracious and ancient residences that line the roadside as we head north up the A508.

Going back in history a bit, Northamptonshire found itself prey to successive invasions: Romans, Saxons and Vikings took turns to leave their mark on the landscape. Over in the west, Towcester, the county's oldest town, began its existence as a Roman fort called Lactodurum. Legionnaires used to march through as they passed along Watling Street on their way from London to Chester.

We're coming into a little village called Brixworth, which contains the most remarkable Saxon church in England. According to one commentator, All Saints is 'the most imposing architectural memorial of the 7th century north of the Alps'. The setting isn't bad either.

'You don't expect to see villages like this in Northamptonshire, do you?' John exclaims of Brixworth itself. 'You expect them in France, but not in Northamptonshire!'

As I mentioned before, John used to work in marketing so I'm interested to draw on his professional expertise and come up with a new advertising pitch for the local tourist board. Northants needs a good marketing line to counter the nothingy clichés of *North by Northamptonshire* and show that it isn't just good for chlamydia and high-definition TVs.

'Perhaps that would work as an advertising catchphrase for the county,' I propose tentatively. '"Northamptonshire villages – a little piece of Provence deep in the heart of the English countryside." How about that?'

John's silence speaks volumes.

We're now drawing towards lovely little Lamport, home to the grand Lamport Hall, which contains portraits by Van Dyck and Lely. And that's not all.

'They've got the oldest gnome in the world in there,' John says in passing.

'Really?' I press for details.

'You can look it up on the internet,' John brushes away my inquiry. 'I'm not that interested in gnomes. All I want to know is that I've got a gnome to go to.' He laughs. John is famous in the family for his dedication to telling bad jokes. Normally he's unstoppable but today it's taken him a full three hours to produce his first one. *That's how seriously he's taking this.* I feel an overwhelming sense of gratitude.

(I did look up the gnome business subsequently, and he's right: 'Lampy' is supposed to be the oldest surviving garden gnome in the world. He was imported from Germany in the 1840s by Sir Charles Isham, who is said to have been an 'eccentric spiritualist' – so who knows what he wanted Lampy for. Apparently Sir Charles's daughters hated gnomes and later banished his collection. Lampy was secreted in a crevice, however, and survived the purge.)

John is tempted to turn the car east towards Wellingborough and Wollaston, home to Dr Martens boots as well as a Roman-era vineyard. Then again he's also tempted to keep heading north, to Market Harborough, a lovely market town just on the other side of the Leicestershire border where Denise likes to come for coffee (she can't stand Milton Keynes, naturally), or to Naseby, where the Parliamentarians routed Charles I and effectively sealed victory in the Civil War in 1645, or to Fotheringhay Castle, where Mary, Queen of Scots lost her head in 1587. There's no shortage of Big History around here.

'It was in Ashton, just up the road, that the World Conker Championships were first staged,' John proffers. 'Don't giggle.'

I wouldn't dream of it. The World Conker Championships are no laughing matter. When the competition was first established in 1965, it was held on Ashton's horse chestnut tree-shaded village green. Since then, it's grown in scale and importance to such an extent that it's had to be relocated to a larger venue, where one Sunday in early October gladiators mount a series of white podiums to do battle armed only with a nut and a bit of string. It makes for a stirringly picturesque and extremely English spectacle; you won't be surprised to hear that there are plenty of morris dancers in these parts too.

And clowns. Nicolai Polakoff, aka Coco the Clown, is buried in St Mary's churchyard in Woodnewton, in the north-east of the county. Coco was an auguste, which means that as part of his routine he was on the receiving end of endless rounds of custard pies and buckets of water courtesy of a whiteface clown. Regular 'Clownfests' are held in the village in his memory, to raise money for charity.

In the end, John decides to turn west and, after negotiating a series of winding country roads, we come to Althorp, the grandest stately home in Northamptonshire and the ancestral home of the Spencers. In the summer you can take a tour for a fee, but the estate closes to visitors in the autumn. To afford us a better view of the house, John drives round to the point where the perimeter wall is most sunken.

'The first Spencer was a sheep farmer,' he begins. 'That was back in the sixteenth century. They've expanded their interests a bit since.'

Althorp is more or less synonymous now with Diana, Princess of Wales, late twentieth-century Britain's regal sweetheart and tragic queen-in-waiting. Diana's family has resided at Althorp for the past four or five centuries and it is here, on a small island in the middle of a lake – like a modern-day Arthur, another much-mythologised royal who reshaped the sensibilities of his nation – that her body lies. The 'People's Princess' was a folkloric figure with the instincts of a Robin Hood or Lady Godiva, whose life was given ultimate form by her bitter conflicts with the Establishment and the ways in which she didn't quite fit in. In that sense, the People's Princess was also the definitive Midland Princess.

A 4x4 – all the cars around here seem to be 4x4s – emerges from the estate gates. Could it be Diana's brother? I wonder.

'Not at this time of year, I shouldn't think,' John says. We peer nosily into the departing car and fail to recognise the driver.

We head off. As we do so, John points to the avenue of trees that line the route from the house to the local village. In more distant times the Spencer family would have ridden along it in their carriage to get to church. As we drive past the village post office, he adds: 'Diana could regularly be seen here. That was before she was married, of course.'

England has few statelier stately homes to show than Althorp, but if all you know of the county is the Spencers' great estate you won't have captured its essence. Half a century ago H.E. Bates said as much: 'Rich though Northamptonshire is in great and lovely houses it is more the transition from red-brick, factory and chapel to the broad serenity and dignity of noble estates that, I fancy, has left so imperishable an impression on me.' And today it's still the way the statelies sit cheek by jowl with those old 'boot and shoe' villages and the larger industrial settlements that really arrests the imagination. That being the case, my uncle really has a duty to show me a town or two, I think.

At last John gives in and deigns to take me to Northampton. If it's really so awful, I must see it, I tell him. As we approach, he insists on continuing to point out favourite spots and sights such as Stoke Bruerne, the 'child of a canal' and home to the Canal Museum ('Just along the way there's the longest canal tunnel in the country, I believe,' he says with his familiar rising intonation), and one of the Eleanor Crosses, made of the same Weldon limestone used in King's College Chapel and erected to mark the route taken by the funeral cortege of Edward I's beloved queen as it passed from Nottingham to London in 1290.

It would be misleading to describe Northampton town proper as distinguished. But it's not that bad, either. One of the big problems is how anonymous it is: as you come in past the huge Halfords, Matalan and Homebase stores, it looks like pretty much everywhere else in the country. But you have to blame planners nationally for that, not just the Midland ones.

'Have you noticed how many heavy goods vehicles there are on the roads here?' John asks. Some mix-up with the post caused him to do some sniffing around a few years back and he discovered that quite a lot of the stuff you order through Amazon emanates from around here (it's amazing what senior citizens get up to in their free time).

He takes me to the home of the Northampton Saints, one-time winners of the Heineken Cup. John is a season ticket holder and has a great admiration for the club's smart commercial exploitation of the site. He's outraged that some of their plans have had difficulty getting past the council, though, and – of course – he doesn't much appreciate the fact that they play some of their biggest matches down the road in Milton Keynes either.

Still, at least the Saints are good at rugby – internationally renowned, even. In stark contrast, the local football team don't add much to the town's lustre. At the time of my visit Northampton Town FC are making a valiant downward dash in League Two to try to secure non-league status for themselves. They're known locally as 'The Cobblers' – let's face it, you're never going to be world-beaters with a nickname like that. (Little-known fact: comedian Alan Carr – you know, the camp one with the specs and the funny teeth – is the son of former Northampton Town manager Graham Carr. I wonder how that sort of thing plays in the dressing room, football being such an open, gay-friendly profession?)

As we pass a disused gas works, John grunts. 'Can you believe it – there are actually people who want to preserve this as part of Northampton's heritage!' he says, appalled.

Nearby stands the altogether more prepossessing Carlsberg Brewery, which was opened by some Danish princess or other in 1974. The company apparently chose the site because the water in the Nene is very similar in composition to that found in Denmark.

'I know!' I exclaim, another light bulb flashing on in my head. 'We could market Northampton as the Copenhagen of England. That would get the tourists flocking here. I once had a brilliant holiday in Copenhagen.'

'Yes, it's just like Copenhagen, only without the "Wonderful, Wonderful" bit,' says John, alluding to the famous song. 'I've always thought that Carlsberg could use "Probably the best lager brewed in a non-city" as a slogan for their Northampton lager.'

Ah yes, the prickly issue of Northampton's non-city status. I should explain that, despite its considerable size and population, Northampton remains nominally a town, and that its non-city status is a source of great irritation to many locals. 'Nobody appears to have the drive to have Northampton made into a city,' John sniffs. Back to that lack of ambition and vision thing again.

On Abington Street, Graham Ibbeson's bronze statue *The Cobbler's Last* (1986) serves as a symbol of the footwear industry. The town also holds jolly St Crispin Street Fayres to celebrate the birthday of the patron saint of shoemakers, when floats of Hush Puppies and Church's brogues pass in a hallucinatory procession along the streets of Northampton and giant balloons in the shape of Doc Martens hover above the heads of the massed St Crispin-loving merrymakers. (My description of proceedings is entirely non-fact-based.)

In the distance the old Express Lift Company's testing tower dominates the landscape. 'Now that *is* iconic – Terry Wogan used to call it the Northampton Lighthouse,' John says proudly.

The cultural life around here isn't bad at all, and I'm not just talking about the world-class collection of historical footwear that you can stand and gaze at to your heart's content in the Northampton Museum and Art Gallery. The work of the great architect and designer Charles Rennie Mackintosh is celebrated at 78 Derngate, and not long ago the revolutionary theatre company Headlong emerged from Northampton to conquer the world – well, London and New York (sort of), which in theatrical terms is pretty much synonymous with global dominance.

And, of course, if you're really stuck for something to do, Northampton isn't so far from London, so you could zoom down the M1 or catch a train for a fun time in the metropolis. Not that the trains are particularly good. John explains to me that the paucity of service results from the fact that Northampton is on a loop rather than a main line. Work to improve communications with the capital has been ongoing for a very long time. How come? I ask. 'Because it's Northampton,' sighs John. 'No ambition.'

Property developers are always keen to stress Northamptonshire's proximity to the capital, of course. To the consternation of some locals, one developer even went so far as to rebrand the area 'North Londonshire' in a marketing campaign in 2010. There was a radio ad voiced by Sandi Toksvig, and an online viral showing metropolitan pigeons relocating to an idyllical suburbia resembling Rushden or somewhere similar. The message – not very exciting when you think about it, but very Midlands – was basically: 'Northants: the perfect place to go to sleep.'

We don't tarry long in town as John is keen to show me Billing Aquadrome, a holiday park that hugs the reservoir. He tells me that a lot of gravel extraction went on around here prior to the opening of the M1 in 1959. 'It's good cycling country too,' he affirms. 'Up, down and around, it's interesting.'

This part of the country is dotted with handsome reservoirs. Suddenly I have an idea: 'Let's rebrand Northamptonshire as "The Artificial Lake District",' I suggest. 'We could launch it as the Midlands' answer to the overhyped beauties of Windermere. Much easier to get to than the North-West given the quality of the road network too.' Truly I am inspired today.

'I'll tell you what,' John says, ignoring my suggestion completely. 'I don't know about attracting tourists, but *I'd* like to come on holiday here! I might suggest it to Denise.'

Perhaps that's the way the tourist-board campaign should go then: 'Northamptonshire – The Number One Holiday Destination

For People Who Already Live There.' It's just the kind of thing the characters in *North by Northamptonshire* would come up with.

Denise is waiting for us when we get back to the house – and she's smiling. Very alarming.

'Right then. I asked Brian,' she announces.

'Huh?'

'You know, our neighbour. About being a Midlander.'

I am on tenterhooks.

'He was born here and has lived here all his life,' Denise begins. 'He says he's not a Southerner, and he's definitely not a Northerner.'

So far so good, I say to myself. And …

'But like me he says he's not a Midlander either because that's Birmingham. He'll say he's from the East Midlands if he's pushed, but he doesn't like being pushed – he's a big fella, too, so I'd advise you not to try to push him. What he tells people is he's from Northamptonshire and that's it. Coffee?'

Oh Lord, I whisper, please let me meet a real Midlander soon – someone who has no hang-ups about identifying themselves as such and who understands what it means to be part of the bigger Midland tribe. Just one will do. *Please.*

* * *

I had a fear when I set out on this adventure that my attempt to uncover a broader Midland consciousness would be an essentially artificial exercise: that is – not to put it too bluntly – I would have to make it up. There's no gainsaying the view that the counties of the English Midlands are widely and unfairly underrepresented in the broader national consciousness. It's easily proved too. But that's not the same thing as showing that those same counties constitute a self-defining bloc, with shared traditions and perspectives that bind them together, in the way that the city-states of the North appear to. So, here goes with the six-million-dollar question: is there such a thing as an overarching Midland identity? Do Midlanders actually exist? Or are we just people from Northamptonshire and people from Leicestershire and Granthamites and Newarkians, etc, with nothing in common beyond the fact that we live in neither North nor South?

Though he's best remembered now as the author of *The Darling Buds of May* which exults in the beauties of the South and was made into a successful television series starring David Jason and Pam Ferris, and introduced Catherine Zeta-Jones to a thoroughly undeserving world, H.E. Bates was from Northamptonshire. The rural idyll evoked in the Larkin family books may notionally be 1950s Kent, but Bates was a Northants man through-and-through (he was born in Rushden) and much of what he describes in *The Darling Buds* (a phrase taken from a sonnet by the greatest literary Midlander of them all – but more on him in the next chapter) is derived from his own youthful experience of Northamptonshire rural life. (Isn't it odd that arguably the finest English nature writers of the twentieth century – H.E. Bates and D.H. Lawrence – both hailed from the supposedly unremittingly industrial and unpicturesque Midlands?)

Bates wasn't just from Northants. He was also avowedly a Midlander. His memoirs are littered with reflections on specifically Midland types and traditions, not least relating to the shoe-making trade. 'I was born, in 1905, into a world of leather and shoemakers,' he recalls at the outset of *The Vanished World*. This local manufacturing tradition has been traced back to the reign of King John, who had a pair of boots made for him when he was staying at Northampton Castle in 1213. By the nineteenth century there were dozens of 'boot and shoe' villages, whose populations devoted themselves exclusively to the production of high-quality footwear. As a result Northamptonshire could lay claim to the title of 'Bootmaker to the Empire'. These 'boot and shoe' settlements have gone now – Bates dates their decline to the eve of the Great War: 'The day of the hand-craftsman was virtually over; the machine was inexorably advancing' – but they produced people of a distinct character: quintessential Midlanders in fact, Bates suggests. 'The impression I really get is of a dry, droll, unshaven independence and it is not at all an unlikeable quality,' he notes in *The Vanished World.* 'The shoemakers of the Midlands have long been noted for their pride, political acumen, sturdy independence of mind and an ability to talk sense under conditions where others often signally fail. It is in fact from this same generation … that there sprang, to their abiding credit, an industrial arbitration system that has virtually kept the boot and shoe industry in England free from any kind of serious dispute or stoppage for over half a century.' None of that North/South them-and-us stuff, in other words. If you're looking for the key to the role played by the Notts men and women in the miners' strike in the 1980s, it lies in this same Midland tradition of sturdy independence of mind.

Throughout *The Vanished World*, Bates demonstrates a rare sense of the tribal distinctiveness of Midlanders. For instance, he describes his grandmother as 'a proud, very beautiful girl in that pure mould for which the Midland valleys of England are justly famous. Not only are the people of these valleys, from Ouse to Trent, the best looking in all England; they are probably some of the handsomest in all Europe.' Contemporary mass migration may have made a nonsense of such generalisations about age-old physical types, but Bates's notion of Midland particularity is striking all the same. He isn't always a fan of the region's defining characteristics either, speaking for instance of 'that harsh Midland red brick which equally oppresses heart, soul, eye and senses'. The main point is that, for Bates, the Midlands is utterly distinct from North and South.

Alongside soap operas and football teams, food is one of the great keys to regional identity. Lunch is for lightweight Southerners; noonday dinners are for salt-of-the-earth Northern working types, runs the logic. Sitting down to your main meal in the middle of the day therefore automatically makes you a Northerner – according to Northerners, at any rate. If someone out there wants to brand Midland mealtimes, Bates may well hold the key. Here he is describing the Sundays of his youth: 'Always, in the true Midland tradition, we ate pudding first and meat afterwards, a practice my father insistently continued all through his life. (My grandfather maintained that in his day the pudding was eaten from the underside of the plate, after which the plate was turned right side up for the meat.)'

So that's how you recognise a true Midlander: they eat their rhubarb crumble before their lamb chop and – with scrupulous economy of means – they use both sides of a single dish to do so.

Anxieties of a lone driver, men in tights swinging from ropes, and the revealing strangeness of the Authorship Controversy

I'm not a good solo traveller. Sitting alone at the wheel, I always manage to persuade myself that there's something wrong with the car. Is it beginning to list to one side? Do I need to change the tyre? (And if so, how do I do that exactly?) What was that noise? Is that smoke I can smell? I hope the engine isn't about to burst into flames! Travelling alone can be an alarming business.

The journey from Northampton to Stratford-upon-Avon in lovely, leafy Warwickshire – a county my friend Elizabeth considers far too rural to be authentically Midland – couldn't be simpler but I still manage to get lost, taking an unplanned detour through Milton Keynes. I have no innate sense of direction, you see. I always mean to research my route thoroughly before setting off but I never do. Why not: male pride? Laziness? A secret love of getting into a sweaty panic as I realise, once again, that I haven't the faintest idea where I am or where I'm going? Whatever the cause, there's an important knock-on effect: journeys take a lot longer than they should and, under pressure to make up for lost time, I foolhardily ignore the increasingly insistent urgings of my bladder and drive on past a series of service stations, until, on the point of wetting myself, I pull the car over in a hysterical rush and end up having to urinate on the side of the road. Perhaps my propensity for pissing on the public highway is evidence of my Mansfield genes. You can take the boy out of Mansfield, etc.

Today, I relieve myself somewhere between Staverton and Shuckburgh. I think it was probably the sign for the tormentingly named Bishop's Itchington that did for me on this occasion. It's a shame I couldn't have held on ten minutes or so longer, until I was out the other side of Royal Leamington Spa (the town drops the 'Royal' in less formal moments, but you can tell it's got real pedigree from the fact that it's twinned with not one, not two, but *three* Continental towns; that's breeding, that is). For here, on the border with Lillington, is found the Midland Oak, or its 1988 replanting, to be precise, which is said to mark the centre point of England. Had my bladder allowed me to, I would have been proud to add my own measure of moisture to the surrounding soil to ensure that it never goes thirsty.

Anyway, moving swiftly on, my destination today is Stratford-upon-Avon, which lies just a few miles beyond the Midland Oak. Stratford, of course, was the birthplace of William Shakespeare, World Literature's Greatest Genius™, and it seems appropriate that the writer who has done more than any other to define English identity across the past five hundred years should have emerged from the county that seems to stands geographically at the very centre of the country. From John of Gaunt's 'this England' speech ('this scepter'd isle, / This earth of majesty, this seat of Mars, / This other Eden') in *Richard II* to King Harry's pre-Agincourt rallying cry ('we happy few, we band of brothers') in *Henry V,* the Man from the Middle has provided the country with the most resonant language in which to express itself in times of both joy and trouble, providing Establishment and radical voices alike with their scripts at critical moments in our history. It seems more than mere coincidence that Shakespeare's birth and death dates are usually given as 23 April – St George's Day, England's National Day. You could almost say that the Bard, in all his variety, *is* England.

He is also a global figure, of course. It's reckoned that at any time of day or night a theatrical group somewhere in the world will be performing *Hamlet,* a play that like many of Shakespeare's other works appears to enjoy universal relevance. The great German polymath Johann Wolfgang von Goethe said: 'Shakespeare meets with the spirit of the world. He enters the world as its spirit.' Meanwhile the great French writer Victor Hugo – author of *Les Misérables* and a noted literary nudist – declared: 'After God, Shakespeare created the most.' More recently, the great US critic Harold Bloom has gone so far as to declare that Shakespeare 'invented the text of modern life'. Unsurprisingly, Shakespeare was voted Man of the Millennium in a major national poll in 1999. (Mind you, in a subsequent, more local poll, Midlanders rated Shakespeare only the second Greatest Midlander. R.J. Mitchell, the inventor of the Spitfire, came top, with Edward Elgar in third place. Midlanders love an outside bet.)

* * *

My driving-related anxieties only increase when I finally arrive in Stratford. I don't enjoy the business of locating somewhere to park and I enjoy the act of parking itself even less – I like to have at least three bays to aim at. In Stratford I head for a quiet-looking multistorey, which appears to have enough empty space to park a 747 in. Result! But when I go to pay, the machine will only accept cash – I don't have any, naturally – and special 'Stratford cards'. Can that be right? What about those more universally recognised credit cards – *everyone* accepts those, surely? Not in Stratford, it would appear. I sigh and set off in search of another car park.

Eventually I find one – I don't mean to suggest there's any lack of car parks in Stratford, there are plenty; there are just too many cars in most of them for my liking – where I successfully berth the motor, as no one I know likes to say, and head over to the pay-and-display machine. Result! This time it accepts Visa.

But not *my* Visa, it seems. When I put my card in, the machine responds by angrily spitting it back out and then huffily switching itself off. Suddenly I am assailed by a vision of spending the whole day in Stratford just going from car park to car park. That's the drive-through counties for you – they make it more or less impossible for you to stop in them.

I stand before the machine in mute perplexity until I hear a fruity female voice at my shoulder.

'Have you broken it?'

I'm wearing a leather jacket, I realise. The woman probably thinks I'm a hooligan. She's probably calling the police on her mobile. I'm going to end up spending the night in a cell in Stratford police station! On the plus side: perhaps that would make a better book – *Banged Up in the Middle: A Tour of Midland Jails*. I turn to try to defuse the situation.

'No … At least, not deliberately,' I begin, but there's no need to go on as she's laughing. She doesn't think I'm a vandal after all.

I explain about the problem with my card as we wait for the

machine to revive. In the meantime a queue has begun to form behind us.

'I've got a couple of pounds in my purse if you need them,' the nice lady says. She really doesn't think I'm a vandal, then; she thinks I'm a vagrant. Probably thinks I made the credit card story up. Other ladies, overhearing our conversation, begin to get their purses out too.

Nice people, Stratfordians.

You won't be surprised to learn that there's a high degree of theatrical theming in Stratford. My route into the centre of town, after I finally finish negotiating with that ticket machine and take leave of my Stratford girls, carries me past a nightclub named Chicago's, which is advertising a 'Last Fling before the Ring' hen night – that's not a Shakespearean quote or allusion as far as I'm aware, but it's almost the only thing you'll see written on the shop fronts here that isn't. After all, Shakespeare's home town is the Midlands' only major international visitor attraction, and what tourists want to see when they come here are traces of the life and works of World Literature's Greatest Genius™: in short, evidence that *Shakespeare woz 'ere*. Most obviously fulfilling this brief is the Royal Shakespeare Company, which occupies a prime piece of real estate by the river, and offers a rolling programme of Jacobethan revivals and newer work to please both cognoscenti and casuals. But the Bard colours just about every other aspect of Stratford's cultural and commercial life. The route through Bard's Walk shopping arcade leads you to the tourist office, which is stuffed with information about Shakespeare-related sites and activities: Anne Hathaway's Cottage, where Shakespeare's wife lived before their marriage; Mary Arden's House, his mother's childhood home; and so on. In the tourist-office window there's a poster for a 'No Holds Bard' tour of Stratford. Bad – or, should I say, *Bard* – puns are more or less de rigueur amidst Stratford's half-timbered loveliness, and there are some delightfully incongruous commercial borrowings from the Big Book of the Bard. The suavely attractive and highly rated Othello's Bar Brasserie is presumably where jealous types gather, while Iago, one of the greatest villains in the Shakespeare canon, has a jewellery store named in his honour. One thing's for sure: it must be hell to live here if you hate the sodding theatre.

In truth, there are only two essential destinations on any Stratford itinerary. (There used to be three, but Gyles Brandreth's Teddy Bear Museum tragically closed its doors to visitors in 2006.) One is the RSC, and the other is Shakespeare's Birthplace, and it is with the latter that I begin my visit. You enter via a thoroughly contemporary brick building and exhibition space, where Will – a major contributor to the movie industry this past century – is given a suitably Hollywood-style build-up, with video clips and a portentous disembodied voice announcing: 'You are about to enter the house in which he was born, where he spent his early adult life, the home which helped to turn him into a genius' or some such, before you're finally ushered into the wattle-and-daub dwelling once occupied by the Shakespeare family. (The Victorians took over the house for the nation in 1847 and coated the exterior with concrete, but underneath it's still just twigs and mud.)

'You're walking on the original floor, the one that William and his wife would have walked on,' a tour guide informs me reverentially as I cross the threshold into this most sacred of Shakespearean shrines. He speaks with a marked Brummie twang – as, unsurprisingly, do many of the locals around here, since we're only thirty miles from Birmingham; Shakespeare himself would probably have sounded more like Lenny Henry or Jasper Carrott than Laurence Olivier. I – along with a gaggle of other visitors, visibly drawn from all points of the world compass – am next directed into the parlour, which is dominated by a big bed. The Shakespeare family would mostly have slept on mattresses scattered on the floor, we are told, while the impressive four-poster was intended to serve as a showpiece for visitors. 'It's a bit like buying a big car and parking it ostentatiously on the drive so that everyone can see it,' the guide explains.

Then – inevitably – the niggling Authorship Controversy rears its ugly head. Our guide isn't impressed by those who would contend that Shakespeare didn't really write the Works of Shakespeare. 'One of the arguments is he had no education,' he says. 'And it's true he didn't go to university. But they put in long hours at the local grammar school and when he left he would have had the equivalent of a Classics degree today!' The crowd oohs and aahs delightedly at this robust rubbishing of the anti-Shakespeareans. 'Sorry, I'm getting propagandist now,' the guide excuses himself, although he surely knows that he's only telling us what we want to hear. After all, if you've spent time and money making a pilgrimage to the Birthplace of World Literature's Greatest Genius™ the last thing you want to be told is that Shakespeare didn't actually write the plays and that Stratford's claim to cultural significance is a sham.

* * *

No one doubts that the Elizabethan theatrical impresario William Shakespeare hailed from the rural Midland redoubt of Stratford-upon-Avon. Equally, no one seriously questions that the Collected Works of William Shakespeare represent the highest literary achievement in the English language. What some people do wonder, however, is whether the two Shakespeares are one and the same person. These sceptics, usually known as 'anti-Stratfordians', suggest that the works were actually written by someone else – someone less provincial, someone better educated, probably someone more aristocratic – who, for whatever reason, chose to hide his (or her: Queen Elizabeth I has been suggested as a candidate) true identity behind that of William Shakespeare. The latter, after all, was a mere 'stupid, ignorant, third-rate play-actor' according to the founding anti-Stratfordian Delia Bacon, who proposed her namesake Francis Bacon as the 'real' Shakespeare. The fact that Ms Bacon subsequently had to relocate to an insane asylum should in no way deter you from giving her theory full credence.

There's much that is strange about the so-called 'Authorship Controversy', not least that the most favoured candidate for having written the Collected Works is Edward de Vere, the 17th Earl of Oxford, who was first proposed as the 'true Shakespeare' by J. Thomas Looney (the clue, as has often been pointed out, is in the name) in 1920. No matter that de Vere died in 1605, before a number of the most famous Shakespeare plays were written and performed: the earl would have had intimate first-hand knowledge of court dealings and a proper university education, which, in the view of many 'Oxfordians' (including Sigmund Freud), makes him much more likely to have written the plays, with their impressive learning and deep knowledge of statecraft, than 'that Stratford fellow' who had only a grammar-school education and no direct experience of government. Old Bailey judge Christmas Humphreys summed up the general feeling of the antis in 1955 in his introduction to Miss Hilda Amphlett's *Who Was Shakespeare?*: 'It is offensive to scholarship, to our national dignity, and to our sense of fair play to worship the memory of a petty-minded tradesman while leaving the actual author of the Shakespeare plays and poems unhonoured and ignored.'

The Oxfordians aren't going away either. A 2011 film making the case for de Vere as the true Shakespeare – entitled *Anonymous*

– recently generated fresh publicity for the anti-Stratfordians. It was directed by Roland Emmerich, creator of Hollywood blockbusters such as *Independence Day*, and featured among its cast Mark Rylance, a noted anti-Stratfordian who was – of all things – formerly artistic director of Shakespeare's Globe in London. In light of the fact that de Vere can attract supporters of such prominence and influence, it's by no means inconceivable that, in the manner of former Wakefield MP David Hinchliffe and his Robin Hood-related rant, the Member for Oxford East will one day be heard issuing dire warnings to Parliament that Oxfordians are becoming so angry about the signs at the Warwickshire border that welcome you to 'Shakespeare's County' that they're going to start pulling them down. You know, what with Shakespeare so obviously being a front for the Earl of Oxford and all.

Significantly, the Authorship Controversy did not begin until two hundred years or so after Shakespeare's death. His contemporaries had no trouble accepting that the 'boy from Stratford' (as Charlie Chaplin, another notable Shakespeare-denier, referred to him derisively) was genuinely the writer of the works that were performed in his name. For instance, Shakespeare's old friend and rival, the well-known playwright Ben Jonson, penned a moving poem in his honour, 'To the Memory of my Beloved, the Author Master William Shakespeare, and what he hath left us', the title of which alone, with its use of the word 'Author', especially in the context of its appearance in the 1623 First Folio of Shakespeare's works, seems to banish all doubt as to who really wrote the plays. Nonetheless, such seemingly incontrovertible evidence was insufficient to stop some people – a tiny minority, it's true, but a very passionate and vocal tiny minority – around the end of the eighteenth century from beginning to question the role of Shakespeare in writing his own plays. Why did it happen then, and not earlier?

Shakespeare's apotheosis – the moment when he metamor-
phosed from an ordinary if much-favoured playwright into the
Immortal Bard and was adopted as the English National Poet –
took place in the course of the eighteenth century, which deserves
in many respects to be known as the 'Midland century'. His elevation was sealed by the agency of two fellow Midlanders. Samuel
Johnson and David Garrick hailed originally from the so-called
'City of Philosophers', Lichfield in Staffordshire, situated only thirty
miles or so from Stratford, but by the mid-eighteenth century
they had established themselves as two of the most influential
cultural figures in London. In 1755 Johnson published his famous
Dictionary, a work of extraordinary intellectual reach and influence which revolutionised lexicography and began the process
of giving definitive, standardised form to the English language.
According to one commentator, 'by the end of the century every
educated household had, or had access to, the great book', and as
a result those same households found themselves imbibing quotations from Shakespeare, by far the most frequently quoted author
in the *Dictionary*. When users wanted to know authoritatively
what a given word meant or how it might be used, they found
that the examples chosen by Johnson were regularly drawn from
Shakespeare's works, a practice that confirmed the Bard's seminal
importance in the development of the English language. Today the
Oxford English Dictionary contains in excess of thirty thousand
Shakespeare quotations.

If Johnson immortalised Shakespeare as one of the great beget-
ters of the English language – as the *Dictionary* emphasises with
its supporting quotations, we owe so many of the basic building
blocks of our everyday language, from 'bated breath' (*The Merchant
of Venice*) to 'wild goose chase' (*Romeo and Juliet*) and 'too much
of a good thing' (*As You Like It*), never mind the more highfalutin

stuff, to the Bard – it was the celebrated actor and theatre manager David Garrick who returned Shakespeare's work to pre-eminence on the stage and, no less importantly, restored a sense of the Bard's geographical rootedness. In September 1769, with the full support of the local council, who were seeking funds to refurbish their town hall, Garrick organised a Shakespeare Jubilee in Stratford-upon-Avon. Though much satirised at the time, this three-day extravaganza drew a large, fashionable crowd from London into the wilds of Warwickshire – whither, it's reasonable to presume, most had never strayed before. Dr Johnson refused to attend, but his biographer, James Boswell, was happy to lend his support and even wrote an account of the splendid proceedings for *The London Magazine*:

> My bosom glowed with joy when I beheld a numerous and brilliant company of nobility and gentry, the rich, the brave, the witty, and the fair, assembled to pay their tribute of praise to Shakespeare … The jubilee began with an oratorio in the great church at Stratford … The procession with music from the church to the amphitheatre, led on by Mr Garrick, had a very good effect. The amphitheatre was a wooden building, erected just on the brink of the Avon, in the form of an octagon, with eight pillars supporting the roof. It was elegantly painted and gilded. Between the pillars were crimson curtains, very well imitated as hanging over each recess.

There, a picture showed 'Time leading Shakespeare to immortality', while guests further honoured the Bard's memory by wearing, 'hung in a blue ribband at our breasts, a medal of Shakespeare, very well cast by Mr Westwood of Birmingham. On one side was the head of Shakespeare, and round it this inscription, "We shall not look upon his like again."'

The Jubilee celebrations – fireworks, public addresses and much more besides – didn't pass off without incident or misadventure. A planned procession of Shakespearean characters had to be abandoned when the heavens opened and rained on Garrick's parade, both metaphorically and literally, half-submerging his shrine to Shakespeare in the process. Metropolitan visitors complained that local shopkeepers gouged them mercilessly – 'Much noise has been made about the high price of every thing at Stratford' – while Boswell himself admitted that the transport might have been better planned: 'Towards the end of the jubilee many of us were not in very good humour, as many inconveniencies occurred, particularly there not being carriages enough to take us away but in detachments, so that those who had to wait long tired exceedingly.' That's a situation that has hardly improved in the last 250 years, as anyone who has tried to escape home by train after watching an evening performance at the RSC will know.

But overall Boswell declared the celebrations a success. 'I laughed away spleen by a droll simile: Taking the whole of this jubilee, said I, is like eating an artichoke entire. We have some fine mouthfuls, but also swallow the leaves and the hair, which are confoundedly difficult of digestion.'

The aftermath could hardly have been more dramatic, not least for the fate of Stratford itself. As has been observed: 'The whole future history of the borough stems from Garrick's decision to hold his Jubilee there.' The previously sleepy provincial town was transformed into the centre of a developing global Shakespeare 'industry'. Today, thanks to the 1769 Jubilee, Stratford has little economic or cultural *raison d'être* beyond its connection to the Immortal Bard, which has turned it into one of the world's great tourist destinations.

Curiously, it was only after the Bard's geographical origins had been so explicitly laid bare by Garrick and his fellow worshippers – when Bardolatry had become akin to a religion and the pilgrimage to Warwickshire had become an important rite of passage for all literature lovers – that the great Authorship Controversy got going. As visitors started to grow familiar with provincial Stratford and its environs, including a rapidly industrialising Birmingham, sceptics began to say: *if the historical William Shakespeare really came from here, if he really was just a middling Midlander, then there's no way he could actually have written those plays.*

There are only two characters in the Shakespearean dramatic canon who bear the name of William: one is a grammar-school boy, the other is a tongue-tied country bumpkin who is said to have been born in the Forest of Arden (there was a Forest of Arden near to Shakespeare's birthplace in Warwickshire) and who loses his beloved to a smooth-talking courtier in *As You Like It*. The role, which may originally have been played by Shakespeare himself (he was an actor too, of course), is interpreted by more sophisticated commentators as a deftly ironic self-portrait. The prime movers in the Authorship Controversy, on the other hand, take it as the unvarnished truth, a revealing jibe at the nominal author of the Works of Shakespeare made by the concealed 'real' author.

Shakespeare was hardly the only important Renaissance dramatist to lack a university degree or formal court connections. Ben Jonson's education similarly stopped at the grammar-school stage, but despite the high degree of learning evident in his plays no one has ever suggested that their author was anything other than the Cockney son-of-a-bricklayer that the standard biography suggests Jonson to have been. Thomas Kyd wrote the linguistically high-flown blood-and-thunder stage smash *The Spanish Tragedy* (an important source for *Hamlet*) without attending Oxford or Cambridge, but again no scholarly hue-and-cry has ever been set

141

up to prove that Kyd was merely a front for a better-educated nobleman. Perhaps that's because, like Jonson, he was born and raised in London. Cultural commentators understand London and the South; they understand the North too – the regions' respective PR machines ensure that they do. Had Shakespeare hailed from Yorkshire or Liverpool, the Authorship Controversy would never have taken hold.

But what's most crucial here – though it's never said – is that no Northerner or Southerner *could* have written the Collected Works. They are beyond the sympathies and imaginative reaches of both. Shakespeare's plays are products of a recognisably Midland consciousness or state of being. Much of the doubt about the identity of their author ultimately stems from the difficulty of inferring much about him and his attitudes from the plays. As the nineteenth-century critic and essayist William Hazlitt wrote, Shakespeare was 'the least of an egotist that it was possible to be'. More than their sublime language, it is the plays' openness to different interpretations, their inherent *adaptability*, that has made them so enduring. Their 'meanings' are hard to pin down because they are properly dramatic, and not simply vehicles for Shakespeare's authorial voice. Take *Henry V*, which dramatises England's victory over the French at Agincourt and is usually thought Shakespeare's most overtly patriotic play. Even here, different directors have used the action to offer radically different interpretations of Shakespeare's words: at the Old Vic in 1937, Laurence Olivier's Henry conveyed a pacifist message; a few years later, Olivier's film of the same play, dedicated to the men who had liberated Europe from the Nazis, offered a wildly conflicting message; Nicholas Hytner's 2003 production at the National Theatre drew critical parallels with Britain's interventions in Iraq. *The Taming of the Shrew* has been staged as both a misogynistic rant and a feminist tract. The plays are both left-wing and right-wing, socially conservative and politically progressive, cosily pro-Establishment and full of radical fury. This extraordinary openness grows out of their author's lack of egotism, as Hazlitt had it, or out of his poetical selflessness, as John Keats characterised it. No true son of the North or comfortably conformist Southerner could have written with so little ego, so little bias or *parti pris*, with an understanding of and sympathy for all points of view. That's right: if you look at the Works carefully, you'll see that they *must* have been written by a middling Midlander rather than a Southern Establishment figure or Northern rebel. They were written by the quintessential shape-shifting Midlander, in fact.

As previously mentioned, those who question Shakespeare's role in the creation of the Collected Works are known as 'anti-Stratfordians': their beef is avowedly with the playwright's place of origin. Most of them would surely agree with Jilly Cooper about the Midlands being 'beyond the pale'; and Shakespeare is nothing if not a typical Midlander. His father, like Margaret Thatcher's, was a small businessman, 'careful of property and propriety', who worked as a glover and later occupied the post of town alderman. Like Dick Whittington before him, in quitting small-town life in the West Midlands and heading for London, Shakespeare *fils* became a symbol of social mobility and adaptability. Sniped at initially as an 'upstart Crow' by the group of Southern writers who dominated the Elizabethan stage in the early 1590s, he rose to pre-eminence in the London theatre while those same 'university wits' – Robert Greene, Thomas Nashe, etc – died prematurely and in penury. Other aspects of his biography have come to outrage later commentators, in particular signs of his bourgeois social conformity. Shakespeare obtained a coat of arms and motto for his distinctly lower-middle-class family – how *nouveau*! – then, in due course, prepared for John Fletcher to replace him as writer in chief to his company, the King's Men, and, like some middle manager with a decent pension pot, *retired*, leaving the capital to spend his final years in tranquillity in his Midland birthplace. How could Shakespeare, the author of the greatest works in the English language, have been so *provincial*?

There's a more general moral to be drawn here. As an artist Shakespeare may have been exceptional, but as a Midlander he was in many respects typical. Certainly, the pseudo-scholarly response to Shakespeare the man – which has been to suggest that the biographically anonymous Stratfordian's works must have been ghosted by Christopher Marlowe, Francis Bacon or the Earl of Oxford (all metropolitan Southerners, please note) – is typical of the response to high-achieving Midlanders generally: that is, they are to be appropriated at all costs for the North or the South instead.

It doesn't have to be this way, if only the Midlands was a bit better at celebrating its own achievements. The prosaic Midland accent decried by both Cooper and Maconie (the latter describes it variously, but always deprecatingly, as 'sing-song' and 'yokel cockney') has shaped the language of our poets since time imme-morial. The two greatest early English poems, the eighth-century epic *Beowulf* and the later alliterative classic *Gawain and the Green Knight*, were both written in what appear to be Midland dialects. The identities of the poems' authors are unknown – anonymity being the natural state of the Midlander – but from 'Hwæt! We Gardena in geardagum' to 'Siþen þe sege and þe assaut watz sesed at Troye', the Old and Middle English poetic traditions seem to have been dominated by distinctively Midland voices.

That metropolitan poet Geoffrey Chaucer, often credited with being the first court writer to demonstrate the superiority of the

English vernacular over French and Latin, wrote in an East Midland dialect which, by the fourteenth century, had been adopted as the language of the court and universities. As a result, the standard English spoken today is Midland in origin. Reader, your tongue is a Midlander.

The list of great Midland poets goes on. England's most popular nineteenth-century versifier, Alfred Tennyson, was from the Midlands. Universally celebrated for his *Idylls of the King*, a rendition of that body of Arthurian legend that serves as one of the key founding myths of the nation, Tennyson was also responsible for immortalising the eleventh-century Midland noblewoman Godgifu, or Lady Godiva. And in 2003 the Poetry Book Society named another Midlander – Philip Larkin – as 'the nation's best-loved poet'. Born in Coventry, and then a resident of Leicester (where he might have bumped into a teenage Joe Orton, the most anarchic and morally subversive of all English playwrights), Larkin is another classic Midlander, shyly preferring the provincial shadows to the metropolitan limelight. Naturally, he's regularly been claimed by the North.

The Midlands has been no less prodigious in its output of novelists. In addition to Alan Sillitoe and H.E. Bates, twentieth-century greats include D.H. Lawrence, Arnold Bennett and Henry Green. You've probably never heard of Green, although you're sure to be familiar with his only serious rival for the title of England's Greatest Modernist Writer – Virginia Woolf. The famous Bloomsberry has the Southern mythmaking machine to thank for her overinflated reputation, whereas Green combined his literary pursuits with a career as an industrialist, studiously avoided the spotlight and, like Shakespeare, one day simply stopped publishing work. A typically retiring and unstarry Midlander, in other words. Though the PR machines of North and South make a deal of noise in claiming otherwise, the best things in life tend to come from the middle, as H.E. Bates noted: '[Higham Ferrers in Northamptonshire] is not only very nearly plumb in the middle of England, but if you take a pair of compasses and draw a circle of fifty or sixty miles with the little borough at its centre you will find yourself enriched by a truly remarkable company of famous men,' he noted in *The Vanished World*. His list of local writers includes Dryden, Bunyan, Milton, Cowper, Clare and, of course, Shakespeare. 'This indeed is the old Kingdom of Mercia, cradle of so much of literature and of the Standard English we know,' he concludes. This is just the sort of staggering stuff I've been looking for. Why don't more people already know about this?

* * *

No visit to Stratford is complete without the pleasure – sometimes the purgatory; sometimes, let's be honest, the hell – of seeing a performance by the RSC. The main show today happens to be a new play called *The Heart of Robin Hood*. 'Oodie is an appropriate subject for the RSC: not only is he a Midlander like Shakespeare, but both men are inextricably linked with the mysterious and magical forests that used to dominate the landscape of so much of this part of the country. Robin and his Merry Men resided in Sherwood Forest, while Shakespeare appears to have spent much of his childhood in the Forest of Arden. In his plays, it's in the woods that the most remarkable transformations take place – think of *A Midsummer Night's Dream* or *As You Like It*. For many, it has become a cliché that the Midland landscape is unvaryingly industrial, but the forest is central to the region's history and mythology. Merrie England – that utopian kingdom of pastoral contentment – is synonymous with Robin Hood and the Midlands.

Before the show, I eat in the theatre's Rooftop Restaurant, which, as you might expect, can't resist a little Shakespearean theming. My bottle of sparkling water bears a quotation from *Macbeth*. (Isn't it bad luck to mention that word in a theatre? Shouldn't the bottle identify it as 'the Scottish play' instead?) The words seem appropriate enough for use on a bottle of fizzy H_2O – 'The earth hath bubbles, as the water has' – although when you remember that they're spoken following Banquo and Macbeth's first encounter with the three Weird Sisters, a meeting that carries them swiftly to their graves, the general implication seems a bit grim. I decide not to drink the water.

Food-wise, it's a toss-up between the Cotswold chicken and Gloucestershire cheese and potato cake. When the waitress comes over to take my order, I tell her – it's irritating of me, I know – that I'll go for the authentic Midland option, thank you very much. She's Eastern European and looks nonplussed.

'You see, we are in the Midlands here, which a friend of mine has compared to Belarus,' I begin to explain, adapting Elizabeth's words slightly to serve my purposes. 'We're caught in the middle between North and South or, in the case of Belarus, between East and West. Now, the Cotswolds are in Oxfordshire, which is considered Southern, whereas Gloucestershire, like Warwickshire, is part of the Midlands. Thus, when I said …'

I can see that I've lost her attention, if I ever had it. I decide to cut to the chase. 'I'll have the cheese and potato cake, please.'

Having savoured every last mouthful of my Gloucestershire-sourced repast, I continue my drive to promote Midland consciousness when I go down to the theatre and purchase a programme for the show. I point to the poster above the programme seller's head which describes Robin as an 'English legend'.

'You've missed a branding opportunity there,' I say. 'You should have called him a *Midland* legend.'

'Yes,' the young man replies uncertainly. 'Absolutely.' He looks relieved when I decide not to explain myself further. The RSC no doubt attracts its fair share of pedants and nutters.

The show turns out to be pretty good. It's certainly highly acrobatic, with actors making athletic entrances via a huge, grassy slide at the back of the stage or down ropes from a tree that looks much more imposing than the real Major Oak, at least in the latter's current state. It was written by a bloke from Surrey (David Farr) and directed by another fella who describes himself as Icelandic with a large helping of Irish (Gísli Örn Garðarsson), and accordingly it shows little of what you might call Midland sensibility. The opposite, in fact. At one point, wicked Prince John refers to the forest as being in 'Middle England', blurring social and geographical categories that have little or nothing to do with one another. The characters are seemingly incapable of uttering the place-defining phrase that would be most appropriate here – the Midlands. By contrast, a place name they're very keen to pronounce is that of York, synonym of the North. Scenes take place at York Castle and York Minster, while plucky Marian is identified as the daughter of the Duke of York. When she first encounters Robin of Sherwood, he's the sort of mean-spirited outlaw who will mug a passing monk just for fun. It's the feisty Northern lass who, turning the age-old values of the 'Yorkshireman's Creed' on their head, teaches him to give to the poor. By the end of the evening, Robin has grown into the iconic robs-from-the-rich-to-give-to-the-poor outlaw of legend – and in the process he's also become an honorary Yorkshireman.

Subtly, at the edges of public consciousness, that revisionist campaign to transform 'Oodie into a Northerner is beginning to grip. Mark my words: unless the Midlands learns to fight back, in a hundred years' time no one will remember that he used to be Robin of Sherwood. Instead, children will be taught that the famous Northern outlaw was distantly related, via the bloodline of Sir Russell of Crowe, to the great Barnsley broadcaster Michael Parkinson.

TO COVENTRY

A flag to gather under, Olympians and Scouts, and the age-old allure of Coventrisation

Before I set off for Coventry, I receive two messages.

The first is in the form of an email from my cousin Dean, who has kindly agreed to be my guide for the day and whose teenage children are supposed to be setting the agenda. 'We have finally worked out Ed and Sarah's busy social calendars and they will both be "in" on Saturday, so do come then,' he writes. 'Re: what we're going to be visiting, Ed says he cannot think of anything good about Coventry but I am sure he does not mean it. Sarah has picked somewhere – you'll need to bring walking boots! Speak soon, Dean.' Ominous, that bit about walking boots. I don't know much about Coventry, but isn't it supposed to be a 'concrete jungle', as that song by local band The Specials has it? Where are they planning to take me?

The second message arrives from my friend Jerry, the one from

Bread-and-Lard Island. He's far too much of a traditionalist to send texts or emails; his words of wisdom are handwritten on a postcard showing the graveyard where he'd like to be interred. I told him that I was about to go West, news that he appears to have taken with the utmost gravity. On his personal map of the Midlands, the western portion is obviously marked with the words 'Here be monsters'. He recommends the route I should take so as to get the earliest and clearest possible indication of the difference between East and West: 'You should drive down the A46,' he says. 'Very important, the A46. It's basically the Fosse Way, which was an ancient communication line before the Romans turned it into a road. You start at Newark, which is the easternmost point of the Midlands. You go down through the Nottinghamshire wolds, rolling countryside. Then you can see Nottingham off to the right, this great wen sucking everybody in. After the Soar Valley and Leicester, you're down to Coventry. That's where things start closing in. It's the beginning of the Birmingham conurbation, and the little pockets of countryside are under siege. Suddenly, it's all people with orange tans driving Jaguars – it's just different over there.'

For Jerry as for my Aunt Denise, the East/West divide within the Midlands is as important as the North/South one nationally. No wonder Midlanders have such an image problem when they won't even agree that they come from essentially the same place. It's a problem that's built into the very name 'the Midlands', which, as my dictionary informs me, can function as either a singular or a plural noun: Midlanders live in a place of indeterminate number – one or many. There are no such problems with the names of North or South, of course. There's only one true North! And despite the historic rivalries between the proudly independent-minded city-states of Manchester, Liverpool and Newcastle, Northerners generally manage to subscribe to a single common identity. Why can't Midlanders do the same? Partly it comes down to that binary business: Northerners find common ground by defining themselves against their binary opposite, Southerners; Rebels versus the Establishment. It also explains why the North feels it can make so free with the Midland heritage: having no binary partner, the Midlands doesn't, *can't*, really exist, so taking from it isn't really stealing. There's only the North and the South, and though never the twain shall meet, nothing shall be allowed to stand between them on the map either.

To foster Midland unity, what we need is a symbol, a metaphorical Midland flag, that we can all gather under. Actually, how about a *physical* Midland flag? There are already separate East and West Midland flags: what we need is one that unites us. It's been suggested that wily old Alex Salmond plumped for a 2014 date for the Scottish referendum because of the numerous national pride-boosting photo opportunities that the Commonwealth Games are going to offer. Chris Hoy with the saltire draped around his shoulders: what could be better calculated to get people voting for Scottish independence? The Midlands should do something similar. If we had a flag of our own, we could get Rebecca Adlington, Kenneth Clarke MP, Adrian Chiles and other famous Midland athletes to pose for the cameras wrapped in it. But what should this putative flag look like? The Isle of Man triskelion (the one showing three legs going round and round in a circle) perhaps? As state symbols go, it's a bit Monty Python and can give people funny notions: personally, whenever I meet anyone from the Isle of Man I always expect them to be tripedal. But it's memorable, and that's what counts when you're trying to create a sense of identity.

After a little reflection, I have decided that the Midland flag should be based on what's distinctive about the region: the fact that it's in the middle. 'Midlands by name, stuck in the middle by nature,' could be our slogan. So what we need is a flag that's all middle, right to the edges, so that – conceptually at least – *it has no edges, it's all middle*. No North above it, no South below. Now all that's required is to work out how to design something that's all middle and then we can really get that unity campaign rolling.

* * *

Weather has a huge impact on our experience of place, but at the moment the landscape is wrapped in such a thick blanket of fog that the approach to Coventry remains a bit of a mystery to me. Is it really all 'closing in' out there, as my apocalyptic pal Jerry suggested? I can't tell. As I near my cousin Dean's house, a couple of miles from the city centre, the fog finally begins to clear, but only thanks to the arrival of heavy rain – 'Arkattit,' I sigh in homage to my Notts forefathers – which poses its own challenge to visibility.

Dean is from Mansfield or, more precisely, the satellite village of Rainworth. In other words, he's a guttural East Midlander exiled in the sing-songy West Midlands. Still, at least the locals in these parts can understand what he's saying. That wasn't the case when he was training as a teacher on the outskirts of West London a couple of decades ago. 'When you're doing teaching practice, if the kids can't understand you straightaway, you lose them for good – as I quickly found out,' he recounts. The London kids and their trainee teacher only grew up about a hundred miles away from each other, but the language gap proved more or less unbridgeable. Not that Dean is hard to understand – he doesn't speak in thick Mellors-the-gamekeeper dialect or anything. Inevitably the adult Southern binarists on his course gave him the nickname of 'Northern'. How he laughed.

He met his wife, Jane, in London while he was doing his teacher training. How does this Southerner fare with interpreting Dean's East Midland grunts?

'Oh I've got used to them,' Jane says, looking at her husband affectionately. 'His dad's accent, on the other hand …'

Dean smiles. 'In the early days, my dad would say something and she'd look at me as if to say: Translate.'

Jane now works in a school in Coventry, where she helps Key Stage Oners to master phonics. To pronounce words in the approved West Midland manner, she finds herself having to shorten her 'a's – 'bath' not 'baarth', etc – and making other concessions to the local accent. One day she'll sound like an authentic Midlander if she's lucky. But she'll probably become a twangy Westerner rather than a throaty Easterner.

Children are very sharp about such matters, of course, and Dean and Jane's super-bright offspring are both keen musicians with good ears, so I ask them about the differences between the way their parents speak.

'I haven't really noticed anything,' says fourteen-year-old Ed, stretching his six-foot frame almost horizontal on the sofa.

'We don't have an accent,' chimes in sixteen-year-old Sarah cheerily.

I explain that everyone has an accent of some sort. Sarah looks displeased by the idea; Ed seems to have fallen asleep.

'Well, sometimes you don't talk properly and I have to ask you to say things again,' their mother chides them gently.

I suggest mischievously that Ed and Sarah sound a bit like Brummies. After all, Coventry is only twenty miles from Birmingham and the local accent certainly has a bit of Western sing-songiness about it.

That gets a reaction from comatose Ed. 'No way! Brummies drag their words on, and their pitch goes up and down,' he says with surprising animation. Sarah does an exaggerated Jasper Carrott (or similar) impersonation and pulls a face as if to say: Don't accuse me of talking like *that*! Even Dean is keen to disavow any connection with Yowyows or Yamyams ('Yow all right?' 'Yam' – as they variously say in Birmingham and the Black Country). No one, it seems, wants to be associated with the way people from Brum or Dudley sound, not even their closest neighbours. Midland unity clearly isn't going to be achieved overnight. And definitely not without a flag.

* * *

It turns out that Sarah's favourite place – where our tour is to begin – is Rough Close, home to the Coventry Scouts. Now Scouting is very important to Dean's family. The terminology is elaborate but I think I've grasped it sufficiently to be confident in saying that Sarah is an Explorer Scout, Ed is an ordinary Scout, while Dean is an Arkela or Cub Scout leader. Jane used to be a Girl Guide but is currently inactive. 'I've got a bright-pink sweatshirt with "iScout" on it, though!' she says.

Yes, even the Scouts do branding.

I ask to see their uniforms.

Sarah's Scout shirt is a patchwork of badges. She takes me through them: First Aid, Navigation … 'I'm rubbish at navigation,' she comments, 'but I've still got the badge. I've also got my Fifty Nights Away, but I haven't sewn that one on yet,' she says.

'You mean "which your mum hasn't sewn on yet"', laughs Jane.

'I thought Scouting was supposed to encourage independence,' I smile at Sarah. 'You mean you've been to Sweden, Germany, the Czech Republic and all these other places but you can't sew on a simple badge!' What a vile old crumblie I am.

'Do – you – sew – your – own – badges – on – Ed?' I ask, enunciating exaggeratedly. (Ho-ho-ho, I really am amusing around teenagers, aren't I?)

No answer comes there from the elongated form on the couch.

Once Dean has shown me his woggle and leadership wood beads, it's time to head out, so he and his children step into their walking boats while I pull on my wellies.

Rough Close is a forty-three-acre campsite on the western outskirts of Coventry that serves as the county Scout HQ. I am told – and I absolutely believe – that it's beautiful here on a warm summer's day, and probably pretty nice even on a merely fair-to-middling autumn day. Unfortunately, it's chucking it down at the moment and the ground is awash with mud, with the result that the spectacle that greets us is a rather bleak one. There's been so much rain recently the wood on one of the camp buildings has even begun to buckle.

As we get out of the car, Dean hands his children an umbrella. Sarah opens and breaks it immediately, although Dean manages to fix it. Ed is much taller than his sister but insists on Sarah holding the umbrella, with the consequence that he keeps bumping his head against it, causing him to complain. Much mirth and some irritation are the result as we wander around the woodland site.

They tell me about a recent event here, when Scouts gathered in their thousands to welcome their Chief, Bear Grylls. Expectations were high but in the event the telly adventurer buzzed in in a helicopter and only stayed fifteen minutes. Ed clearly wasn't impressed. He prefers Ray Mears to Grylls anyway.

We go to stand under the dripping eaves of one of the Scout huts. Both Ed and Sarah have spent many happy nights here, although they are typically laconic when I ask for details. Happily, Dean is freer with his words, enthusing about a recent 'Bugs and Critters

Camp' for Cubs. 'You know the sort of thing: we set jam jars in the ground and in the morning we see what we've caught overnight. Then we spend the next day identifying and drawing them.'

I ask Sarah what the summit of her Scouting career has been so far. 'I don't really know,' she says, not unreasonably. *Who is this silly man and why does he keep asking me silly questions?* she must be thinking to herself, though fortunately she's too well brought up to actually say it. With a little prompting from Dean, she ultimately decides on the Sweden Selection Camp as her best moment, when she was chosen as a Jamboree representative for the UK.

At this point there begins a gentle argument between father and daughter about Sarah's Jamboree itinerary.

'You were in Belgium to start with,' says Dean.

'Dad, what are you talking about? It was Denmark.'

'Was it?' He seems mildly surprised. Sarah does a 'whatever' roll of the eyes.

'And you, Ed? What's the best thing you've done as a Scout?' I ask.

'I've learned to make fires,' he offers mysteriously after a pause. What is he telling me – that he's a pyromaniac? He doesn't look the type. 'Oh, and I slept in a cardboard box,' he adds, no less mysteriously. (To raise money for a homeless charity, I subsequently discover.)

Dean isn't wearing his woggle or wood beads but he is every inch the Arkela as he strides off towards the Camp Fire Circle, a permanent wooden amphitheatre in the forest where Scouts gather on a warm summer's evening – so not on a day like today, obviously – for songs and skits.

What sort of songs? I ask. Not 'Ging Gang Goolie' by any chance?

He considers for a moment. If they do still sing 'Ging Gang Goolie' he obviously doesn't fancy going into details. I don't blame him.

'Silly songs like "The Crazy Moose", you know,' he offers breezily.

'I'm afraid I *don't* know. Could you sing it for me?'

Dean clears his throat and tries a line or two.

'That's definitely not it,' deadpans Sarah, the Explorer Scout. 'You're completely wrong, Dad.' And she pulls another face.

* * *

To return to the binary conundrum: what is the opposite of the middle? What can the Midlands, furnished with that fantastic new all-middle national flag, define itself against?

It strikes me that there *is* a binary model that could be adopted: that of centre and periphery. This spatial metaphor typically crops up in descriptions of imperial systems of rule, the advanced, authoritative middle doling out intellectual and material benefits to a network of comparatively backward provinces. And there is no question that, geographically speaking at least, the Midlands is positioned at the centre of England. Indeed, with my new centre-periphery model in mind, I had thought of beginning my Coventry trip in symbolic fashion with a visit to the nearby village of Meriden, where a sandstone pillar carries the following announcement: 'This ancient wayside cross has stood in the village for some 500 years and by tradition it marks the Centre of England.' The Ordnance Survey doesn't agree – it thinks the geographical heart of the country is eighteen miles away, at Fenny Drayton in Leicestershire; and of course that oak tree I almost pissed on back in Leamington Spa stakes a claim to the title too. But, however you calculate it, the centre of England is somewhere around here.

So Coventry more or less marks the geographical centrepoint of England. But can it claim to be the centre in any other sense – in a way that satisfies the terms of the centre-periphery model?

What cultural, intellectual or administrative benefits has it historically been responsible for dispersing to the English periphery (i.e., London, Manchester and other benighted corners of the country)?

Well, it's given us bikes, cars and aeroplanes for a start. Coventry was a clock- and watchmaking centre in the eighteenth and nineteenth centuries until the Swiss became dominant and the skilled Coventrian workforce, suddenly finding itself at a loose end, had to turn to manufacturing bicycles. The inventor James Starley – he came up with the differential gear, if that means anything to you – set up shop in the city and developed the Rover Safety Bicycle with his nephew, John Kemp Starley. Far superior to the penny-farthing, the Rover famously 'set the pattern to the world'. Indeed, so great was its renown the younger Starley renamed his company in its honour. You can probably guess what happened next: in line with developments elsewhere, Rover began to produce motorcycles and then cars, putting Coventry at the heart of the British motor industry. Daimler, Triumph, Massey Ferguson and Jaguar are among the other major companies to have historic associations with the city. By the 1950s, powered by West Midland knowhow, the UK had become the world's largest exporter of cars, and was second only to the US in terms of overall volume produced. The Midlands was at the centre of the UK *and* the global motor industry.

The decline was comparatively sudden and vertiginously steep. By the end of the last decade Britain was only the twelfth-biggest producer, turning once-thriving Coventry into something of a ghost town, to echo another Specials song. Jaguar still has its headquarters here, although its production is no longer centred on the city, and the distinctive London black cabs are built here, but otherwise the story is a disheartening one. In classic post-industrial fashion, instead of big factories and a busy workforce, Coventry now has an award-winning museum celebrating what the city *used* to produce. The Transport Museum has the largest collection of British-made road vehicles anywhere in the world, including the world speed record-breaking Thrust2 and ThrustSSC.

The area has been a major sporting centre too. As you drive across the city today you can spy the hulking Ricoh Arena, or the 'City of Coventry Stadium' as it was briefly renamed during the 2012 Olympics when a handful of football matches were played there. The Midlands didn't get much of a look-in with the 2012 Olympics, despite the fact that the modern Games were essentially invented here. London had nothing to do with the latter process; ancient Greece didn't have much input either. After all, the modern Olympic Games have almost nothing to do with the ancient Olympics. For one thing, there are a lot more events now and, for another, athletes no longer have to be fluent Greek-speakers to compete (a mandatory requirement back in Astylos of Croton's day). In fact, the connection between the two is virtually nil. Baron Pierre de Coubertin, the French aristocrat who founded the International Olympic Committee (IOC), admitted as much in his memoirs when he described what had really influenced him and his colleagues in shaping the first modern Olympics, in Athens in 1896: 'It was to [Thomas] Arnold that we turned, more or less consciously, for inspiration.' Arnold was the headmaster of Rugby School – just down the road from Coventry – which in the nineteenth century pioneered the role of sport in education. Coubertin was so impressed with the athleticism and moral uprightness of the students when he visited in the 1880s that he decided on the spot to adopt Arnold's Rugby as his model for the new Olympic movement.

Actually, I'm overstating the case for Rugby's influence. The school can't take *all* the credit for inspiring the modern Olympics.

No, it has to share the kudos with William Penny Brookes's Wenlock Olympian Games, held in Much Wenlock in Shropshire – which also happens to be in the West Midlands. Coubertin met Brookes in 1890 and shortly after founded the IOC. It's no coincidence that one of the London 2012 mascots was called Wenlock.

And it's not just the Olympics: innumerable important sports and sporting events can trace their origins to the Midlands in one way or another. To take one example: it was at Rugby School (again) that the sport of rugby – there's a clue in the name – was born after some knucklehead who was supposed to be playing football got confused, picked up the ball and started running with it. Rather than telling the poor chap he'd got the rules wrong, his pals played along and in the process invented a new sport. Now that's the classic Midland spirit of innovation for you.

* * *

'It's not a pretty place, is it?' grins Dean as we drive into the city centre afterwards.

Well, no. Not immediately at any rate.

'It's known as the "City of Three Spires", and on old images of Coventry you always see three spires. In the past travellers knew they were getting close when they could see them,' he explains. 'But there are so many high-rise buildings now you can't see them any more.

'That huge grey concrete skyscraper is the HQ of the council's planning department. It says a lot, that does,' he continues. 'Concrete, concrete and more concrete. It's a concrete jungle.' Back to that Specials song.

Sarah is a good singer and has been posting her work on YouTube. She says she's had seventy-two views over the past few days and an email from an admirer who says he thinks she's much better than the wannabes you get on the pop charts. Dean furrows his brow. 'Hmm. That's very nice but don't arrange to meet him,' he says.

Dean doesn't drive a Jag (and he isn't orange) but he did once work for the company in its design engineering department. As such, he's spent a good many hours trying to fathom what focus-group participants mean when they say things like a particular design element feels 'right' or 'cheap'. Are they referring to the sound, the appearance, the touch, the operation? Dean says it's important to avoid questions with simple yes/no answers when you're conducting focus groups. Start general – 'What do you think of the styling of this vehicle?' – and only gradually home in on more precise matters – 'How does that key feel in your hand?' That's the approved method, apparently. You certainly have to be careful how early in the process you start asking questions about tactility – 'otherwise people start stroking switches,' he laughs, 'and that's not normal behaviour': 'normal' behaviour being the assessors' holy grail, obviously.

As we drive around he points out where all the big car factories used to be. 'The only trace of a lot of them now is in the road names. Look at that,' he points as we pass a sign for Vanguard Avenue. 'That's all that's left of the old Vanguard car factory.' In quick succession we pass Herald Avenue (Triumph Herald) and Renown Avenue (Triumph Renown). Coventry is coming like a ghost town, as The Specials put it so resonantly.

Sarah announces that a lot of her friends call Coventry 'Chaventry'. I'm not sure whether this is intended to express disapproval or its opposite. Probably both. Twenty-first-century language's slipperiness is so generous in that po-mo/Blairite Third Way manner: no longer does it have to mean *either* x *or* y, instead it can mean *both* x *and* y – not to mention z if you want it to.

Dean points out where the drive chain for the *Titanic*'s engine was made, in a factory just off the ring road. Given its distance from saltwater – its defining quality, after all – the Midlands isn't renowned for its seafaring genius. If you want nautical lore and legend, you'd be better off in Greenwich or Portsmouth or Liverpool. But I can't resist mentioning in passing that it wasn't just the *Titanic*'s drive chain that was made in the West Midlands. No, Captain Edward Smith was made here too – in Hanley in Stoke, just on the other side of the Black Country. Let's begin by getting a few things straight. First, *it wasn't Smith's fault that the ship sank*. Nor was it Smith's fault they made that god-awful film starring Leonardo DiCaprio and Kate Winslet about the incident. (If, on the other hand, you regard the 1997 James Cameron movie as a cinematic masterpiece, or you chose the strains – I use the word advisedly – of Celine Dion's 'My Heart Will Go On' to accompany you in the first dance at your wedding, then you must award Midlander Smith at least some of the credit for these miraculous artistic achievements.) Anyway, Smith was a captain of the old school, valiant in getting his passengers to the lifeboats before determinedly retiring to the wheelhouse to go down with his ship. As one witness informed the *New York Herald*: 'I saw Captain Smith on the bridge. My eyes seemingly clung to him. The deck from which I had leapt was immersed. The water had risen slowly, and was now to the floor of the bridge. Then it was to Captain Smith's waist. I saw him no more. He died a hero.' A Midland hero, lost at sea. As the boat was being engulfed by waves, Smith is reported to have urged his crew, 'Be British, boys!' – a phrase that is engraved on his memorial in Lichfield – although some sceptics think the papers may have dreamt that bit up. After all, they argue, who could possibly have witnessed him speaking these words and survived to sell the story to the press? I'm tempted to suggest that the *News of the World* tapped Smith's mobile and was listening in to him on the blower to his wife as the ship began to sink, and that's how they got the exclusive. But what do I know?

(I also choose to believe that what the good captain actually said was: 'Be *Midlanders*, boys!')

* * *

'The number of people you could kill in an afternoon driving around Coventry,' murmurs Dean as he swerves to avoid a suicidal multitasking road-crosser, apparently too deep in conversation on his smartphone to notice that there's a stream of traffic headed directly at him.

It's not just unaware phone users who are doing their bit to add spice to the Coventry road experience. The City Council has started to introduce so-called 'shared spaces'. These are four-way junctions without traffic lights or kerbs or crossings, which turn selected car/pedestrian intersections into a bit of a free-for-all. It sounds to me like the scheme was dreamed up by someone who wants to keep the population numbers down, but the official line is it's intended to improve traffic flow and safety. Time will tell.

A lot will no doubt depend on how drivers conduct themselves. The signs aren't that promising. Dean points to a set of bent railings at the (non-shared-space) junction ahead. 'See that? That's a result of "drifting". In Japan it's a sport,' he explains. 'It's what you do when you drive very fast in restricted spaces: to get round tight corners at speed, you pull the car round sharply and flick the back end out.'

So that's why you see ripples in railings everywhere – drifters! Who knew?

'There's a Japanese film about it, isn't there, Ed?' says Dean.

'Yeah,' eventually comes Ed's drawled assent from the back seat.
'What's it called again?' Dean asks his son.
Silence. Then, finally: 'Dunno.'

* * *

Back to the centre-periphery model and the intellectual and cultural centrality of the Midlands. If you think about it, the word 'Coventry' enjoys a curious linguistic centrality; it's been disseminated to the periphery in a way that few other place names have. Of course, the names of towns and cities often carry associations of some kind – the word 'Manchester' might make you think of, say, rain or conjure images of MUFC surrendering abjectly to Barcelona in the Champions League final in 2011. Nothing positive, obviously. But Coventry has managed to turn itself into both an idiom and a verb that can be applied to anywhere or anyone, without geographical prejudice or predetermination. This is an unusual accomplishment. You can't Liverpoolate a car, can you? Or, despite the county's extraordinary resonance in matters of cosmetic beauty, Essex a face. Not linguistically, anyway. Now, I probably shouldn't crow too much about Coventry's verbal currency, since in neither case is the meaning particularly positive. All the same, the city's name is inscribed into the English language. Let's begin with the most famous usage: the expression 'send someone to Coventry' appears to date from the time of the Civil War, when locals refused to speak to Royalist prisoners held in the city, and means to ostracise someone by not speaking to them. And, as I pointed out before, you can send someone to Coventry wherever in the Anglophone world you are, from Melbourne to Manhattan. (As it so happens, the phrase does also sum up what most people feel about Coventry: a deeply unfashionable place of exile from mainstream society – when you go there no one wants to talk to you any more. But that's another matter.)

Then there's the verb 'to Coventrise' (or 'Coventrate'), which enjoyed a brief period of furious fashionability in the mid-twentieth century. The city – a centre of arms manufacture in World War II – was repeatedly targeted by the Luftwaffe, with the worst damage being inflicted on 14 November 1940, when the cathedral was bombed and much of the medieval part of the city was laid waste. The Nazis enjoyed the experience so much, they made up a verb to celebrate it – in German, *koventrier* means 'to annihilate'. The term briefly caught on with English-language newspapers and press agencies who, as the bombardment of the country intensified, ran headlines such as 'Nazis "Coventrize" Central London' and 'Nazis "Coventrize" Bristol'. It's time this forgotten verb was exhumed and put back into currency, in slightly modified form ideally. Next time you find yourself having to report a scene of destruction, see what sort of reaction you get if you say 'he Coventrised his motor' instead of 'he totalled his car'. If we all pull together, we might even be able to popularise it as a synonym for 'getting drunk'. Rather than 'hammered' or 'leathered' (both of which terms have similarly violent connotations), why not say 'I got so Coventrised on Friday night I woke up in the Black Country on Saturday'? If we make a big effort, we can move the word 'Coventry' from its current destruction-and-exclusion position on the word-association chart and reposition it firmly at the centre of the linguistic map of fun and entertainment. Yes, we can!

* * *

As we approach Millennium Place, two huge lengths of steel bend themselves into an arch in front of Coventry's celebrated Transport

167

Museum. If you squint a bit and carry out a quick mental trans-formation of the forms before your eyes, you might think that they look a bit like a pair of wings. I'm not feeling very imaginative, though, so to me they just look like a couple of bits of twisted metal. Dean tells me that I am gazing upon the celebrated Whittle Arch. He's clearly not that impressed, either.

'No doubt it looked *fantastic* on the designer's sketchpad,' he sighs.

Still, the project has won lots of awards and commendations, and you can certainly see that it's state-of-the-art, the sort of thing that could only have been achieved by means of the most sophisticated methods: CAD imaging, avant-garde materials, all that. In a sense you could say it's Coventry's answer to the Bilbao Guggenheim. If only it had a more obvious visionary or imagi-native element it would probably be as big a tourist attraction as Frank Gehry's fantastical titanium creation. That's a big 'if', obviously.

Aesthetics aside, it's only proper that the name of Whittle should be commemorated. If the Midlands managed to sink the *Titanic*, Coventrian Sir Frank Whittle made up for his native region's gaffe at sea by helping mankind to conquer the skies. (I should mention again that the man who created the Spitfire and there-fore – sort of – won the Battle of Britain, R.J. Mitchell, was also a Midlander, from Staffordshire, which is just up the road. But since we're in Coventry at the moment, I'm going to stick to discussing local boy Whittle's soaring aeronautical contributions here.) It's ironic that the man whose pioneering work would carry air travel ever higher was initially refused a place in the Royal Air Force on the grounds that he wasn't tall enough. But little Whittle did not give in. Oh no. Early on in his career he realised that, to enable them to travel further and faster, aircraft would need to fly at higher altitudes in order to reduce air resistance. The kinds of piston engine then in use were plainly inadequate for the task, so Whittle set about developing a new kind of engine that would carry air travel beyond the sound barrier. The result was the turbojet, first developed in the late 1930s, and Air Commodore Whittle – as he would eventually become – has not unreasonably been dubbed the 'father of jet propulsion', securing for himself a place in the history of aviation as seminal as that of the Wright brothers. Today, a statue of Sir Frank, appropriately posed gazing skywards, stands in front of the Transport Museum beneath the Whittle Arch. Visually it's fairly banal but it does at least reinforce the message: If it moves, it was probably made in Coventry or by a West Midlander. Well, *used* to be, at any rate.

* * *

Modern-day Coventry is a concrete jungle; I think we've established that much. But did you know that until recently the city boasted one of the most eye-catching medieval districts in Europe? Its historic loveliness appears to have been one of the main reasons – the fact that it was also churning out war munitions was another – why Hitler decided to launch the 'Coventry Blitz' in November 1940. The Führer famously decided to spare passably pretty Paris but seemingly he just couldn't bear the thought of supremely comely Coventry surviving: it was just too lovely to live. So the Luftwaffe let fall its bombs and devastated the city's historic heart.

The postwar response to the wartime destruction wasn't up to much. 'They reckon that the ring road destroyed more houses than the Luftwaffe,' comments Dean. There's a school of thought that the authorities might have done better to reconstruct the city in the same way that the Germans rebuilt Dresden, where many historic

169

buildings were painstakingly reconstructed after their devastation in the Allies' wartime bombing campaign. Instead, the powers-that-be decided to start again, adopting the plan proposed by Donald Gibson, Coventry's first City Architect and Planning Officer. This involved the creation of the premier major pedestrianised shopping precinct in Europe, separating motor traffic from foot traffic (those new 'shared spaces' represent a reversal of Gibson's policy). Coventry's urban regeneration scheme was considered positively avant-garde at the time. A lot of cheap temporary housing was thrown up – again, I use the term advisedly – and then the authorities conveniently forgot that it was only intended to be temporary. Much of it is still there.

Meanwhile, the surviving medieval bits of the city retreated en masse – brick by brick if necessary; whole buildings were moved – to Spon Street, the historic thoroughfare linking Oxford to Birmingham which was cut in half by that highly destructive, city-reshaping ring road. Spon Street's sudden concentration of Tudor buildings, overlooked by Coventry's defining concrete towers, has an air of unreality about it today.

We're standing now in the roofless ruins of the old St Michael's Cathedral, destroyed by Hitler's bombs. The outer walls of the fourteenth-century building survived the Blitz, as did the spire, and they have been left to stand, unrestored, as a monument to the horrors of war. By all accounts the spire is very impressive when you can see it, but at the moment it's curtained off behind scaffolding. If you look in the other direction you'll see Sir Basil Spence's famous replacement cathedral, to which the ruins of the old one are connected by a canopy. Spence's unabashedly modern St Michael's contains artistic masterpieces in the shape of Graham Sutherland's *Christ in Glory* tapestry and Jacob Epstein's statue *St Michael's Victory over the Devil*. There are few more significant Modernist assemblages in the UK.

Sarah is complaining about being cold; Ed, completely motionless under their umbrella, seems to have frozen solid. Churches are usually damp but the absence of a roof makes the old St Michael's particularly nippy. I try to warm the teenagers up with my conversation.

'Do you know the expression "Sent to Coventry"?' I ask them. They shake their heads minimally. The rain continues to fall.

Perhaps they don't use the expression in Coventry. On reflection, why would they? After all, it wouldn't make much sense to send someone who was already in Coventry *to* Coventry, would it?

Stupid question.

So cancel what I said before: there is a place in the Anglophone world where you cannot use the phrase 'sent to Coventry' with any meaning, and that place is Coventry. Obvious, really.

Just along the way there's a reminder that all the best folk heroes hail from the Midlands. Seriously, what has either the North or the South got to offer that can compare with Robin Hood, that celebrated 'man in tights', and Lady Godiva, that barely less fêted (if much less Hollywoodised) woman out of her tights? Lady G was an eleventh-century Coventry noblewoman who, according to legend, stripped naked and cantered through the city centre on horseback in order to get her husband, Leofric, Earl of Mercia, to lower the taxes. Along with Robin Hood's robbing from the rich to give to the poor, Godiva's selfless act of stripping for social justice provides one of the defining myths of the Midlands (the selflessness-in-pursuit-of-social-justice bit, not the nudity). The good burghers of Coventry appreciated the gesture and respectfully averted their eyes – with the exception of one local muppet named Tom, who allowed himself to gaze upon Godiva's uncovered loveliness and was struck blind for his trouble. He also entered the language as a consequence: yes, as well as 'sent to Coventry' and 'Coventrised', the city has provided the national tongue with its most resonant – and most thoroughly

English – term for *voyeurs* (which is a French word, of course): 'Peeping Tom'. Coventry, home of spying pervs. They should make more of that in the tourist-office bumph.

There's a statue of Godiva on Broadgate, a few strides from the cathedrals in the commercial heart of the city. It's overlooked by a clock, from which, on the hour every hour, Peeping Tom peeps out at a blushing Godiva in the buff. Dean explains that Broadgate used to be popular with newlyweds, who liked to be photographed in the gardens around the statue. 'But then our wonderful planners decided that we didn't need the gardens any more and slabbed the lot.'

Oh, you naughty town planners.

* * *

Coventry was the first city to take a 'twin': Stalingrad (now Volgograd), during the Battle of Stalingrad. The gesture, made at the height of the Allies' misfortunes during World War II, was designed to show unity with the suffering Soviet city. Since then Coventry has twinned up with more than two dozen others, including the similarly war-damaged Dresden. It's no coincidence that it now identifies itself as the 'City of Peace and Reconciliation' – the experience of war has left a deep impression on Coventry.

Musically the city has done a neat line in the sound of war and conflict. One of the masterpieces of the twentieth-century classical canon, Benjamin Britten's *War Requiem*, was written for the opening of the new Coventry Cathedral in 1962. And then there's The Specials, conflict-scarred Coventrians to the core. (Fittingly, the band's original name – The Automatics – referenced the car industry.) 'From this unpromising town, still getting over Hitler's bombs, emerged a musical movement that gripped Britain in the run-up to the explosive riots of 1981,' wrote one of the band's trio of frontmen, Neville Staple, in his memoir, *Original Rude Boy*.

That movement, of course, was 2 Tone. Named after the label set up by The Specials' keyboardist, Jerry Dammers, it married the energy and aggression of punk to the rhythms and sounds of the Jamaican ska and rocksteady genres. But where punk was nihilistic, 2 Tone was socially progressive, actively promoting racial harmony, although no band simultaneously better captured the melting-pot unease of late 1970s England than The Specials: no song more accurately sums up the mood of Britain's cities around the time of the 1981 riots than 'Ghost Town'. In the case of 'Too Much Too Young', the band also promoted the use of contraception. Based like many 2 Tone tracks on a Jamaican ska original (in this case Lloyd Charmers's 1969 song 'Birth Control'), 'Too Much Too Young' shot to number one when it was released as a single – although the accompanying video tended to be cut short when it was screened on *Top of the Pops*, so missing out the references to methods of pregnancy-avoidance. This was also the band (in its later incarnation as The Special AKA) that wrote 'Nelson Mandela', hitting in the process the keynote of popular politics in the 1980s and providing the soundtrack to the emerging global political consciousness. The song went top ten in the UK and was even adopted as an anthem by the ANC in South Africa.

Political engagement aside, ska revivalists were also intensely style-conscious: the name 2 Tone has been taken to refer not only to the music's message of unity between black and white, but also to the two-tone rude-boy suits and porkpie hats adopted as something of a uniform by the movement's followers. Concrete it may be, but Coventry still has *style*.

* * *

Later, as I'm about to leave Dean's house, an unusually lively-looking Ed confronts me. 'You've been recording us, haven't you?' He may be only fourteen but he's already several inches taller than me. Fortunately, he's smiling.

'Erm, yes.' Suddenly I feel a total sneak. I stammer some lame explanation that I hadn't wanted to make them self-conscious by putting a recorder on show or making an announcement when I started to tape them. (I did ask them in advance whether they were willing to be featured in the book, though – I'm not that much of a sneak.)

'I thought so,' Ed nods. 'It was the way you were holding your phone. I noticed how careful you were not to cover the microphone.'

I feel like saying: But, Ed, weren't you asleep the whole time? What would be the point, though? The answer is only too clear.

Beware these seemingly slumbering adolescents: they're really smart and, contrary to appearances, *they're watching your every move.*

Time to go and get Coventrised.

The propaganda value of a £50 note, baltis and Brum-bashers, and a moment of Stendhalian delight

Birmingham is Britain's Second City and, as is only appropriate given this elevated status, it is forever coming top of national polls. As far as most Midlanders are concerned, the fact that these polls are negative in nature – designed to establish the worst rather than the best that Britain has to offer – is neither here nor there. Unlike most other towns and cities trapped in the largely overlooked no-man's-land between North and South, Birmingham is somewhere people have at least heard of. It's a start.

So what exactly does the Man on the Clapham Omnibus – or the Woman on the Newcastle Shuttle – know about Brum? Two things principally, if persistent press reports are to be believed:

1. The people there have the worst – the most irritating – accent in the UK. 'Nasal', 'monotonous', 'miserable', 'ugly', 'dull',

'droney', 'whingey' and 'annoying' are the words non-natives generally use to evoke it. Research suggests that talking like a Brummie will give listeners the impression that you are unimaginative and of low intelligence. Apparently, having a Yorkshire accent will make those same listeners think you're clever like Geoffrey Boycott or Kimberley Walsh. For some probably not unrelated reason, in the land of advertising the Brummie accent is indissociable from the way pigs are thought to speak. One recent survey found that, as a consequence of all this negative stereotyping, men from the West Midlands are less likely to pull on a night out than males from other regions of the UK. 'The results won't come as a surprise to West Midlanders like TV's Adrian Chiles,' commented *The Sun* feelingly. 'Adrian was linked to BBC *One Show* co-host Christine Bleakley, but she fell for Chelsea ace Frank Lampard.' If only he'd pretended to be a Cockney – or, better still perhaps, to come from Barnsley – he'd have stood a better chance, runs the logic. Unless perceptions of Brummies' terminally unappealing tones change, you might conclude that natural selection is likely to see a significant population decline in Birmingham and the West Midlands generally in the coming generations.

2. The city is home to the most notorious and derided stretch of road in the country. Roads, like accents, are an unending source of fascination to the English, so this is no small matter. Opened to great public fanfare in 1972, Spaghetti Junction was the first free-flowing traffic interchange in the UK. Linking three different motorways and featuring not a single roundabout or set of traffic lights, it was indeed a pioneering piece of engineering. Alas, its wild tangle of looping, intertwined strands of highway – the

source of its Italo-exotic nickname; its official moniker is actually Gravelly Hill Interchange – has been judged to be lacking in aesthetic appeal. Another complaint concerns the practicality (or otherwise) of its design: according to some, Spaghetti Junction is little better than 'a motorway junction masquerading as England's largest car park'. The justice of these clichés is of little importance. The crucial point is that Birmingham's most instantly recognisable landmark is a road system designed to get you through or around the city as quickly as possible. In that sense, Spaghetti Junction is the Midland site *par excellence*, Mercia *in excelsis*, the perfect embodiment of what the region means to everyone who doesn't live there: an irritating, sprawling concrete eyesore that exists merely to be negotiated as you make your way to somewhere that's actually worth visiting.

* * *

A West Midland friend of mine – he likes to call himself Tone (Tony), although he will forever be Sticky Fingers to those who shared accommodation with him in his uni days – once told me that Brummies resent Manchester's elevated national profile. 'It's always treated as Britain's Second City and that's not right because *we're* Britain's Second City,' he complained.

He's right, of course. In terms of scale, Birmingham is second only to London. There are over a million Brummies and barely 500,000 Mancunians, even when you count all those new recruits courtesy of the Beeb's move to Salford. But, as a recent poll confirmed, these may not be the most vital statistics when it comes to national perceptions: most people *think* of Manchester as the

UK's Second City, whatever the statistics say. That probably has a lot to do with Manchester United having won the league more often than Aston Villa (twenty to seven), but it's not just football. There's a reverence that characterises the discussion of all things Manc – cultural, political, even architectural – that's noticeably absent when people talk about the wonders of Brum.

Take the following example. A couple of years ago the influential newspaper the *New York Times* named Manchester among the top twenty 'must-see' places in the world. Surely the designation of the capital of the rainy old English north-west as a tourist destination of global merit would provoke an outburst of mirth on this side of the Atlantic? Not a bit of it. The news of Manchester's *NYT*-approved apotheosis was hailed with solemn approbation by 'design guru' Stephen Bayley, who kicked off an article in the *Daily Telegraph* with a classic piece of Manc misinformation: 'Manchester was Cottonopolis, the dirty, sooty, thumping heart of the Industrial Revolution' (actually it was Birmingham that was the thumping heart of the Industrial Revolution – more on this in a moment – but we've already noted the Northern habit of appropriating Midland history whenever it suits, so we shouldn't be surprised by this). Next Bayley recites a few of the favoured pieties about the city's great contributions to national and international politics and commerce: 'Never mind that Engels was a Manchester businessman and that Rolls did his deal with Royce near the site of the Peterloo Massacre' (we've already covered the overhyping of Peterloo's place in national history and we'll return to *The Communist Manifesto* in a moment; for now let's just note that Rolls-Royce's great spiritual and physical home is in fact Derby in the East Midlands and that the UK's great twentieth-century 'motor city' was actually Birmingham – or Brum, as it's aptly called – and its environs).

Finally, at the end of this dense trail of allusive half-truths, the article arrives at its main theme: 'But [Manchester's] place in global history, especially in global design history, is no less important just because it is less well-known … the fabulous (and intimidating) physical presence of Manchester buildings diverted the story of architecture and design.' Bayley then (very briefly) traces the influence of the factories of Cottonopolis on the German architect Karl-Friedrich Schinkel, and through him 'on the Gropius family, then on Mies van der Rohe and the Bauhaus', concluding that as such 'Manchester was an inspiration for the Modern Movement'. There's good reason why this story isn't terribly well known, of course, hinted at in Bayley's deployment of the indefinite article: Manchester was *an* inspiration – you might think that 'an infinitesimal, more or less entirely insignificant inspiration' would have been a more accurate way of phrasing it, but let that pass. Ever noticed the similarities between dismal old Manchester and glorious, soaring Chicago? No? Let's say no more about it then.

Bayley then mentions the wonders of *Coronation Street* and Factory Records (the label behind New Order and Happy Mondays – decide for yourself how significant a cultural 'achievement' that is) and extols the splendours of the city's Northern Quarter, which, he alleges, 'makes the Sohos of London and New York appear as sleepy as Bath'. There's a whiff of desperation – not to mention gross misinformation – about another of his proofs of Manchester's greatness: 'Bob Dylan went electric in the Free Trade Hall in 1966.' Is the implication here that the great US folk troubadour was overwhelmed by the crackle of futuristic metropolitan energy on his arrival in Cottonopolis and decided to plug in and go electric on the spot? If so, the facts – as usual – don't quite fit the frothing hyperbole: Dylan first went electric in 1965, initially on his album *Bringing It All Back Home* and then – as has been very well documented – at the Newport Folk Festival in Rhode Island, USA. Indeed, the Manchester gig is primarily remembered for the audience response, which included the famous denunciatory cry of 'Judas!' Properly told, it's hardly a story that unambiguously illustrates Mancunians' fearless modernity.

But Bayley saves the best for last. 'The word "tourism" was coined by Stendhal, whose name was appropriated by an Italian psychologist to describe a syndrome where a traveller faces such a variety of experience that a state of dizziness occurs,' he explains. Can you guess what's coming next? 'Florence and Venice cause Stendhal's Syndrome, but so too does Manchester. Rightly understood, as Disraeli knew, it is at least the equivalent of the capitals of the Renaissance and classical worlds.'

Holy chutzpah, Batman! I don't think I've seen such a blatant mixture of hyperbole and delusion since, oh, I don't know … since I last read an article about the glories of the North.

Now compare Bayley's encomium with the inexplicably mean swipe at Birmingham taken by the *Guardian* when the city was jockeying to be named the 2008 European City of Culture. Such an ambition on the part of a city 'made nationally laughable on account of its adenoidal accent' was pure hubris, suggested an article in the newspaper formerly known as the *Manchester Guardian*. Rather than 'presume to join a list of truly great cities such as Paris, Florence and Amsterdam', it should 'write a letter of apology for its crimes against civilisation'.

'More than half of Britain's new patents come from Birmingham, making it Britain's most creative city,' acknowledges the writer, Stuart Jeffries, before running through some of the not inconsiderable cultural attractions cited by Brum's PR team: 'The Be In Birmingham 2008 campaign … suspects you'll know already about Symphony Hall, the Birmingham Royal Ballet, the Pre-Raphaelites in the city art gallery, the fact that Edward Burne-Jones was born in Pershore Street, that Tony Hancock was from Hall Green … It won't let you forget that Dvorak, Elgar and Mendelssohn made Birmingham the most musically exciting British city, and more recently that Simon Rattle has engineered its unexpected classical music renaissance.' The achievements are impressive – at least as impressive as those of Manchester – but the tone in which they are quoted is typically disparaging. How *dare* Birmingham boast about its accomplishments, Jeffries seems to be saying – not a sentiment you hear expressed very often about the infinitely more vainglorious city-states of the North, Manchester and Liverpool. What's even more astonishing is that Stuart Jeffries is himself a West Midlander – what's that all about?

To get a further flavour of the two cities' contrasting attitudes to their own greatness, compare www.prideofmanchester.com, which proclaims its mission as 'celebrating life in the rock'n'goal capital of the world!', with www.birminghamitsnotshit.co.uk, whose name and self-professed 'mildly sarcastic' approach to local matters say it all really. When I logged on, the former was full of breathless claims of the following kind: 'Why so many, if not most, of the country's top comedians have come from the region is a question many have tried to explain. On these pages we celebrate the comic legends and tv series to have emerged from the comedy capital – Manchester, England!' The claim is laugh-out-loud funny, even if Manchester's comedians aren't. The Birmingham website, meanwhile, more modestly declares its love for the city's 'people, arts, animals, buildings, parks, grass verges, factories and bus stops'. Wherever you look in Birmingham and the West Midlands generally, the spirit of self-deprecation reigns.

You get a further sense of this from the cities' respective soap operas. Recorded in Birmingham and set in the fictional West

181

Midland county of Borsetshire, *The Archers* has been stirring the nation's passions in that quiet, regionally anonymous way so typical of the Midlands for half a century, eschewing narrowly regional characterisation in order to be simply and inclusively *English*. Little better encapsulates the difference between the histrionic, hyperbolic North and the more mature, emotionally centred Midlands than the contrasting anniversary celebrations for *Coronation Street* and *The Archers* at the end of 2010. To mark the former's fifty years on the air, multiple inhabitants of Weatherfield were killed off in an improbable accident involving an exploding bar, a collapsing viaduct and a suddenly-trackless tram. The excitable drama didn't end there, either: one character proposed marriage then promptly had a heart attack, another was hit with a hammer. Is that really what they think of as entertainment up North? The residents of Ambridge, meanwhile, were celebrating their sixtieth anniversary. A major, earth-shaking storyline was promised. 'There had been rumours of a traffic pile-up, a church steeple collapsing, a shooting spree or an out of control fire,' one newspaper reported. 'In the event, a man fell off a roof.' Classic. The Midlands don't need over-wrought Northern hoopla to keep the rest of the nation tuned in.

* * *

I call my old friend.

'Hi there, Sticky! It's Robert.'

'Oh hello. And don't call me that. I've moved on. You wouldn't like it if I still called you …'

Unfortunately the line begins to break up so I am unable to hear what he says next – and therefore cannot transcribe it for you, dear reader. But I take his point.

Tone grew up in well-to-do Sutton Coldfield, which is to the north of the city centre, and now lives – alone – on the edge of Bournville, a nineteenth-century model village created by the Cadbury family for its factory workers; according to Tone, it smells of chocolate. In classic Brum fashion, my friend has a slightly lugubrious, sing-song accent, and in some transmogrified cartoon or claymation ad-land universe he could easily be reimagined as a talking pig – albeit an empathetic, intelligent and attractive one.

'Now look,' I say, getting down to business. 'I want to pick your brains about something. I've just been reading something about the *New York Times* according Manchester "resort" status. What do you think about that? Outrageous, no? Makes you hopping mad and all that?'

'Dunno really. I quite like Manchester.'

'But years ago – don't you remember? – you told me how much you hated Manchester because of the Second City thing.'

'"Hated" is a bit strong.'

That's one thing about Brummies – they don't readily do anger.

I decide to try another tack. 'Well, look. Don't you think the *New York Times* should accord Birmingham resort status too?'

'Erm … not really.'

'But architecturally, culturally, politically, industrially, Birmingham is at least as distinguished as Manchester.'

'I still wouldn't recommend it as a "city break" sort of destination. If friends wanted to visit, I could take them on a little whizz-bang tour, but it's not particularly set up for tourists. I mean, if you like places that smell of chocolate, Bournville's tops, but, erm … you can have a nice weekend in Birmingham if you really have to – but, like I said, I wouldn't recommend it.'

'Blimey. No wonder no one takes Birmingham very seriously if that's the best a true-born Brummie can do.'

Tone sighs. 'Anyway, what are you calling for?'

'I'm trying to write something that definitively proves Birmingham's superiority over Manchester.'

(Deep silence.)

'Are you still there?' I am eventually moved to ask.

'Erm, when was the last time you actually came to Birmingham?' Tone finally says. Is he laughing?

'I don't know. I think it was probably in 1986, to see Metallica play at the Odeon on the Master of Puppets tour. What a great gig that was. My head hurt for a whole week afterwards. Why?'

'Well, I have to tell you that it's just possible that Birmingham *isn't* better than Manchester.'

'Don't be silly. Of course it is,' I say with slightly forced cheer. 'Birmingham is in the Midlands, and the Midlands is better than the North, *ergo* Birmingham is far superior to Manchester. That's the basic argument of my book.'

'Good luck with that then.'

Oh dear. It seems that Tone – in common with the rest of the country – has been hypnotised into believing Manchester's idea of its own magnificence. Is he dating a Mancunian girl, perhaps, who ties him up and forces him to recite mind-numbing mantras about the wonders of the North before she'll bestow her sexual favours on him? He's very suggestible, is Tone. He certainly developed some odd opinions around the time he was seeing that Thai ladyboy; perhaps it's happening again. Anyway, whatever the cause, it's bad news. I'm relying on him to show me the beauties of Brum.

Gathering up my courage, I explain the role I have already allocated to him in my mind. Before he can refuse it, I ask him where we should start our tour when I visit next week.

'Off the top of my head, erm ... we could try Moseley Bog,' he suggests.

'It doesn't sound particularly promising.'

'It's nice. It was one of Tolkien's inspirations for *The Lord of the Rings*.'

'It makes sense that he thought of that pile of crap while he was in a bog,' I say. Boom-boom! I've never been a fan.

'All right, then. If you fancy having an "ironic" good time, we could start in Cadbury World.'

'What's that?'

'It's a theme park "where chocolate comes to life", or so they say.'

'What, literally? It gets up and starts walking around?'

This is beginning to remind me of the sorts of conversation we used to have in our university days.

'Will you be driving up?' says Tone, interrupting my extraordinary comic flow. 'If so, let's meet in the Balti Triangle. We can have lunch there.'

'The Balti what?'

'Don't worry – I'll email you the details.'

* * *

It just so happens that my visit to Birmingham coincides with the launch of a new £50 note bearing the image of the great Brum-based engineering-entrepreneurial team of Matthew Boulton and James Watt. As I drive up the M6 I've got my radio tuned to a phone-in on BBC WM (West Midlands). Judging by what's being said, the good burghers of Birmingham aren't overplaying the honour. The cheery presenter declares herself a 'credit-card girl' and says she never draws out more than £40 in cash, which means that she has never actually seen a £50 note. Nor has anyone who calls in, apparently. In Manchester they'd have a ticker-tape parade to celebrate this sort of honour; in Birmingham it just provokes a shrug of amused indifference.

Brummie understatement notwithstanding, we need to get this Industrial Revolution stuff straight before we go any further.

Britain entered the eighteenth century an agricultural nation and left it the world's foremost industrial power – almost entirely thanks to Midlanders.

The story of the Lunar Society has a fairytale ring about it. Once a month, on the Monday nearest the full moon, the members of the Society – assorted Midland entrepreneurs, enthusiasts and inventors – gathered at one of a series of locations in and around Birmingham. (This particular point in the lunar cycle – which gave the group its name – was chosen to ensure that members had as much light as possible to travel home by afterwards; this all happened before the introduction of street lights.) Matthew Boulton, the greatest of all Birmingham entrepreneurs, was the central figure, and one of the places where they met was Boulton's Soho House. In his article on Manchester's glories, Stephen Bayley compares the city's Northern Quarter with the Sohos of London and New York, but Manchester has nothing to compare with Birmingham's Soho – that being the name not only of Boulton's home but also of his revolutionary manufactory, which was the scene for the development of so many of the innovations and inventions that drove the Industrial Revolution. It was at the Soho Foundry that James Watt's revolutionary improved steam engines were manufactured. 'I see here, Sir,' Boulton announced to James Boswell at his Soho Works on Handsworth Heath, 'what all the world desires to have – Power.' You can say, without a hint of overstatement, that Birmingham's Soho changed the world.

The Lunar Society counted among its members many of the most innovative thinkers of a particularly innovative age: not just Boulton and Watt, but the great chemist and freethinker

Joseph Priestley (he discovered oxygen – that's right, thanks to him we all started to breathe more easily), Erasmus Darwin, Josiah Wedgwood … These are major figures not just of the Industrial Revolution, but of the wider, globe-reconfiguring Enlightenment. Their individual contributions were at least as significant as those of Voltaire and Goethe and Benjamin Franklin, so it's only fitting that the Brum-based movement has been honoured with the geographically specific designation of the Midland Enlightenment. London had nothing to compare with it.

But how did so many brilliant minds find themselves gathered together in a cultural backwater such as was mid-eighteenth-century Birmingham? Well, in the first place, Midlanders, from the East and the West alike, just *are* cleverer than the rest of the population – get over it. That aside, there are a few other factors that may have contributed to the extraordinary density of inquiring and capable minds in the region at this time. The 1662 Act of Uniformity had banished Nonconformist religious groups – basically anyone with beliefs that fell outside the orthodoxies of the Anglican Church – from the metropolis and excluded them from membership of the Establishment generally. Many Dissenting families thus relocated to the Midlands, where, denied entry to the traditional professions, they were encouraged to develop their entrepreneurial skills. The Cadbury family, who created that model village at Bournville that smells so deliciously of chocolate, were Dissenting Quakers, as was leading 'Lunartick' Josiah Wedgwood's family, as was Abraham Darby, whose iron-smelting experiments at Coalbrookdale laid the technological foundations of the Industrial Revolution. This was a non-Establishment revolution, led by men excluded from the centre of national cultural life by their religion. The result, as travel writer Arthur Young pointed out in 1791, was that Birmingham became 'the first manufacturing town in the world'.

* * *

Birmingham has been responsible for the creation and manufacture of a wide variety of foodstuffs over the last couple of centuries: Typhoo tea, HP Sauce and (I think I may have already mentioned this one) Cadbury's chocolate, to name only a few of the better-known brands. But nothing says contemporary melting-pot Brum quite like the balti, a hugely popular style of curry served in a distinctive pressed steel bowl.

The so-called Balti Triangle, centred on Sparkhill a few miles south of the city centre, is the best place to taste this local speciality. It's also a regular haunt of Tone's, a fact that's eloquently attested to by his bulging waistline. We're on our way to lunch but he wants to stop en route at the Lahore Juice Bar to pick up a kulfi cone.

'You'll spoil your appetite,' I tell him, sounding like his mother. Well, not quite: I can't do the accent.

He can't resist the jalebi, Lahori falooda and the like that light up the windows of the sweetshops on Ladypool Road. It's not just the confectionery that's colourful around here either: women in bright saris browse in dress shops advertising new Eid collections.

For a culinary hub, the Triangle is rather quiet at lunchtime: most of the restaurants only open after five. Still, Tone has found somewhere that can accommodate us. It's a large and airy establishment with an open tiled kitchen where we're met with images of Barcelona footballing legend Lionel Messi on a huge plasma TV screen and Asian pop on the sound system. That's cultural fusion for you if you like.

Terminally unambitious where food is concerned, I go for the simplest chicken dish on the menu and a mango lassi, or 'Asian beer' as some like to call it. My friend is more adventurous – he likes a meal with a little heat in it, he says – and is soon sweating profusely. They don't serve alcohol but Tone has brought a few cans of beer to counter the effect of the chillies.

As we're waiting for our meals, he waves a newspaper clipping in my face. 'Have you seen this?'

'What is it?'

'It's a restaurant review. It's pretty rave.'

'And it's a review of this place?'

'No – of one just down the road.'

'It doesn't work like that, you know. Just because the place next door has got three Michelin stars doesn't mean the grub here'll be any good. You are naïve, Sticky.'

'Tone.'

'Sorry. You are naïve, *Tone*.'

'That wasn't what I meant. I thought what the article had to say about the area was interesting. Look at what they write: "In aesthetic terms it lacks the impact of Manchester's Curry Mile ... Yet the Balti Triangle has the stronger claim to be the heart and soul of Anglo-Indian cuisine." It compares us with Manchester and – sort of – says that, actually, we're better. That's a national newspaper saying it too. You may want to quote that in your book.'

'I may indeed. Though it still says Manchester has greater "aesthetic" impact.'

'I don't know why, but people like to treat Manchester as this tremendous cultural centre,' Tone says with sneering vigour. This is a good sign: I had feared he was going to spend the day singing the praises of the North. Perhaps that Manchester girlfriend I dreamed up has dumped him. Who knows, perhaps *he* dumped *her*, for pushing her kinky Northern propaganda games too far. If we get sufficiently drunk later, I may ask him about it.

'Birmingham has had its share of cultural significance too,' he continues, 'but you'd hardly know it from the way people talk about it. Take music. Manchester bands seem to get lauded higher and higher, while Birmingham bands seem to get pushed into the background: Dexy's, Duran Duran, even Led Zeppelin somehow don't seem to have the place in the pantheon of music that you'd expect. And then look at Oasis!'

'Don't talk to me about sodding Oasis,' I say. 'Worst band in the world. No sooner do they give us all a break by splitting up than the Stone Roses re-form. One step forward, two steps back. It's not fair. Anyway, tell me something positive about Birmingham.'

'Well, I'm very, very proud of the steam engine. I was taught so much about it at school, I can't not be really. We were forever being told: "You're from the Midlands and the Industrial Revolution was born here." I hate the way Manchester has usurped all that about the Industrial Revolution. Other than that I don't really know … Oh, I know – the music of the Moody Blues, who invented psyche-delic rock, of course. If you listen to the opening of their albums, their drummer – I think his name's Edge, but I might be wrong – reads a psychedelic poem at the beginning of a couple of them as a kind of introduction: "Be it sight, sound, smell or touch …"'

'Super … Anything else you can say in favour of your native city?'

He sighs wearily and opens a second can of beer. 'No, not really. I've been exposed to so much anti-Birmingham propaganda. You have no idea what it's like.'

He looks as though he's going to cry. I excuse myself and go to the loo. Thankfully, by the time I return Tone has composed himself sufficiently for our interview to continue.

'Right then: if you weren't a Midlander, would you rather be a Northerner or a Southerner?

'A Northerner,' he responds unhesitatingly. 'It really means something to come from the North. Not necessarily something *good* – just *something*. You meet grammar-school kids from Manchester who still feel they have to be a bit tasty. They think they have something to live up to. Northerners generally feel they have something to live up to, all that "Soft Southerners" blather. I don't know what Birmingham kids have in that way. And when I meet them, I like Northerners generally. I suppose I prefer that feeling of being a little outside the corridors of power and the mainstream. That's very Midlands. I don't quite identify with Southerners. I think what Brummies share with Northerners is a hatred of pretension and what they share with Southerners is a dislike of making a scene.'

'But do "Southerners" actually exist? I don't think anyone has ever introduced himself to me as a "Southerner" as such. It's other people who talk about "Southerners". Northerners principally.'

'Oh I think they exist,' he nods. 'They like horses. Southerners like horses. And they don't live in the real world. They don't really get that there's a world out there at all.'

'Okay then: so what is a Midlander? And I don't want any more of this half-Northerner, half-Southerner bit. What are we like, in and of ourselves?'

He sits silently for a moment and for once doesn't use the pause to stuff his mouth with more food.

'I think a general cynicism, a sceptical nature, might be the hallmark of being from the Midlands,' he begins eventually. 'You can see it in our best comedians. Frank Skinner and Stewart Lee both do a great line in pulling everything down around them. Tony Hancock – our greatest comedian according to a BBC radio poll in 2002 – was from Birmingham, and his humour was all about tugging at illusions, dynamiting self-delusion. We're masters of self-deprecation – not something you'd say of Mancunians or Northerners generally. Personally I think it's a major virtue – and very English, obviously – but it can cut both ways. I'm sure it's one of the main reasons why the Birmingham identity hasn't imposed itself so much on the national stage.

'The school humour of my time was very negative – bitterly sarcastic,' he continues. 'Not in that very aggressive mockney-cockney London way. There was a certain despondency about life that was reflected in wanting to mock everything. That could just be teenage boys, of course. But friends of mine from school said that when they got to university they went on joking in the same way they had at school and other non-Brummie kids would say to them: "Why be so negative?" So maybe it really is a Brummie thing, to question everything, to tug at illusions.'

'So you're proud to be a Brummie?'

'Well, it does have certain negative connotations.'

'That would be an example of the famous Brummie under-statement, I think.'

'It used to be the case,' he carries on, 'that if you ever saw a Brummie in a sitcom on TV he'd be the thick character. And not just thick but also quite cynical and money-oriented. Timothy Spall's character in *Auf Wiedersehen, Pet* was thick and ended up, if I remember correctly, as a rather self-centred and fenced-off property developer, something like that. In *Our Friends in the North* all the evil property developers are Brummies too.'

'Typical anti-Midland propaganda,' I say encouragingly. 'This is what we need to fight back against.'

'Yes, only I think there might be some truth in it.'

Oh dear. He's starting to waver again. That Manchester girlfriend must have really got into his head. He's going to need to go into therapy again.

'I'm going to switch my recorder off if you keep talking in this way,' I say.

He carries on regardless. 'I think there's a connection in this country between Brummies and mindless exploitation of the environment. Certainly if you walk around the city centre, the damage that we've done to our own city in the name of Brutalist architecture and every other kind of architecture that came after it … it's worse than any other city, any other great city, that I've seen.'

'Ooh, I'm *really* looking forward to my tour now.'

He shrugs and stuffs his mouth with naan.

'Well,' I say mischievously, 'you could put it another way and opine that Birmingham refuses the temptations of elegance, remaining impressively unsentimental and tough.'

'If you were a bit of a prick, you might.'

'I knew you'd say something like that, Sticky my dear. I was in fact quoting Stephen Bayley on his beloved Cottonopolis: "Manchester refuses the temptations of elegance, remaining impressively unsentimental and tough." You can get away with that sort of thing if you're talking about the North. You can say it and people will still want to go there – they'll think: "Fantastic, it's ugly and really rough, I must book a holiday!" Why doesn't that approach work with Birmingham?'

Tone is chewing hard.

'We just can't take ourselves that seriously,' he spits out eventually.

Undone by our own sense of humour: that's the history of the Midlands in a nutshell.

* * *

'Boulton and Watt's steam engine had not only given power a new economy, it had acted as the midwife of a new society,' writes Roger Ward in his fascinating book *City-State and Nation* (2005). That's hardly an exaggeration. The nineteenth century saw a revolution in British politics driven by the great manufacturing towns of the Midlands and the North. If Britain emerged from the so-called 'Age of the Provinces' with a re-energised and newly democratised constitutional order, it was largely due to the reform movements spawned in Manchester and Birmingham. As the capital of the Lancashire cotton district and thus of Britain's biggest export industry, Manchester exercised a major influence over the nation's economic policy: the 'Manchester School', of course, was the great proponent of free trade. But in other respects – democracy, education, social and industrial innovation – Birmingham was far more influential.

Here's what Richard Cobden, the great nineteenth-century political reformer and leader of the Anti-Corn Law League, had to say about the contrast between the two towns: 'The social and political state of [Birmingham] is far more healthy than that of Manchester; and it arises from the fact that the industry of the hardware district is carried on by small manufacturers, employing a few men and boys each, sometimes only an apprentice or two; whilst the great capitalists of Manchester form an aristocracy ... The former state of society is more natural and healthy in a moral and political sense. There is a freer intercourse between all classes than in the Lancashire town, where a great and impassable gulf separates the workman from his employer.'

That is, Manchester was a much more divided society, with the toiling many ruled over by a few big plutocrats. By contrast, Birmingham's 'workshop economy' – much more skills-based and diversified in its output, and much less conflictual in terms of workplace relations – gave rise to a greater sense of social unity, making it the engine of parliamentary and civic reform in the 1830s and then again in the 1860s and 1870s. As a result of its programme of municipal improvements, Birmingham was declared 'the best governed city in the world' in the latter period, and under leaders from Thomas Attwood to Joseph Chamberlain it wielded a political influence in Britain unmatched outside London. Nineteenth-century Birmingham, concluded the Congregational minister Dr Robert Dale, was capable of deeds 'as great as were done by Pisa, by Florence, by Venice in their triumphant days'.

One of those deeds worthy of the great Renaissance city-states was the passage of the 1832 Great Reform Act, which laid the foundations of our modern electoral system. Shortly after our current glorious Coalition Government assumed power, Nick Clegg promised the 'biggest shake-up of our democracy since 1832'. Little Nicky has delivered nothing of the sort, of course, but it was good of him to remind us all of a *genuinely* defining event in British politics in the modern era. The foremost public campaigner was the visionary Brum-based economist Thomas Attwood, who founded the Birmingham Political Union (BPU) and played a crucial role in securing the reform of the franchise in the 1830s. As Lord Durham declared: 'The country owed Reform to Birmingham, and its salvation from revolution.'

In his paean to Cottonopolis, Stephen Bayley drops out in passing that 'Engels was a Manchester businessman', as if to suggest that the city was thus responsible for writing *The Communist Manifesto*. In a sense it was: the inequalities and misery that Engels observed in Manchester helped inspire the ideas contained in that revolutionary pamphlet. But is that really something to boast about? Birmingham didn't give rise to any such document principally because it was a far less unequal and much more creative

195

society. William Hutton described charter-free Brum as 'a town without a shackle' in the late eighteenth century; its citizens were certainly less shackled. It didn't need *The Communist Manifesto* because its natives already enjoyed a significant degree of social mobility and were busy dreaming up a series of more modestly progressive manifestos – those industrial patents Stuart Jeffries is so dismissive of in his *Guardian* article, but also practical social and political innovations – designed to make the world a better place. On a practical, everyday level, Birmingham has given us a lot more that we should be grateful for than Manchester.

* * *

Thankfully we don't have to negotiate Spaghetti Junction to get into central Birmingham after our balti experience, but the endless girdles of ring roads still make the journey a challenge.

We park up by Aston University, where the clustering of looming high-rise buildings is enough to give you vertigo, and walk round to New Street Station where the natty, clear-glass Tourist Information booth is located. Inspired by the launch of that new £50 note, I suggest that we organise our tour of the city around the Boulton–Watt partnership, so Tone approaches one of the attendants to ask for advice. I listen in to their conversation, which sounds as though it's being conducted in some sort of local patois. 'Yow' this, 'Yam' that. And apparently it's not just nonsensical 'rhubarb' talk they're engaged in; *they can actually understand one another*. Astonishing. Eventually Tone returns with a 'Matthew Boulton City Centre Walk' brochure.

'I'm a bit worried about not being able to understand the locals,' I tell him as we leave. 'I'm an East Midlander so I don't know the lingo. I hadn't a clue what you were saying to that boy back there. Can you teach me a few dialect words so I can blend in more effectively?'

'Don't be a berk,' Tone snaps.

'I don't think "Don't be a berk" counts as Birmingham dialect,' I say. 'People have said it to me all over the country. Come on. There must be something I could drop into my conversation to make myself more *simpatico* to the natives.'

'The best advice I can give you if you want people to like you is to just keep your mouth shut,' he says.

'Come on, Sticky, talk Brummie to me.' I make big eyes at him.

He sighs deeply. 'All right then. "Bostin'" is a good word to use, as in: "That's totally bostin." It means something's great, brilliant. I use it quite a lot. Ironically, of course.'

'Of course. You Brummies don't like to get too excited, do you?'

'No.'

'Right then. So I can now say "Bostin'". Perfect. Any other words I should know?'

'Yeah. "Bab."'

'What? Bap? Meaning a soft bread roll or, more colloquially, a woman's round, springy breast?'

'Ba*b*. It's how a grandmother might address a young person. "Yow all right, bab, how are yow?"' The Brummie accent he adopts to utter the last sentence is so unexpectedly strong that it makes me jump.

'"How are yow today?"' I mimic him when I've recovered my sang-froid. '"Bostin', thanks." Yep, sounds perfect for dropping into small talk with shopkeepers and the like. Let's hit the road, bap!'

'It's "ba*b*",' Tone corrects me before striding on ahead. I don't think he wants to be associated with me any more.

There are seventeen stopping-off points on the Matthew Boulton City Centre Walk. The first, appropriately, is the blue plaque that marks the site of the great man's birth up near Colmore Circus. The area has changed a good deal since 1728, but Boulton – a forward-thinking sort of guy, after all – probably wouldn't disapprove too much of its high-tech makeover. It's guarded over by the huge, ultra-modern Wesleyan Building, home to the Wesleyan General Assurance Society (founded 1841), whence we set off down The Priory Queensway to stopping-off point number two, Old Square. Apparently the latter used to be the finest Georgian square in Birmingham, before it was laid waste in Joseph Chamberlain's slum clearances in the 1870s. There's an attractive engraving of the way it looked in 1732 in the tour brochure. It doesn't look so hot in the present day.

Stopping-off point number three, just around the corner from where Joseph Priestley sparked four days of rioting in 1791 after he made a speech in favour of the French Revolution, is St Philip's Cathedral on Colmore Row. Boulton was christened in this Baroque treasure box in 1728, just three years after the building's completion. Its designation as a cathedral only followed in 1905, some sixteen years after Birmingham had finally attained city status.

I'm impressed and even a bit moved – not least by the lovely Pre-Raphaelite stained-glass windows, designed by local-boy-made-good Edward Burne-Jones in the mid-nineteenth century – but Tone says he prefers the city's other cathedral, St Chad's, the first Catholic church to be built in England after the Reformation. He would say that, of course, because he's a Catholic and used to sing in the choir there. He assures me it's an example of Gothic Revivalism at its finest – the architect was A.W.N. Pugin, who also helped to design the Houses of Parliament. Unlike St Philip's, it has no direct connection to Matthew Boulton but we should get to see it when we reach stopping-off point number eleven, which is in the city's esteemed Jewellery Quarter. I can't wait.

Actually, I can wait *a little*. Before we proceed any further, we decide that we are in urgent need of a drink. A ten-minute refreshment break shouldn't seriously affect our progress. We dive into a pub and, as they don't serve lassi, I have my first pint of the day. Tone is on to his third already. I pay the barman and begin to say 'Thanks, bap' but the last word dies on my lips.

I must say, I really am warming to Birmingham; I'm even looking forward to seeing the notorious Bull Ring shopping centre later. Birmingham's harsh materialism and 'defiant absence of beauty' have been constant themes in commentaries on the city since the nineteenth century, its reputation for ugliness being reinforced by the fact that it became a testing ground for British architectural Brutalism in the 1950s. I haven't seen much cold concrete and nature-banishing angularity today, though. I can't imagine why that Stuart Jeffries was so mean about it, especially as – did I mention this before? – he's a West Midlander himself. I decide to lay the matter before my friend and relate the contents of the *Guardian* article to him.

'What's the name of the writer again?' he says as he tears open a packet of crisps and burrows his snout into it like a truffling pig.

'Stuart Jeffries.'

'Oh yes. I like him. He's a good writer.'

'I didn't say he wasn't good – brilliant even; he's from the Midlands, after all. But why was he so nasty about his own birthplace?'

'Where was he born exactly?' asks Tone.

'I don't know. I'm not his mother. The West Midlands. You know: somewhere around here.'

'It could be important.'

We look him up on Tone's smartphone.

'That explains it!' exclaims my companion, crisp mush tumbling from the sides of his mouth.

'What does?'

'He's from Wolverhampton. Went to school in Dudley.'

'So? That's basically Birmingham, isn't it?'

'Nooooo! Wolves is in the Black Country. That's one of the worst insults you can give a Brummie, to say he's from the Black Country. And vice versa, of course.'

'There's intense local rivalry between the two of you, you mean?'

'You could say that. I don't really think of people from the Black Country as having anything in common with me. The Black Country and Birmingham feel like two entirely different areas. Most Brummies would rather be mistaken for a Scouser than for someone from *Dud-lai*.'

'Gosh.'

'That's how people from Dudley talk, by the way: *Dud-lai*,' he explains rather otiosely, half-yodelling the word. 'When we're feeling a bit blue about something, people in Birmingham put on a Black Country accent and go: "Our accent might be awful but the *Dud-lai* one is infinitely worse." It's a consolation.'

He pauses to take a long draught of his beer. 'Not that there's anything really wrong with the Black Country,' he says, returning to his theme. 'I rather like hot pork sandwiches. That's what they eat there, you know.'

There's no answer to that.

'So you think that's why Stuart Jeffries could write something like that about Birmingham?' I resume. 'Because of the rivalry?'

'Yes.'

'I must say, West Midlanders lack much sense of tribal loyalty. No wonder we have an image problem if near-neighbours are so unkind to one another.' I sigh and drain my glass.

Tone nods and looks solemn. 'Though Lancashire and Yorkshire have this massive rivalry, people from both will both happily say: "I'm Northern." They'll happily agree on having this larger shared identity. But not in the Midlands. It's London's fault. We feel its pull more and that ruins any wider sense of tribal belonging. Have you seen that graph that shows areas of the country whose economies are more than 60 per cent dependent on London?'

I signal that I haven't.

'Well, it extends as far as Rugby [where the modern Olympics and rugby football were both born, remember]. So London really does encroach on the Midlands, far more than it does on the North. The Midlands has always remained caught in the middle, really. And that's why there's no sense of a unified, separate identity.'

'Exactly!' I exclaim, the booze beginning to have an effect on my mood. 'But that's what I'm trying to do with this book – raise Midland consciousness! Start a revolution!'

'I'm not sure Brummies are going to be much help to you there,' Tone begins, discouragingly. 'We're too ready to raise an ironic eyebrow.'

'Bugger irony. If we could just …' I begin, my fingers automatically bunching into a fist of revolutionary intent, but Tone has disappeared in the direction of the loo.

* * *

An hour and a half later, vision a little fuzzed, we've climbed up to Victoria Square. There's a huge boxy plasma screen pumping out a mixed programme of news and pop videos, while a handful of Occupy protesters have set up tents opposite the Council House. It doesn't look as though they're about to ignite anything to rival the Priestley Riots.

We clamber up and round into Chamberlain Square, which bears the name of the renowned Birmingham political dynasty – the great one, 'Brummagem Joe', orator, statesman, Liberal reformer, Colonial Secretary, the greatest prime minister Britain never had; and the dismal one, Neville, the 'Peace in our time' appeaser, perhaps the worst prime minister Britain ever had. A bronze figure holding a quill pen lies elegantly sprawled across some steps. This is Thomas Attwood, of Great Reform Act fame. Above him are written the words 'Prosperity, the Vote, Reform', while the paper he holds is inscribed 'Prosperity Restored'. History – big history, English political history, world-shaking history – is all around us.

We pile into the Birmingham Museum and Art Gallery for stopping-off point number four, which involves us looking at various collections dating from the period when Birmingham was 'the great toyshop of Europe' (toys being small metal products) and Boulton and his partners were plotting the Industrial Revolution. Most eye-catching are the fine Portland Stone sphinxes salvaged from the landscaped grounds of Soho House.

'The Staffordshire Hoard's supposed to be in here somewhere. Should we have a quick look at that too? That's a major Midland coup,' I call to Tone as he dashes down the museum stairs.

'No time!' he calls back. It appears Tone has decided we need to pick up the pace.

Stopping-off point number five is across Chamberlain Square, at the Central Library, home to the Boulton and Watt archive. We don't have time to examine its several million letters and other documents just at the moment, but it's good to know that someone's looking after it. Outside the library stand statues of Boulton's fellow Lunarticks Watt and Priestley. It's nice that they've not been forgotten.

Then higher still we climb, hurrying through the retail hell of the grossly misnamed Paradise Forum to emerge at the top of the city. This is Centenary Square. I must say, I'm beginning to develop a bit of an East Midland inferiority complex. My beloved Nottingham only has one proper square; Birmingham seems to have *hundreds*! Our stopping-off point here (number six) is in front of William Bloye's disconcertingly bright gilt statue showing Boulton, Watt and fellow engineer William Murdoch examining the plan of a steam engine. But Centenary Square is so spectacular it's hard to know where to look first – the Hall of Memory, built for the fallen of the two world wars, Symphony Hall, the International Convention Centre, Birmingham Rep or the new Library of Birmingham, with its curtain wall of glass and metal. The civic and cultural energy is irresistible.

'Wow! This is really something,' I say. I feel almost solemn.

'S'pose,' grunts Tone.

For stopping-off point number seven we need to drop back down the hill to Brindleyplace, a contemporary canalside development named for the engineer James Brindley. Our brochure wants us to think about how Boulton's wares would have been shipped around the world from the wharves that used to be located here, but our concentration is fading. It's getting dark, and the lights strung across the canal make it all look very Christmassy. An All Bar One winks at us in sexy come-hither fashion from across the bridge.

'Late autumn's a stupid time to go travelling around the country,' says Tone unhelpfully. 'The days are too short.'

'I'm beginning to think you might be right.'

We shake our heads and say that we don't like drinking in chain pubs, but then agree to make an exception on this occasion. The Boulton tour brochure is tucked into my bag; stopping-off points eight to seventeen are destined to remain unexplored today. I'll be back, though.

By the time we re-emerge, several hours later, it's very dark. Tone is singing 'Nights in White Satin' by his beloved Moody Blues.

Brindleyplace looks positively Continental under its seasonal lights. It could be Amsterdam, Venice even.

'You know, Birmingham's really not bad at all,' Tone says.

'I think it's *splendid* actually,' I reply with a hiccup. 'Yes, I'm glad you've come to your senses and dumped that Manchester girlfriend of yours.'

He peers at me uncomprehendingly.

We make our way back across the canal to begin the climb back up to Centenary Square.

'Do you know what the derivation of the word "Manchester" is?' Tone suddenly blurts.

'No – surprise me.'

'Well, it comes from its Roman name, *Mamucium*.'

'Very nice.'

'And do you know what that means in Latin? Well, I'll tell you. It means "breast-shaped hill".'

'So –' I am fuddled so it takes a moment for the penny to drop. 'So you mean Manchester means "Tit Hill"?'

'Yes!'

We both begin to whoop with delight.

'Tit Hill! Tit Hill! Tit Hill's got nothing on Brum!'

Back in Centenary Square, I suddenly think: What an extraordinary palimpsest Birmingham is! Birmingham isn't Britain's Second City at all – it's the cultural, political, industrial capital of the country, our First City. My head is beginning to spin with the superabundant density of it all: the Chinese quarter, the back-to-backs, the Bull Ring. Birmingham: birthplace of gas lighting, custard powder, Brylcreem, the magnetron, surgical radiography; nursemaid to poets from W.H. Auden to Benjamin Zephaniah. All the highs and lows of English history are piled up higgledy-piggledy one on top of the next. I look over towards Newhall Hill, where Attwood took the country to the brink of civil war in 1832 before securing the passage of that Great Reform Act, then turn to face Smethwick, home to the Soho Foundry and that new social model, where Christabel Pankhurst – daughter of the great Suffragette Emmeline – so narrowly failed to become the first woman MP in 1918, where future British Union of Fascists founder Oswald Moseley sat as Labour member from 1926 to 1931, and where the great comic actor Julie Walters was born. And here, I tell myself as I look around, stood Darwin, and here stood Wedgwood, and here stood Watt; and that is where the orator and classical scholar Enoch Powell made his 'Rivers of Blood' speech in 1968. The best and worst of England, all mixed together … Overcome with the richness of it all, I experience a sudden vertigo – a dizziness before the sheer profusion of historically resonant experience that can only be described as 'Stendhal's Syndrome' – and I think to myself: *Birmingham, bab, you are totally bostin'.*

But perhaps it was just the booze talking.

TO LICHFIELD

The sound of heavy industry, philosophers in denim and leather, and the evolution of Dr Darwin

The early-evening drive from Birmingham to Wolverhampton proves nightmarish – two and a half hours to cover all of eighteen miles. It's made worse by the fact that I subject myself en route to commentary of a Manchester City European Championship match on the radio. Fuelled by all that Emirates oil money, the Northern team are a sure bet to get their hands on the big European prize soon. The Midlands doesn't even have a representative in the competition at the moment and doesn't look likely to be able to muster one again this century. Oh for the spirit of Cloughie to rise up and lead the Midlands back to European footballing eminency!

When I finally get to Wolves it's raining and the car parks are all full near the Civic Hall, which is where I need to be in the next twenty minutes if I'm not to miss the start of the big treat I've decided to give myself: Motörhead in concert. I drive back out beyond the Wulfrun shopping centre – Wulfrun was an Anglo-Saxon noblewoman who founded a convent at nearby Tamworth; 'Wolverhampton', a word so wonderfully evocative of general Dark Age hairiness, may be a corruption of her name – and end up leaving the car down a dark backstreet. I anxiously dictate detailed notes into my voice recorder about how to find my parking location again after the gig. I can just imagine having to tell a policeman that I've lost my car, and no, I can't remember the registration number or even what kind of car I drive. Why don't I know the make of my own car? Am I subnormal?

So I'm keyed up when I get to the Civic Hall. Thankfully there's something very reassuring about Motörhead; this is music you can really relax to. The band made their mark on the national consciousness thirty years ago with their brilliantly bracing homage to life's gamblers, 'Ace of Spades', and, although individual members have come and gone since, their sound and shtick have varied very little in the intervening period. (Though frontman Lemmy, a man of legendary drug and booze intake, has adapted the lyrics of 'Ace of Spades' to reflect his own, perhaps surprising longevity. When he sings the line 'I don't want to live forever,' he now adds: 'But apparently I am.' It's one of the most touching reflections on ageing in the whole canon of rock and roll.)

The show begins in time-honoured fashion, with sirens wailing and lights raking the huge Marshall stacks that line the stage as the trio thunder into 'Bomber'. And suddenly there, at the centre of all this confusion and racket, is revealed Lemmy. He's of pensionable age now but he's never varied from the one true path of rock and roll – he's never been tempted to put out a crossover album with Beyoncé, for instance. 'This is one for all the family. It's called "Rock Out With Your Cock Out",' he chuckles from under his black cowboy hat. There's a strong element of panto about it all, and actually he's not wrong that what he's serving up is family entertainment. There are plenty of women and children as well as the more traditional tribe of hirsute men in attendance. Many are wearing T-shirts emblazoned with the motto 'Everything louder than everyone else', so when the guitarist instructs the audience to 'put your hands up in the air if you want it even louder', they obediently raise their arms and the decibel level increases significantly for the next number. The classics just keep coming – 'Orgasmatron', 'Killed by Death', 'Iron Fist', the inevitable encores of 'Ace of Spades' and 'Overkill' – until finally the stage goes dark and it's all over. Afterwards I stumble back out into the sodden Black Country night, shirt glued to my chest with sweat, deafened, blinded and voiceless. If it's catharsis (and a hearing problem) you're after, Motörhead put on a show every bit as powerful as anything old Sophocles managed.

* * *

Metallica's 'Black Album' was recently declared the biggest-selling US release of the past two decades. With in excess of 15.5 million units shifted, the 1991 American heavy metal masterpiece had managed to pip Shania Twain's much more obviously middle-market-friendly *Come On Over* to the top spot. Now don't tell me that don't impress-a you much.

The question remains, though: what has Metallica's vast American – indeed, global – success got to do with the Midlands? The answer: pretty much everything.

My hair fell out when I was in my twenties, and with my luscious locks vanished any last lingering hope I had of fronting a hard rock band to worldwide fame and glory. Rock singers – 'shouter' is probably more accurate in my case – can't be bald; not until they're on their thirtieth-anniversary reunion tour anyway. At about the same time, my songwriting partner quit to become a Sensible Dad, which sounded the death knell of our band, ECT (which stands for Electro-Convulsive Therapy, and is not to be confused with 'ETC' or 'etcetera', as dyslexic stage announcers regularly mis-announced us during our short gigging career). So I put away my playing ambitions and became a bit of a music journalist instead. These days I write mostly about jazz. (I can hum all twenty-seven minutes of the original studio version of Miles Davis's iconoclastic fusion masterpiece 'Bitches Brew' backwards.) But even now, nothing gets me stirred up quite like the sound of heavy metal. NWOBHM – aka the New Wave of British Heavy Metal – was happening as I came to musical consciousness in the late 1970s, and, drawn on prematurely by the tastes of my older brother, I fell in love with the likes of Angel Witch and the Tygers of Pan Tang (that y-for-an-i spelling is just *so* NWOBHM). We even had our own local NWOBHM heroes in Mansfield, Witchfynde (see what I mean about the y-for-an-i thing?). Their guitarist was the mysteriously monikered Montalo – Trevor to his mum – and the twin pentagrams on the cover of their debut album, *Give 'Em Hell*, gave them an occultish allure. Not that I've ever been into Satanism – or spandex, for that matter. But as I've got older and started moving in different circles (not least, jazz ones), whenever things have started to get too comfortable, I've always enjoyed telling people that my favourite band is Motörhead. 'You're being ironic, right?' comes the furrow-browed rejoinder. Not really, no. And not least because there's nothing quite like the feeling – that very Midland feeling – of not quite belonging, of being an outsider.

I don't really understand the prejudice against heavy metal. Music writer Erik Davis characterised one early strain of the genre as 'morbid' and 'contrary to nature'. Frankly, can you think of qualities that are more appealing to a teenager, and indeed to the teenager in every adult? At the very beginning of the metal phenomenon, another journo complained: 'Because it doesn't swing, it doesn't set the audience dancing; it aims for the temples, not the feet, and its total effect is one of stupefaction.' That's meant as a criticism, of course, but why does music have to make you want to move your feet in a traditional rite of sociability? We don't all want to live in a Jane Austen novel, you know. What's so wrong with anti-social mental pulverisation, at least as a recreational strategy?

So heavy metal was the sound of my youth, and, no matter how many times I listen to Purcell's great tragedy of regal passion and divine duty *Dido and Aeneas*, it's probably Motörhead's insistently hummable 'Love Me Like A Reptile' that I'll have on my lips at the moment of my decease. There's nothing I can do about it, and I don't regret it. You see, as a Midlander – with all that that entails – I have metal in my genes.

In the Eighties, English heavy metal musicians were rarely out of the headlines in the USA, and for all the wrong reasons. The most notorious was Ozzy Osbourne, a hellraiser of the first water, who hit the front pages serially for biting the head off a dove, then a bat, and then for getting drunk, dressing up as a woman and relieving himself on the Alamo (this resulted in his arrest – the Alamo is a national shrine).

Then there were fellow metal men Judas Priest, who found themselves in court after it was alleged that they were responsible for the self-inflicted gunshot wounds of two fans. On 23 December 1985, having spent hours consuming alcohol and marijuana and, allegedly, listening to music by Priest, 20-year-old James Vance and 18-year-old Raymond Belknap set off for a playground in Reno, Nevada. They were armed with a 12-gauge shotgun, which they intended to use to kill themselves. In the event, Belknap success-fully blew his head off, whereas Vance failed in his suicide attempt, leaving the bottom half of his face badly disfigured – the gun had seemingly slipped from his grasp at the crucial moment, probably because it was covered in Belknap's blood. Very heavy metal.

The case came to court in 1990, when it was suggested that Vance and Belknap had been driven to suicide by a subliminal message – 'Do it, do it, do it' – embedded in a track on Judas Priest's *Stained Class* album. 'It was like a self-destruct that went off,' Vance recounted to a newspaper between his much-reported suicide attempt with a gun and eventual death from a painkiller overdose three years later. 'We had been programmed. I knew I was going to do it. I was afraid. I didn't want to die. It was just as if I had no choice.'

The high-profile case had Constitutional ramifications. 'It was the first time there had been a judicial determination of whether subliminal messages were or were not protected speech under the First Amendment,' the presiding judge later commented. The conclusion he came to was that they were not so protected: 'Because speech is basically the expression of thoughts and ideas that a person can reflect upon and accept or reject, but a subliminal message is a surreptitious attempt to influence the subconscious and, therefore, is not something you could reflect upon and accept or reject.' Though judicially of great importance – Judas Priest helped clarify the First Amendment! – the judge's pronouncement had little bearing on the outcome of the trial at hand, since pros-ecutors failed to provide conclusive evidence of the existence of any such deliberately planted subliminal messages in the music. An expert witness for the prosecution claimed to have found backwards messages of 'Fuck the Lord' and 'Try suicide'; Priest singer Rob Halford countered by saying that he had likewise played the record backwards and had found the rather more anodyne messages of 'I-I-I asked her for a peppermint / I-I-I asked for her to get one', while guitarist Glenn Tipton said he had heard 'Hey mom, my chair's broken'. That deadly 'Do it' turned out to be the sound of the singer exhaling. Faced with this evidence, the judge found in the band's favour that any apparent 'messages' were phonetic accidents and the case was dismissed.

After the trial, Halford reflected with typically dry Midland wit that, if Judas Priest had ever dabbled with putting subliminal commands in their music, they were unlikely to have inserted ones ordering their fans to kill themselves, given that that would have been tantamount to the band committing commercial suicide. They were far more likely to have included positive, upbeat messages – such as 'Buy more of our records' – instead.

This wasn't the only time the band found themselves flirting with the American Constitution. Priest also had a run-in with Tipper Gore – the then-wife of saintly US politician Al Gore – after the Washington-based Parents' Music Resource Center (PMRC) decried 'a sick new strain of rock music glorifying everything from forced sex to bondage to rape'. The organisation listed Priest's 'Eat Me Alive' at number three (just below Sheena Easton's 'Sugar Walls') on its 'Filthy Fifteen', a chart of the songs it deemed most objectionable. PMRC co-founder Tipper complained that the Priest tune was a violent ode to oral sex conducted at gunpoint. Was she right, or was she indulging in a spot of feverish 'Rorschach audio', as parents have a habit of doing when they listen to their children's record collections? Well, the song's opening lines – about 'wild vibrations got me shooting from the hip' and a growing urge to 'let rip' – do appear to confirm that it's basically about sex and probably more specifically about getting a blowjob, and the subsequent 'I'm gonna force you at gunpoint' does indeed seem to

213

point to a threat of force (although some might see in such weapon imagery little more than phallic symbolism – elsewhere in the tune Halford apparently refers to his penis as a gun-like 'rod of steel'). Of course, at a Constitutional level, the question was less whether Tipper's interpretation was valid and more whether recording artists had the freedom to say whatever they jolly well pleased, no matter what nannying parents made of it. In the event, legislation was avoided – amend the sacred First Amendment just because skinny little homunculus Prince had sung about 'Darling Nikki' (number one on the PMRC's 'Filthy Fifteen') masturbating with a magazine? *Puh-leez!* By way of compromise, the record industry agreed to put 'Parental Advisory' labels, or 'Tipper's stickers' as they became popularly known, on any release likely to cause offence.

As for the Priest song, you probably think it sounds a bit primitive, and perhaps it is. But a consideration of the wider political and artistic context endows it with an altogether grander cultural significance. This was, after all, late 1980s Reaganite America, where a new battle in the ongoing national 'Culture Wars' was about to be joined when Federal funding was withdrawn for a travelling exhibition of homoerotic work by photographer Robert Mapplethorpe. Among other edgily fetishistic works (all delivered with Mapplethorpe's cool aestheticising classicism), the artist's self-portrait showing him with a bull whip inserted in his anus caused particular outrage among conservatives, who questioned whether public money should be spent promoting material that seemed so at odds with traditional family values. At the same time, other taboo-testing works – such as Andres Serrano's *Piss Christ* (a photograph of a plastic crucifix immersed in the artist's own urine) – drew the ire of the religious right, which won support from successive Republican presidents Ronald Reagan and George Bush Snr. The situation exploded at the height of the AIDS crisis

(Mapplethorpe himself fell victim to the disease in 1989), a context that galvanised liberals and gay rights activists who were dismissive of Washington's handling of the pandemic. The result was a resounding victory for the social progressives, with improved rights and representation for minority groups generally.

Now, Priest fans had been nudging one another for years about lead singer Rob Halford's high-pitched vocals, taste for S&M-ish leather outfits and predilection for playing with whips on stage. Might he possibly be … *gay*? When Halford's homosexuality was confirmed a few years later, 'Eat Me Alive' was transformed from a song about oral sex at gunpoint into a song about *gay* oral sex at gunpoint, with the blowee almost certainly dressed in bondage gear, and perhaps even with a whip up his arse – just the sort of scene that Mapplethorpe might have photographed, in fact. Now here's the clincher: such information recasts the song from a piece of paternalistic Neanderthal misogyny into a pioneering and bravely outspoken liberal celebration of alternative lifestyles. In other words, Judas Priest and 'Eat Me Alive' are part of the post-AIDS global consciousness-raising avant-garde. They're progressive. *Hell, you could probably even call them PC.* Thanks to Priest – and, of course, a few others who also spoke up in defence of the socially and politically marginalised and their favourite hobbies and pastimes during this period – Western society is a much more tolerant place today. So there.

Aside from a certain notoriety resulting from their American misadventures, Judas Priest and Ozzy Osbourne have a number of other things in common. In the first place, there's the influence both are acknowledged as having exerted on the development of heavy metal. MTV.com, for instance, named Priest the second most important band in the genre's history, just behind the group with which Ozzy began his career and whom *Rolling Stone* magazine dubbed 'the Beatles of heavy metal': Black Sabbath. A second thing that Priest and Ozzy, like the other founding members of Sabbath, share is their place of origin: Birmingham.

Is this mere coincidence, or might there be something that indelibly links heavy metal with the Midlands? Could there really be a degree of geographical determinism at play in the fact that the music's progenitors and greatest exponents, Black Sabbath, came from the region? And is that really why I identify so strongly with it?

Though Ozzy Osbourne is their most famous frontman, Sabbath have had several singers across the course of the last four decades, including an American, Ronnie James Dio. But despite the vocalists' changing accents, the band's signature sound has remained unmistakable throughout. This is because its defining element is the sound of Tony Iommi's guitar. Prior to becoming a full-time musician, Iommi worked in a metal factory – a sheet metal factory, to be precise – in Birmingham, where at the age of fifteen he lost the tips of two fingers on his right hand in a grue-some industrial accident. The left-handed Iommi assumed that his guitar-playing days were over, but a friend encouraged him to reconsider his options by getting him to listen to a recording by Django Reinhardt, the great interwar 'gypsy jazz' guitarist who had also lost the use of two fingers on his fretting hand. Encouraged, Iommi fashioned himself prosthetic finger endings and strung his guitar with extra-light strings. The tension they exerted on his damaged fingers was still too great, however, so he detuned his guitar to relieve the pressure – a move that immediately gave his playing a distinctly darker, doomier feel. When his bandmate Geezer Butler followed suit and detuned his bass too, a new musical genre came into existence. The sound of heavy metal, you could say, was born in blood and mental agony one day in a sheet metal factory in Birmingham.

Speaking today, Brian Tatler, guitarist with the acclaimed Stourbridge-based NWOBHM act Diamond Head, agrees that the histories of Birmingham heavy industry and heavy metal are intertwined. 'If I'd been born by the coast, listening to the sound of the sea, the waves and the seagulls, that could have taken me in a different direction,' he says. 'There's a place called Cradley Heath not far from where I live that was famous for making chains. And in the steelworks in Brierley Hill a few miles away you've got drop forges and blast forges. It's possible that some of the heavy metal sound came from that kind of industry. Working in those kinds of jobs – cauldrons-of-fire kind of jobs – and working with hot metal probably had an impact.' Tatler, the son of a toolmaker and a former doormaking apprentice himself, wrote the riff for 'Am I Evil?', Diamond Head's most famous composition, under the inspiration of 'Symptom of the Universe', a Black Sabbath track whose sound he evokes in industrial terms: 'That was the ultimate riff for me. It was so dark and repetitive. Listening to it was almost like being bludgeoned, it was so relentless.' Heavy metal, you could say, is heavy industry in musical form.

Black Sabbath took their moniker from the name of a 1963 Boris Karloff horror film that was showing at a cinema near the band's rehearsal space. Their preoccupation with Satanic themes seems to have begun with a little innocent market research. Watching punters queue up to see the Karloff film, Geezer Butler noted that it was 'strange that people spend so much money to see scary movies'; shortly afterwards he tried his hand at writing a lyric inspired by the work of occult writer Dennis Wheatley and by Butler's own vision of a hooded figure standing at the foot of his bed ('What is this that stands before me? / Figure in black …'). Coupling Osbourne's unearthly, keening vocal with a doomily gothic, downtuned musical accompaniment that revelled in the use of the tritone – or *diabolus in musica* ('musical devil') as medieval scholars called this most physically unsettling of musical intervals – the resulting eponymous song was in stark contrast to the flower-power sounds that dominated the late Sixties: 'Peace and love was not necessarily our reality ... There wasn't a whole lot of flowers being handed out in Aston,' as Sabbath drummer Bill Ward put it. Impressed with their new direction, the band began to focus on producing songs that were the musical equivalent of horror films, releasing their debut album in February 1970 – on Friday the 13th, to be precise.

This pure, dark aural outpouring of West Midland industrial alienation was an immediate commercial success in the teeth of the peace-and-love Zeitgeist. Mainstream radio stations refused to give it airplay, and hip music critics like Lester Bangs in *Rolling Stone* magazine wrote uncomprehendingly of the album's 'discordant jams with bass and guitar reeling like velocitised speedfreaks all over each other's musical perimeters, yet never quite finding synch'. But the kids loved it. And so the pattern of popular appeal and Establishment dismissal was set for this West Midland form of outsider art.

Rolling Stone has since come round to Sabbath's place in rock history, acknowledging their second album, *Paranoid*, as a release that 'changed music forever'. Even so, the popularity of heavy metal still seems to come as a surprise to many mainstream commentators. When Planet Rock, the hugely successful digital-only radio broadcaster which proudly lays title to being 'Britain's classic rock station', was put up for sale by its owners, GCap, in early 2008 owing to the perceived unviability of DAB, one upmarket British newspaper (oh all right – *The Times*) reacted by publishing a sneeringly *de haut en bas* article professing faux-sympathy for the station's imminent demise. According to the paper, the station's audience, made up of the terminally 'unfashionable' who 'like nothing better than the sound of white men thrashing away at guitars', was soon to be denied its daily diet of Sabbath and Led Zeppelin (singer Robert Plant and drummer John Bonham were also born in the West Midlands). This was sad, the writer of the piece suggested mockingly, but what could you expect when it was so 'cheesy' and 'crass'? Rewardingly, a year later the same paper found itself in the invidious position of having to announce that Planet Rock had not merely survived, thanks to the intervention of entrepreneur Malcolm Bluemel, but was the only national commercial station to have trebled its audience in the past five years: it was even drawing larger audiences than the BBC's digital-only stations, which had seven times the budget to spend on their programming as well as enjoying huge promotional advantages. 'We're a cottage industry, and we still beat [the BBC] in the ratings,' Bluemel commented. Though it's based in London, the success of Planet Rock, built on Brummie heavy metal and achieved in the teeth of Establishment contempt, is a classic Midland David-and-Goliath tale. It's so popular in the West Midlands, it's now available on FM there.

Is heavy metal dumb? A lot of people seem to think so, and it's one of the reasons the middlebrow mainstream feels it can treat the genre with such disdain. While British punk – which, after all, was launched by Johnny Rotten and Steve Jones doing nothing more impressive than saying 'shit' and 'fuck' on national telly – enjoys serious intellectual credibility, metal is regarded as a subject fit only for mockery.[1] Just look at some of the films documenting the scene. For instance, *Heavy Metal Parking Lot* (1986), a short work of *cinéma vérité* by John Heyn and Jeffrey Krulik, is held up as a classic of the genre. This funny, mildly unnerving faux-anthropological study unfurls as Middle American metal fans gather in the venue car park before a Judas Priest concert

---

[1] Why was punk taken so seriously? Because it happened in London, of course.

in Maryland. A bare-torsoed youth sucks on a tube of beer, his drug-dilated pupils dancing wildly in front of the camera as the interviewer tries to find out where he is from. The addled fan begins by responding the West Coast, but then, after a brief confab with his friends, decides to tell us where he is now instead: 'I'm on acid, that's where I am.' Another metalhead teasingly attracts the camera's attention before pointing to the words 'Fuck off!' emblazoned on his T-shirt. Meanwhile a young lady indicates her leg and warns viewers: 'See that scab. Don't ever get it in the car' (her boyfriend had apparently been too rough in seeking paradise by the dashboard light). The fans aren't an especially impressive lot, then, and they're certainly not very articulate. 'Do you like heavy metal?' the roving reporter asks one red-haired girl. 'Hell yeah!' she trumpets back. 'What do you do when you go to a concert?' the interviewer probes further. '*Paar*-dee!' He isn't fazed. 'Are you still at school?' he asks. 'Hell yeah!' And so it continues until the interviewer wraps up his interrogation with: 'Is everybody having a good time?' 'Hell yeah!' How much dumber can you get?

I could quote a statistic here. In 2007 the UK's National Academy for Gifted and Talented Youth revealed that a disproportionately large number of its members list heavy metal as their favourite kind of music. That's right: more bright students listen to metal than to any other kind of music. As Ian Winwood noted on the *Guardian* website at the time, there's a reason for this: there's a strong correlation between being gifted and being a bit inadequate socially, and metal represents the voice of the outsider. 'Popular consensus may have Morrissey or Thom Yorke as poster boys for the lonely hearts' club clientele,' concludes Winwood, a writer for metal bible *Kerrang!* (metal fans really don't care whether you find that title silly or not), 'but it is metal, and it will always be metal, that is the true voice of the outsider. And it doesn't take a genius to understand that.' Now I'm not saying that all Midlanders are exceptionally gifted and/or talented (although proportionally they're way ahead of Northerners and Southerners), but, as everything in this book demonstrates, history has certainly conspired to make them natural outsiders – people who, as Jilly Cooper would have it, live 'beyond the pale'.

Where the powers-that-be in Liverpool and Manchester have vigorously exploited their cities' musical heritages, Birmingham's political representatives have missed important branding opportunities. Councillor Matt Bennett was recently quoted as saying: 'I studied in Liverpool and they do know how to make the most of their music. Yes, they have The Beatles but they do like to go on and on about it. So I say give Ozzy Osbourne the Freedom of the City. He is the most famous Brummie on the planet.' A Black Sabbath Day has been mooted as a way of boosting music tourism to the city. What a great idea.

Of course, at a more grassroots level, metal's Midland rootedness has long been appreciated. There's a regional musical archive, www.homeofmetal.com, while for the past thirty years Leicestershire has played host to metalheads every summer when they come to be sonically bludgeoned in the mud at the pretty historic village of Castle Donington. The festival in question is now called Download, but in its first incarnation it was known as Monsters of Rock. Audiences could be a bit suspicious of foreign bands in the early days. I remember Twisted Sister, a bunch of extremely butch, not to mention ugly, American guys who insisted on wearing frocks and make-up, receiving a mixed reception in 1983. That was a pity, I thought, because I really loved those self-styled 'Sick Motherfuckers' ('You're an SMF,' ran one of their anthemic fanbase-dedicated choruses). I didn't care much for second-on-the-bill act Meatloaf, though, so I wasn't unduly perturbed when the Donington crowd demonstrated their lack of appreciation for his operatic histrionics and the big man tried to hide behind his outsized handkerchief. Hoping to win over the faithful with a show of rock'n'roll defiance/camaraderie, 'Loaf then charged to the front of the stage, raised his middle finger and shrieked, 'I respect you motherfuckers!' No one was impressed, of course, and the bottles of piss – or festival champagne as I prefer to think of it – continued to rain in on his big potato head.

The 1986 Monsters of Rock Festival was notable not only for an appearance by a one-armed drummer (Rick Allen of Def Leppard; if you don't already know the story, it would take too long to explain) but also for the inclusion on the bill of a spoof act – something of a novelty in those days. Born of a Channel 4 comedy show, the delightfully unamusing Bad News (featuring Rik Mayall, Nigel Planer, Ade Edmondson *et al.*) had no trouble living up to their name, but neatly underlined an important point about the music that's equally evident in that documentary of the same year, *Heavy Metal Parking Lot*: it's easy to send up. And no one understands and appreciates that fact better than metal's own biggest followers – no one sends heavy metal up better than metallers themselves. The 'mockumentary' *This Is Spinal Tap*, one of the funniest films ever made, was created by people who love hard rock: innumerable comic details are drawn directly from heavy metal history (that 'miniature Stonehenge' sequence is straight out of Black Sabbath folklore). Metal fans and Midlanders alike know that 'It's such a fine line between clever and stupid', and for the most part we really don't care which side others place us on while we're enjoying ourselves. You see, to be a heavy metal fan, you have to be able to delight in the music's – and your own – absurdity. Metal is a form of Midland philosophy, a joyous, life-affirming statement of the essential absurdity of human existence. Where

France has Jean-Paul Sartre and a bunch of pseudy intellectuals in black polo necks who drag on Gitanes, the Midlands has denim-and-leather Existentialists who will merrily sing along to 'Into the Void'. Though there's certainly a metalhead 'uniform', there's also a wonderfully freeing lack of concern with fashionability or being hip. We really don't care which parka or Fred Perry shirt is 'in' this season. And let me tell you this: self-mocking Midland Existentialism is a lot more fun than the dreary self-regarding cool of Manchester and London bands. It's no accident that Midland metal has achieved a global audience of a size that no bunch of Madchester clowns or London darlings of the press could ever dream of reaching.

Finally, to return to Metallica and what they owe to the Midlands. As we've seen, at the most general level, the music they play was forged in the metal factories of the English West Midlands. But their debt to the region is even more specific. In the early Eighties, Metallica drummer and co-founder Lars Ulrich, the son of a Danish tennis star, became obsessed with the music of second-generation metal gods Diamond Head and blagged himself a week's accommodation on Brian Tatler's floor in Stourbridge (Midlanders are hospitable folk). Ulrich learned a great deal from Tatler and his bandmates, including most of their repertoire: at their first gig, Metallica played nine songs, four of which were written by Diamond Head (including 'Am I Evil?'). Metallica singer/guitarist James Hetfield was even more explicit in acknowledging his band's debt to the NWOBHMites. 'We're a combination of the two Heads, Diamond Head and Motörhead,' he explained simply. And before you ask: yes, Lemmy, the Motörhead leader, also hails from the West Midlands.

To sum up: without Diamond Head, no Metallica; without Black Sabbath, no Diamond Head; and without industrial Birmingham and the Black Country, no Black Sabbath. In other words, without local sheet metal, no global heavy metal. It's a message that Birmingham Council should be vigorously communicating.

* * *

Have you noticed the way coincidences abound when you start looking for them? (But if you're actively seeking them, should you really think of them as coincidences, or should they rather be understood as associated phenomena actively generated by the inquiring intellect?) Anyway, the more I think about the current egregious neglect of the Midlands, the greater the weight of evidence of just that fact seems to force itself on my attention. I'm sitting in a car park in Lichfield, eating a packed lunch (I don't get an allowance for all this travelling about, you know) and leafing through a newspaper. As I scan the radio listings, my eye is caught by a programme on Radio 4 about the attempts of Malmesbury in Wiltshire to brand itself 'The Philosophy Town' on the grounds that the political philosopher Thomas 'nasty, brutish and short' Hobbes was born there. Now you can't blame a town for trying, so I'm not about to begin a fire-bombing campaign in that sleepy Southern redoubt just because it's hoping to attract more, and more contemplatively given, tourists. But everyone knows that if there's a Philosophy Town or City in the UK, it's Lichfield in the Midland county of Staffordshire. It's been known as the 'City of Philosophers' for over two centuries, for Kant's sake; the opening paragraphs of the Wikipedia entry confirm as much.

Surely, I think as I read the item in my newspaper, the writer is going to point that out? No. Instead she lists other towns and cities with strong associations in the public consciousness: 'Blackpool for lights … Liverpool for comedy and Manchester for arts.' She offers a fairly random selection that takes in North and South, and even Wales, but there's not a single mention of the Midlands. Typical. But that's not the worst of it. She has a suggestion for the people behind Malmesbury's Philosophy Town push: 'If only they could persuade Radio 3 to bring them its annual Free Thinking Festival they'd be half way there. So far it's been at Gateshead and Liverpool so it's due a turn south.' 'Oh I see, the North-West and the North-East have had a go, so now it's the South's turn,' I begin to mutter. I'm nodding my head sarcastically as I do so. 'So that's your attitude, is it? Well, how about the Midlands! Aren't they due a turn?' Soon I'm punching the paper and shouting with such violence that it makes the car rock slightly. A passer-by bends to peer in at the window. When I notice him, I rapidly steady myself and give a thumbs-up and mouth 'No problem!' with a forced smile. I do a quick mime with my newspaper as if to say: 'Makes your blood boil, doesn't it? I don't know why I bother buying it!' I'm becoming over-elaborate in my performance, I realise, but somehow I can't stop myself. Eventually a woman stoops beside my spectator, takes one look at me and pulls the man – her significant other presumably – away. As he departs, he takes out his mobile phone. Is he calling the police? The lunatic asylum? Technically I haven't done anything illegal, or that could honestly be said to point to clinical insanity, but just in case I decide to move the car.

In appearance and atmosphere, Lichfield isn't unlike Stratford. It's solidly bourgeois in that half-timbered, olde-worlde way, and although it doesn't attract much in the way of tourist trade – the Garrick Theatre is hardly a draw to compete with the RSC – it is home to another major birthplace museum: that of the eighteenth-century literary titan Samuel Johnson, or Dr Johnson as he was known to his patients (I'm joking; he wasn't *that* sort of doctor). Johnson was the one who dubbed Lichfield the 'City of Philosophers'. It's hard to think of a man of letters whose achievements are better able to stand comparison with those of Shakespeare. And, as I said before, Johnson also played a critical role in establishing the Swan of Avon as the National Poet. Midlanders stick together. They did in the eighteenth century at any rate.

The Birthplace Museum – the house in which Johnson was born and spent the first twenty-seven years of his extraordinary life – overlooks the market square, where there's a large statue of Old Sam in pensive, self-lacerating mode (he once did self-imposed public penance for a wrong he considered he'd done his father). As I'm passing I suddenly think it might be fun to buy some potatoes from the fruit-and-veg stall near sculptural Sam's feet, to show how down-to-earth even our most highfalutin Midland philosophers are. I pay for my half-kilo of spuds, thank the vendor and smile virtuously to myself. And then it strikes me that I'm now going to be stuck with a big bag of potatoes for the rest of the day. Perhaps it wasn't such a good idea after all.

Still, onward. A true Midlander is proud to carry his load.

When you first go in, the museum looks for all the world like a bookshop, and in fact it is. This is appropriate since Johnson's father was a bookseller. The person in charge glances at my bag of potatoes, resets his faces and invites me to browse the stock if I want to, though he has only books and no veg, and advises me that behind a further door is the museum proper: a mixture of objects relating to Johnson, video presentations and some handsomely calligraphed *bons mots* uttered by the man himself. Johnson was a bubbling fount of epigrammatic wit and wisdom, of course. 'Sir, it is no matter what you teach children first, any more than which leg you shall put into your breeches first,' announces the first display quotation that my eye lights on. 'Sir, you may stand disputing which is best to put in first, but in the meantime your breech is bare.' Too many 'Sirs'? Too prolix? (In a battle of the stand-ups, Tim Vine would be on his tenth punchline before poor stammering Sam got to his first.) All the same, you can't help but luxuriate in those wonderful cadences. Try reading Johnson's sonorous phrase-making aloud: the man had *rhythm*. Shakespeare would have approved. Lemmy, a P.G. Wodehouse devotee as well as Nazi memorabilia collector, surely does approve.

The house is a funny shape; the creaking staircase you mount to view the birth room is trapezoidal: Sam's father took against right angles for some reason. You get a good sense of this most sociable of scholars from the items on display, which include table skittles and various other miniaturised pub games. He liked pubs, did Dr J. Another of those Johnsonian *bons mots* is posted on the wall: 'A tavern chair is the throne of human civility.' I don't just admire Samuel Johnson, I decide, I *like* him. Let's spend a further moment drinking in the humour of this great Midland polymath. Sam the pretension-puncturing literary critic: '[Milton's epic poem] *Paradise Lost* is one of the books which the reader admires and puts down, and forgets to take up again. None ever wished it longer than it is.' Sam the down-to-earth art critic: 'I had rather see the portrait of a dog that I know, than all the allegorical paintings they can show me in the world.' Sam the sports commentator: 'Fishing I can only compare to a stick and a string, with a worm at one end and a fool at the other.' Sam the proto-TV chef: 'A cucumber should be well sliced, and dressed with pepper and vinegar, and then thrown out, as good for nothing.' And Sam the marriage-guidance counsellor, reflecting on the wisdom of a widower taking a second wife: '[Remarriage is] the triumph of hope over experience.'

There's a space containing all sorts of informative displays devoted to Johnson's dictionary at the top of the house, but this book isn't the place to rehearse Johnson's many accomplishments in detail. Unusually for a Midlander, they're already well enough established to require no special repetition or underlining here: that unparalleled dictionary, the voluminous essays, the ground-breaking edition of the Bard, the poetry, *Rasselas* and, above all else, the extraordinary, ceaseless flow of *conversation*. Imagine Stephen Fry, only ten times cleverer, fifty times more eloquent and a thousand times more industrious (those dictionary definitions didn't write themselves, you know). Not quite as good-looking, mind. Old Sam was no pin-up. Badly scarred on his face and body as a child by a case of scrofula that also affected his eyesight and left him deaf in one ear, he was so tic-ridden that when the Cockney artist William Hogarth first glimpsed him, 'shaking his head and rolling himself about in a strange ridiculous manner', he assumed Johnson was a care-in-the-community case. Subsequent exposure to the doctor's eloquence convinced Hogarth otherwise, of course, but Johnson's achievements were hard-won: he experienced periods of profound depression, and has been posthumously diagnosed as suffering from both Tourette's Syndrome and Obsessive-Compulsive Disorder. Apparently he couldn't bear to walk down a particular alley without giving every post a knock with his cane as he passed; if he missed one, he insisted on starting again.

It's unfortunate that Johnson's most often-repeated aphorism – 'When a man is tired of London, he is tired of life' – underlines his affection for the capital rather than the Midlands. But he did take his biographer and friend James Boswell – author of the great *Life of Samuel Johnson*, or 'Portrait of a Midlander' as I prefer to call it – to Lichfield to show him, as he wrote, 'genuine civilised life'. Lichfieldians were, he said, 'the most sober, decent people in England' and 'spoke the purest English'. Boswell recorded his friend as retaining the distinctive Staffordshire way of pronouncing certain words too: 'theer' (for 'there'), 'woonce' ('once'), 'poonsh' ('punch'). Johnson was proud of his Midland roots, then. If only all Midlanders who find themselves lionised in London today were equally keen to declare their origins.

* * *

Afterwards I wander away from bustling Lichfield town centre, up Bird Street, between Beacon Park and Minster Pool (an ancient reservoir further evidencing deep-rooted Midland engineering genius), and towards The Close, where I get a first proper look at the magnificent Lichfield Cathedral. Churches with a single spire are ten-a-penny; double-spired churches can likewise be had for a pound-a-dozen. But ones with *three* spires, and no common-or-garden churches at that but venerable *cathedrals* that can be traced right back to medieval times – how many of those can you think of? I'll tell you: there's only one, and it's here. And my, does Lichfield Cathedral have gravitas. It's built on the site of the shrine of St Chad, the Bishop of the Mercians (the medieval name for Midlanders), who died here in 672 from plague or similar and who was noted for his humility – a true Midlander then. If you approach it via The Close – the large grassy precinct in front of the cathedral, hedged about with some particularly eye-catching town houses – the first thing you see is the imposing, time-darkened west front, dotted with more than a hundred statues of kings and biblical figures. There are plenty more fine sights in store for the visitor inside, not least in the chapter house, which contains *Chad's Gospels*, an eighth-century illuminated manuscript, and the Lichfield Angel, a limestone sculptural figure with one hand carrying a sceptre and the other raised in blessing. It dates from

229

around 800 and may have formed part of Chad's ancient shrine. It was only rediscovered in 2003 and sheds important new light on the medieval cultural life of the Midlands.

If Lichfield had nothing more to offer than Dr Johnson and the thrice-spired cathedral and its treasures, it would still be worth a visit. Even my grumpy old *Rough Guide* admits as much, acknowledging the former as 'that polymath of all polymaths' and the latter as variously 'unique' and 'magnificent'. But, even so, I'm yet to mention the best that this 'City of Philosophers' has to offer. It lies hidden away behind the splendid Victorian, Georgian and Tudor houses of The Close. If you follow your nose, up through a fragrant herb garden towards a spacious red-brick town house now known as the Erasmus Darwin House, you will find yourself retracing the route taken by the most influential late eighteenth-century thinkers on nights of the full moon, for this is one of the places where the Lunar Society met.

Born in Elton near Newark, Erasmus Darwin arrived in the market town of Lichfield in 1756, a couple of decades after Samuel Johnson had left. Like Johnson, he was no looker: badly pock-marked, he grew so fat he had a half-circle cut out of his dining table to accommodate his capacious gut, and in ordinary conversation he stammered like a schoolboy called on to deliver an impromptu oration at the UN. But, unlike Dr J, Dr D was mighty appealing to the ladies. He fathered a dozen and more children of his own, and provided a home for even more (his second wife already had a family when they married).

But it's not as an unlikely sex symbol that Darwin rose to eminence. His day job – as a medical man – brought him wealth and respect, not to mention patients from London keen to seek the advice of the Lichfield MD, but it was his extracurricular activities as a leader of the Lunar Society that secured him lasting fame.

As the Lunarticks' biographer Jenny Uglow has written: 'Together they nudge their whole society and culture over the threshold of the modern, tilting it irrevocably away from old patterns of life towards the world we know today.' Their achievements were extraordinary; not that you would think so from Darwin's own pronouncements. He lightly dubbed his circle's experiments 'a little philosophical laughing' – no more. They helped launch a global revolution, however, and move the world from the agricultural to the industrial age. As both a scientific thinker and hands-on physician, Darwin, a giant of the Midland Enlightenment, dedicated his life to the chasing away of the darkness of ignorance and suffering.

His personal gifts were wide-ranging and visionary. As has been noted, though he died before Queen Victoria was born, he foresaw the train and the tank. He was forever imagining and projecting, sketching and building. His many futuristic inventions include a canal lift, a horizontal windmill (commissioned by fellow Lunar member Josiah Wedgwood) and the basic steering system that is still used in cars and buses today. Stepping into the Exhibitions Room at Erasmus Darwin House, the visitor is met by a model of his 'Turning Mechanism', developed to prevent travellers being pitched out of speeding carriages – a big problem on the uneven roads of the late eighteenth century. You also get an eyeful of Darwin's four-foot-long 'Bigrapher', which allows the mechanical reproduction of written documents – a Xerox machine *avant la lettre*. Having carried out an analysis of human speech and concluded that it was made up of a comparatively small number of sounds, Darwin also designed a speaking machine, which featured 'a wooden mouth with lips of soft leather'. According to the good doctor: 'This head pronounced the *p*, *b*, *m*, and the vowel *a*, with so great nicety as to deceive all who heard it unseen, when it pronounced the words *mama*, *papa*, *map*, and *pam.*' It spoke, he said, with 'a most plaintive tone'. Had Darwin hit on Artificial Intelligence? His good friend Matthew Boulton – a shrewd businessman as well as a significant inventor in his own right – wrote a contract in which he said he would give Darwin £1,000 if he could get the machine to pronounce the Lord's Prayer, Ten Commandments and Apostles' Creed as well. As Darwin's biographer Desmond King-Hele points out, the contract was probably intended as something of a joke: as a deist, Darwin would hardly 'have wished to create a robot priest whose novelty value would benefit the Established Church'. Owing to his other competing interests, he never completed work on his potentially world-changing speaking machine – he was just too busy with his other globe-shaking inquiries.

Does that sound like an exaggeration? Well, it isn't one. As a naturalist, Darwin was a pioneer of evolutionary thinking and expounded his theory in rhyming couplets:

> *Organic life beneath the shoreless waves*
> *Was born and nurs'd in ocean's pearly caves;*
> *First forms minute, unseen by spheric glass,*
> *Move on the mud, or pierce the watery mass;*
> *These, as successive generations bloom,*
> *New powers acquire and larger limbs assume;*
> *Whence countless groups of vegetation spring,*
> *And breathing realms of fin and feet and wing.*

Darwin posited the idea that all species had evolved from a single common ancestor, forming 'one living filament', and discussed the role of competition and sexual selection in bringing about change in different species. (He had his evolutionary motto *e conchis omnia* – 'everything from shells' – painted on his carriage, but was promptly forced to have it removed by a local churchman who was anxious about the possible consequences of Darwin's ideas for traditional, Bible-based notions of Creation.) Of course, it was Darwin's Midlander grandson, Charles, who made the canonical presentation of evolutionary principles in *On the Origin of Species* (1859). But in essence Erasmus had arrived at the same conclusions some sixty or seventy years earlier. However you look at the evolution of evolutionary theory, it was a Midlander who uncovered and expounded perhaps the most powerful idea to have reshaped the way we live and think about our place in the universe in the past two centuries.

Erasmus Darwin also enjoyed great literary fame. His *Botanic Garden* (1791) was a bestseller that almost saw him named Poet Laureate and exercised a vast influence on the emerging generation of Romantic writers. His object, he said, was 'to enlist Imagination under the banner of Science'. Few if any have ever equalled him in his ability to use poetry as a vehicle for new ideas. The oft-quoted dictum of Alexander Pope (a small-minded Southerner) that 'True wit is nature to advantage dressed, / What oft was thought, but ne'er so well expressed' meant nothing to him: Darwin's wonderfully expressive lines were turned to give shape to ideas that *no one had ever thought of before*. Even if you're a poetry fan, you'll probably never have read a line of Darwin's verse – after the huge success of *The Botanic Garden*, he quickly fell out of favour owing to his radical politics: the French Revolution was getting under way and conservative England was battening down the hatches. But Samuel Taylor Coleridge, author of 'The Rime of the Ancient Mariner', was a friend, and one of his best-known bits of verse, 'Kubla Khan' – you know the one: 'In Xanadu did Kubla Khan / A stately pleasure-dome decree' – was inspired by Darwin. As was Mary Shelley's novel *Frankenstein*. Darwin was a famous figure in his own day, and his experiments and ideas resonated widely: the Midland Enlightenment was widely discussed. In her introduction to the novel, Shelley described the genesis of the story during her stay on Lake Geneva with her husband and the ever-scandalous Lord Byron – another intellectual rebel with Midland connections, of course.

> Many and long were the conversations between Lord Byron and [Mary's husband] Shelley, to which I was a devout but nearly silent listener. During one of these, various philosophical doctrines were discussed, and among others the nature of the principle of life, and whether there was any probability of its ever being discovered and communicated. They talked of the experiments of Dr. Darwin, (I speak not of what the Doctor really did, or said that he did, but, as more to my purpose, of what was then spoken of as having been done by him,) who preserved a piece of vermicelli in a glass case, till by some extraordinary means it began to move with voluntary motion … Perhaps a corpse would be re-animated.

And so, from the experiments of Dr Darwin was born Dr Frankenstein and one of the most resonant fables of the modern world. Darwin's genius was of a broad, generous kind that not only made him a fount of extraordinary notions in his own person but also inspired genius in other people.

Fellow Lichfieldian Samuel Johnson didn't initially want to quit his native Midlands for London; it was only when Edial, the boys' school he had set up near Burntwood, failed that he packed his bags and headed for the Smoke. He went in the company of one of his pupils, David Garrick, the future actor and King of Covent Garden – Midlanders ruled the metropolitan arts scene in the mid-eighteenth century. Not that Johnson made a fortune from his labours: he was arrested for debt in 1756, and it was only after King George III granted him a yearly allowance in 1762 that he achieved any sort of financial equilibrium. Darwin, by contrast, thrived in the Midlands. He was offered the post of physician royal by the same monarch but refused – he felt no need for the capital, he said. When he did leave Lichfield in 1781, it was only to move to Derby. Intellectually the North Midlands gave him all the stimulation he required: the company – Wedgwood, Boulton, Watt, Priestley – could not be bettered in London, and the financial rewards were more than sufficient too.

So there you have him – Erasmus Darwin, eminent poet and naturalist, pioneer of evolution, leader of the world-changing Midland Enlightenment, *bon vivant*, whose literary and intellectual endeavours are imprinted firmly on human history. All in all, a most heroic chap, with a perhaps greater claim to the title of 'polymath of all polymaths' than his fellow Lichfieldian Johnson. And yet he and his splendid house don't get even a passing mention in my *Rough Guide* – a neglect that's almost certainly a result of the great Darwin's refusal to settle in the South and propagate his world-changing ideas from the capital. The anti-Midland bias continues to distort our national history.

Pills 'n' thrills in Mansfield and Stoke, what price an omelette?, and a pilgrimage to the 'Monumite'

I really am worried about Anna. Unless she has a brainwave, and quick, she's going to marry the wrong man. I just know it. Henry is an eligible sort of fella but far too conventional. Young Willie is a much better bet – a potential soulmate, someone who might be able to liberate her from the prison that she's built for herself out of Nonconformist religion and familial duty. She won't listen to my advice, though. She's too … well, *dull*. I've been chattering away at her for the past two hundred pages and, so far as I can tell, she hasn't cocked an ear to my advice even once: 'Sod your old Scrooge of a dad!' 'Help poor Titus – you don't want him killing himself, do you? (Oh dear, too late, he just has.)' 'Screw the sewing meeting. Live your life, girl!' *Nada*. No matter how loud I scream, no response comes there. That's one of the frustrations of being a mere reader.

Anna Tellwright is the heroine of Arnold Bennett's 1902 novel *Anna of the Five Towns*, which I've been reading in preparation for my trip to Stoke-on-Trent. There are few better guides to late Victorian Smoke-on-Trent, as the smog-darkened heart of the Potteries used to be known, than Bennett, who, though a 'realist' in style, nonetheless reshaped his favourite subject – life in his home town – for artistic purposes. For instance, among Stoke-on-Trent's many singularities is the fact that it's the only federated city in the UK: it's actually made up of six different towns. Bennett was born in Hanley, one of those 'Six Towns', but always referred to them in his books as the 'Five Towns', since he thought five sounded better than six. He also tweaked the towns' names a bit: Burslem became 'Bursley', his own Hanley became 'Hanbridge', etc. Fair enough, a dab of artistic licence here and there usually improves a picture. But there's something bigger going on here: Bennett's attitude to his place of origin may stand at the root of – and is at least expressive of – a deep regional identity crisis. He called his first (autobiographical) novel *A Man from the North* (1898) and was given to making statements of the following, binarist kind about himself and his fellow Stokeites: 'We are of the North; outwardly brusque, stoical, undemonstrative, scornful of the impulsive; inwardly all sentiment and crushed tenderness.' For Bennett, if you weren't from the South, you were from the North; there was no Middle (Midland) Way. Judging by that Amazon thread I referred to earlier, many people in Stoke still feel the same way. 'Though perhaps geographically we are in the North Midlands, we are very much a Northern city in spirit, outlook and feeling,' writes one such contributor in response to Maconie's *Pies and Prejudice*.

* * *

In truth, it's not just Anna Tellwright I'm worried about. It's my dad too. I've asked him and my mother to accompany me on my tour of Stoke – when he worked in nearby Leek my father made regular swoops over to Trentham Gardens to attend boxing matches in the company of his friend, the renowned 'crooning flyweight' 'Tiny' Bostock, so he'd be a knowledgeable companion – but he says he doesn't fancy the outing today. Too tired, he says. That's reasonable enough, I suppose: he is eighty. And few people think of a trip to Stoke-on-Trent as a treat. But what's really troubling is that he's not even interested in discussing the route I should take in the car. *My father, who's never happier than when he's behind the wheel himself, unable to raise the enthusiasm even to look at a map and tell me which road to take!* It's not normal. After all, isn't that what dads are for, giving road directions? As a result of his non-participation, I'm sure to get lost en route.

Anyway, Mum is ready to go, or she will be when she's made Dad take all of his pills for the morning. And my, aren't there a lot of pills to sift and swallow around here. Downstairs by the dining table there's a huge silver box file full of them; the overflow supply is contained in a big plastic bag that sits beside it. Dad has a lot of tablets to take these days, and he grumbles over every one. His aversion may stem from the fact that his own father was a bit of an aspirin fiend. 'Shake him and he'd rattle,' my father used to say. Not that all of the pills are for Dad, there are plenty for Mum too; and they're all mixed up together. They claim to know which is which, but I'm sure they swap some days unwittingly; maybe even on purpose occasionally, just for a giggle. They didn't used to take all these pills when I lived here. And they didn't used to have huge jerry cans of detergent scattered hither and thither through the house, either. What do they need industrial quantities of the stuff for exactly? To dissolve bodies in the bath? What goes on here when I'm not around?

'And why are we going to Stoke, did you say?' Mum asks, when she finally emerges from the house. 'From what I remember, it's horrible.'

'You always say that about everywhere, Mum, and then you always change your mind and decide it's the loveliest place on God's earth as soon as we get there,' I reply. 'And even if it is horrible, Stoke-on-Trent is a major Midland city with a distinctive character and history, and it is therefore my duty, as the herald of the Great Midland Renaissance, to go and examine it.'

She grimaces. 'You do go on, twerpie.'

'You don't have to come if you don't want to.'

She grimaces again but gets into the car anyway.

'It's going to be fun, you'll see. First we're going to the Wedgwood Museum … I know, I know, don't bother saying it: You've never much liked Wedgwood … And then we're going to have Omelette Arnold Bennett for lunch, if we can find somewhere that serves it.'

'What's that when it's at home?'

'Arnold Bennett, Stoke-on-Trent's greatest literary son, had an omelette named in his honour. It's basically cheese and haddock. The chef at the Savoy created it for him.'

'La-di-da.'

'I wonder whether it's served much in Stoke nowadays,' I say as I start up the engine. 'I wonder whether Bennett himself is still celebrated there too.'

'I don't care. And I don't like cheese.'

* * *

Stoke-on-Trent doesn't enjoy a very good press. In his autobiography, *A Journey,* Tony Blair recounts a conversation between the Duke of Edinburgh and the politician Joan Walley. Where are you

MP for? Prince Philip asks Walley, who confesses to representing Stoke. 'Ghastly place, isn't it?' comes the Duke's killer punchline. It's one of his less controversial jibes: pretty much everyone seems to agree that Stoke is indeed ghastly. I've been building up a casual collection of examples from the press. Take this recent quote printed on the front of a Sunday newspaper supplement alongside a picture of Slash, the former Guns N' Roses guitarist: 'Meet Slash, the hell-raising, long-haired rocker from ... Stoke.' The implication of such studied bathos being that it's simply incredible that anyone cool and with-it could hail from the Potteries. And then there's this preview – also in the *Telegraph*; doesn't the paper care about the feelings of its readers in Stoke? – for a Radio 4 programme about the birth of verbatim theatre: 'Stoke-on-Trent may seem an unlikely place from which to launch a theatrical revolution but, half a century ago, that's exactly what director Peter Cheeseman and a small group of actors – including Robert Powell and Ben Kingsley – did.' Why? What's so unlikely about Stoke as an artistic launchpad? No one would write that about Manchester. No one would *dare* to write it about Liverpool; they'd have to do a Boris Johnson and make a personal apology to the city. The general message appears to be – Stoke: appalling, risible or utterly negligible. And as that Radio 4 documentary itself reveals, that's the view the locals themselves often express. 'This city has a history of underperforming and underachieving,' runs one typical contribution.

It's not entirely accurate, of course. In fact, you could go so far as to say that it's *absolutely inaccurate*. Modern Stoke-on-Trent was shaped by one of the biggest achievers of any land or age: Josiah Wedgwood. It's hard to overstate the great Lunartick's accomplishments, although the great nineteenth-century British PM William Gladstone had a jolly good try when he declared: 'He was the greatest man who ever, in any age or country, applied himself to the important work of uniting art with industry.' His achievements in Stoke were akin to those of the Emperor Augustus, who famously found Rome a city of wood and left it a city of marble; in Wedgwood's case, the line might be that he found Stoke an agglomeration of small artisan workshops tossing around the local brown and yellow Staffordshire clay to no great effect and turned it into the crockery hub of the world-straddling British Empire. It doesn't quite trip off the tongue like the Augustus line but what it describes is still no mean feat.

This being the case, the Wedgwood Museum in Barlaston – it shares a site with the pottery firm's current factory – is the most appropriate place to begin an outing to Stoke. Before we go in, I take a photograph of my mother standing beneath the statue of Josiah Wedgwood that's placed imposingly in front of the red-brick block. 'I've never really liked Wedgwood,' she says, wrinkling her nose. I knew she was going to say that! But I'll bet she's changed her mind within the hour. She's a woman of very strong, and highly variable, opinions, is my mother.

We sign up for a workshop tour, which gives you the chance to nose around as the firm's craftspeople demonstrate various traditional techniques, from jewellery making to enamelling.

I let my mother slide in front of me as we approach the station occupied by a hand-painter. I'm no good at talking to people – they take one look at me and decide I'm up to no good – whereas my mother is an expert in coaxing information, often of a highly personal nature, out of them.

'Where do you sell most of those?' my mother asks the hand-painter as he dabs at a pot.

He looks up at her over his half-moon spectacles. 'I don't have the exact figures so I can only tell you what I *think*,' he says with the care of one with a practised love of precision. 'But I would say in Australia, Canada … the old Empire largely.'

'That's what I would have said,' my mother agrees. She's getting that look in her eye, the one she gets whenever she thinks about my brother and his family, now resident on the other side of the world. 'I have grandchildren in Australia, you see,' she tells the man. Is she going to pull out a picture of them to show him? Fortunately she doesn't have one with her. Is she going to cry? Probably.

Life is cruel.

We move on to the potter's wheel. It's impossible – impossible for me, at any rate – to watch a pair of hands bury themselves in moist potting material and not be reminded of that scene in *Ghost* where Patrick Swayze and Demi Moore grow increasingly intimate as their interwoven hands caress a lump of sweating, spinning clay into rising phallic life. The Wedgwood potter leading the demonstration today is a paunchy, late-middle-aged bald man, very skilled at his trade but not much like Demi Moore physically, so I do my best to stop thinking about that scene in *Ghost*.

We move on to the next station. Lovely Christmas tree ornaments are laid out like little gingerbread men on a baking tray, in an overt incitement to buy. I can feel my mother reaching for her purse.

'Aren't they beautiful, Robbie?' she whispers. 'Should I get one for the kids in Australia? I do love Wedgwood.'

Bingo. It's taken my mother precisely twenty-six minutes to perform one of her famous volte-faces, passing from chilly disdain to warm approval of all things Wedgwood in under half an hour.

We proceed into the main museum, which is dedicated to 'The People Who Have Made Objects of Great Beauty from the Soils of Staffordshire' and which serves as a repository of eight thousand or so items relating to the history of pottery. It's a remarkable collection.

There's a dessert plate from Wedgwood's 'Frog Service', designed for the Empress Catherine of Russia and her new palace of La Grenouillère, so named because it was surrounded by frog-infested marshes (*grenouille* is French for 'frog'). The service consisted of 944 different pieces of cream earthenware adorned with paintings of English country houses. There wasn't much profit in Catherine's original commission, but Wedgwood was a shrewd businessman who knew how to take advantage of his imperial connections: he had the service put on display in London before it was shipped to Russia so that society hostesses, keen to emulate the Empress, could order copies. The 'Frog Service' was soon all the rage.

There's also one of Wedgwood's 'Am I Not a Man and a Brother?' jasperware medallions, struck in 1787 to express his commitment to the abolitionist cause. The leaders of the Midland Enlightenment weren't just interested in technological progress or commercial success; moral advancement was a core belief too. The anti-slavery campaigner William Wilberforce came to see Wedgwood at his home at Etruria Hall, and the latter's 'Am I Not a Man and a Brother?' design had a significant impact on public opinion after it was adopted for bracelets, brooches, hatpins and other fashion accessories by the metropolitan great and the good. From his base in Stoke-on-Trent, Josiah Wedgwood never struggled to speak directly to tastes and opinions in London, Paris and New York.

Styling himself 'Potter to Her Majesty' after Queen Charlotte accepted a tea and coffee service from him, Wedgwood was a tireless experimenter and innovator. His discoveries – jasperware, the pyrometer – made him a fortune as well as a Fellow of the Royal Society. When he began his career, porcelain imports from China dominated the British market. A decade or so later, he was able to write, humorously, 'Don't you think we shall have some

Chinese missionaries come here soon, to learn the art of making cream colour [china]?' As a result, as the historian and local MP Tristram Hunt has noted: 'The British Empire was serviced from Staffordshire.' It was Wedgwood who put the Potteries on the world map, and gave it its identity.

To achieve such worldwide eminence, he needed to do more than merely design and manufacture plates and cups that the whole world wanted to eat and drink from; he also had to guarantee the means to have those desirable crockery items delivered swiftly and intact to his global customer base. This was no easy task, since Stoke-on-Trent was (and is) landlocked – distance from the sea being, as I keep saying, the defining feature of the Midlands – and, at the time when Josiah was making his first experiments, Stoke's potters remained obstinately dependent on packhorses to get their wares to market. The roads were poor – remember the long hours Erasmus Darwin devoted to designing a carriage that wouldn't go arse-over-tit every time it hit a pothole – and slow, so goods often arrived at their destinations late and/or damaged.

And so it was that Wedgwood became a prime mover in the building of a canal that would give Stoke access to both the Trent and the Mersey and provide it with efficient access to the world market. Enlisting the help of his friends Thomas Bentley and Erasmus Darwin (yes, him again), Wedgwood persuaded Parliament to approve the route of a new canal that would run from the East Midlands to Liverpool via Stoke. In 1766, Wedgwood himself cut the first sod of soil of what would become the mould-breaking Trent and Mersey Canal, and set about building his new state-of-the-art factory, Etruria, on its banks in preparation for the waterway's completion.

The great Derbyshire-born engineer James Brindley, who lived for much of his life in nearby Leek, masterminded the construction as part of his 'Grand Cross' scheme, which aimed to use canals to link England's four great rivers, the Mersey, Severn, Thames and Trent, so creating a great inland network of waterways that would allow landlocked sites to behave as though they were ports. Through their proximity to major rivers and the sea, Liverpool, Manchester, Bristol and London had always enjoyed an advantage over their Midland manufacturing rivals; Brindley's scheme, abetted by Wedgwood, would even things out, to dynamic effect. It was through the development of the canal network in the mid-to-late eighteenth century that Birmingham was able to emerge as the leader of the Industrial Revolution in the early nineteenth century.

Brindley's devotion to the scheme would eventually kill him. In 1771, having completed 365 miles of the visionary canal network, he was caught in a storm while out surveying a new branch of the Trent and Mersey, and was taken ill. He was attended in his sickness by Darwin – who, between suing to Parliament, devising new carriage designs and theorising evolution, still found time to see to patients – but even the great Lichfield medicine man couldn't save Brindley's life.

* * *

It's time to hit Stoke-on-Trent proper. On the way I start to tell my mother about the Lunar Society. She seems interested so I begin to develop my theme, arriving at the subject of Charles Darwin, whose grandfathers – Erasmus Darwin and Josiah Wedgwood – were both key Lunarticks.

'If you think about it, evolution had as big an impact on our sense of our place in the universe as the Copernican revolution had in the early seventeenth century,' I crescendo. 'Ideas that big don't come along very often. And, in the case of evolution, that was a Midland notion.'

I look across to see what impact my presentation is having on her. She's nodded off.

Perhaps that's just as well because I need to stop yakking and concentrate if I'm ever going to find the city centre. Now, I'm delighted that Stoke-on-Trent is a polycentric conurbation; the fact that it grants equal billing to all its constituent parts makes it a very forward-looking, we're all in-this-together sort of place. But as a visitor, I have to ask, with a rising note of irritation in my voice: *Where is the bloody centre?* I have driven here, *with my eighty-year-old mother beside me,* and we are now tracing circles around endless suburban-looking ring roads in the hope of one day discovering the heart of the place. There's no shortage of signage: Tunstall is this way, Longton is that, Fenton is the other. But where's the sign pointing to the reassuring middle bit, the commercial and cultural hub containing all the museums, not to mention the big M&S and John Lewis? The bit where they're most likely to serve a delicious Omelette Arnold Bennett? Eventually I spot a sign for Hanley that's also marked '(City Centre)'. To judge by this, Hanley must be regarded as the city centre – albeit only sort of, in a secondary, parenthetical sense, since in the first place it is itself, everything being equal in egalitarian old Stoke-on-Trent. Am I right? Dunno. To add to the confusion, signs marked 'Stoke' now begin to spring up and these are pointing in the opposite direction, away from the bit previously indicated – in those self-deprecating brackets – as the '(City Centre)'. I pull the car over to the side of the road to consider the question further. After due reflection, I decide that these new signs must mean Stoke, one of the Six Towns, as opposed to Stoke-*on-Trent*, the conurbation as a whole. It's amazing to think that the area has one of the lowest

247

densities of graduates in the country – I'd have thought you need at least a degree in Geography just to find your way home here. (I am not the first to note the potential for confusion in all this competing and clashing nomenclature. There have been proposals to rename the town of Stoke 'Old Stoke', 'Stoke Minster' or even, quite simply, 'Stoke Town', and to dub the central bit of Hanley unambiguously 'Stoke-on-Trent City Centre', without brackets. But no firm action has yet been taken. Clearly Stoke – sorry, Stoke-on-Trent – enjoys discombobulating first-, and probably only-, time visitors.)

Anyway, I finally locate a car park in the centre of Stoke-on-Trent, or Hanley (City Centre) I should say, and wake my mum.

'How long should I get a ticket for?' I ask her.

Still half-asleep, she peers at the unpromising scene outside. 'Ten minutes should be enough,' she declares.

I'm going to mention another Radio 4 comedy at this point. And before you ask, no, I'm not the kind of middle-aged, middle-class stiff who spends all his time listening to Radio 4 – I listen to Radio 3 too. Ho-ho-ho. And Planet Rock, and 5 Live when Richard Bacon – that excellent broadcaster who just happens to be from Mansfield – is on, and Gem106, which provides the best soundtrack you can have to accompany a drive through the East Midlands. (I refuse to listen to 6 Music: too many presenters with overegged Northern accents. I'm not having that propaganda in *my* house.) And in a couple of years I'm going to start listening to Radio 1 again so that I am still able to hold a conversation with my lovely son when he becomes a surly teenager. But anyway, back to that Radio 4 comedy, *Beauty of Britain*, which takes place in Stoke-on-Trent. Unlike *North by Northamptonshire* (see Chapter 5), the setting isn't the punchline of every joke, but it's certainly intended as humorous that the show's Zimbabwean heroine, Beauty, should have come to the UK to 'live the dream' and ended up residing in Stoke, where she cares for the elderly. There's definitely a metaphor of Stoke-on-Trent as a giant old people's home in there somewhere. In one episode Beauty's mother flies in from Africa for a visit. 'I'm enjoying my time in Staffordshire,' she announces. Oh, someone responds, no doubt mildly incredulous, how long have you been here? 'About an hour and a quarter,' comes the answer. And that's the maximum length of time you'd want to stay, is the inference one naturally draws from the ensuing silence. So my mother – who's only come from nearby Mansfield, not the more distant Zimbabwe, and consequently has made less of a personal investment in the success of the trip – is probably about right with her 'ten minutes'.

I would like to say that our subsequent tour of the city centre, or rather (city centre), dispels these first impressions, but it's not true. The Wedgwood Museum encourages you to believe that there's nothing that can't be achieved with and through pottery – including the abolition of slavery – and that, in Barlaston, you're on the threshold of a thrusting metropolis, a world leader in trade and industry and politics. But you're not; not any more, at any rate. Even its biggest fans fail to find beauty in its ruined terraces and retail parks: 'this most superficially unlovely of cities', as Potteries cheerleader Matthew Rice, writing in *The Lost City of Stoke-on-Trent* (2010), calls it.

Stoke, the city that at its industrial peak boasted a skyline of two thousand bottle kilns, was both literally and metaphorically built on pottery. The fact that it sits on readily accessible clay and coal deposits gave it obvious advantages as a centre for ceramic production, and so plentiful and ubiquitous were these materials that the foundations of many of the houses and factories hastily thrown up in the huge civic expansion that followed the Industrial

Revolution were made using shraff, or fired pottery waste. There were still hundreds of pottery companies in Stoke in the middle of the last century; now only a handful remain, and it's not entirely clear what's taken their place. A bit like post-coalmining Mansfield, and indeed so many other post-industrial towns and cities across the country, Stoke is a place in need of a new *raison d'être*.

We hit the streets around the Potteries Shopping Centre in search of an Omelette Arnold Bennett. It all looks a bit dreary and 1974, but who knows what we'll find around the next corner …

'That looks exciting. What is it?' my mother says, stopping suddenly and pressing her nose up against the window of a shop that looks like a local variation on Ann Summers. Not the sort of place Mum usually browses in, so far as I'm aware.

'It's bondage gear, if you really want to know,' I say, determined to tell it like it is. 'Mum, are your eyes all right?' She's always been long-sighted so I'm surprised by the signs of her newfound myopia.

'Oh yes, they're getting better. At least, *I* think they are,' she replies enigmatically.

I wish I'd done more research on places to eat in Stoke before setting out. I'm sure there's a plethora of fine and varied cafés and brasseries, and probably even a few Michelin-starred restaurants if you know where to look. Unfortunately we don't know where to look and it's getting late and we're too hungry to delay further, so we dive into a department store. You can't go wrong with a department store caff.

There's not much food on display when we get there, which is probably just as well since there don't appear to be any staff to serve it anyway. Eventually a woman appears from nowhere and stations herself behind the serving counter.

There's no sign of an Omelette Arnold Bennett on the menu and, somehow, taking into account my impressions of Stoke so far, I can't muster the energy to ask whether they could rustle one up for me. I'm not a fan of lost causes.

My mother, who's momentarily forgotten about the omelette question, fancies the soup. Which is just as well, because soup is pretty much all they have. There are two flavours on offer, though: tomato and something a bit more poncy. I'm a ponce so I plump for the latter. My mother opts for down-to-earth tomato but when the woman tries to scoop it out of the tureen she discovers she only has a half-serving left.

'I'll only charge you for half, lovey,' she promises as she scrapes away.

I don't know – what are the ethical and commercial underpinnings of the exchange here? Either you can serve someone a proper plate- or bowlful or you can't, is the way I see it. Do restaurants usually offer customers the option of halves? Would you like half a steak, Sir? A quarter of an egg? A sixth of a portion of peas? If you went to a restaurant and asked for half a bowl of soup, at half the menu price, what would they say?

Amazingly, my mother goes along with it. 'I'm not very hungry anyway,' she says, and the woman ladles out the miserly serving.

'Look,' I feel like saying, 'we're from Mansfield so our standards aren't particularly high, but this is just unacceptable.' But what's the point? At least the woman gives us a whole spoon each, with no hole in the middle, before she disappears back off to wherever she was hiding when we first came in.

We take our place at one of many empty tables and prepare to tuck into our bowl and a half of soup. 'When that woman comes back, I'm going to ask her about – what was it called again?' my mother says, suddenly remembering our omelette quest.

'Omelette Arnold Bennett.'

'That's right: Omelette Alan Bennett.'

251

'*Arnold* Bennett.'

'Oh yes. Arnold Bennett. That nice Yorkshireman.'

'No, not that nice Yorkshireman. That nice *Staffordshire* writer.' I sigh.

'Anyway, his omelette.'

'I wouldn't bother mentioning it,' I say.

'No, I *am* going to,' she responds with faux-determination.

The woman returns. My mother doesn't move. Nor does she eat her half-bowl of soup.

'What do you think about me getting an iPad?' she says, apropos of nothing, as we're stumping around the streets in search of something interesting to do afterwards.

'Good idea,' I reply. 'But I'd get some new specs first if I were you; iPads aren't much use unless you can actually see the screen.'

'You can download books on an iPad, can't you?' she continues slyly. 'I could read yours on my iPad – if it ever comes out, that is. Have you got a publisher yet?'

That's a painful subject, and she knows it. 'No, not yet, Mum. Most publishers don't seem to think that the Midlands is a real subject. Not like the North, you know.'

She looks at me as if to suggest that they might be right.

There's a pause, so I begin to tell her about my day with Uncle John in Northampton. I say that I need to show him the chapter when it's written up so that he can decide whether he wants me to use his real name. I'll be changing people's names where appropriate or where they ask me to, I explain.

'I hope you're going to change mine,' she echoes back fiercely.

'Of course I will,' I reply. 'I'll call you my mum but spell "Cath" with a "C" instead of a "K" to throw people off the scent. Your friends won't have a clue it's you.'

She raises a hand as if to hit me, but after a brief mid-air hesitation uses it to scrub my cheek affectionately instead. 'My little boy,' she gurgles.

Now she's smiling again, I pose her for a photograph in front of a poster advertising a Staffordshire Hoard travelling exhibition entitled 'Dark Age Discovery'.

'Hey, you're not trying to make it look like *I'm* the Dark Age Discovery, are you?' she asks as I snap away. She raises that hand again but this time she doesn't spare the child.

* * *

I've said that one of the reasons the Midlands registers so faintly in the popular imagination is the region's lack of top football teams. That hasn't always been the case, of course. In fact, West Midland teams used to enjoy international prestige: Aston Villa (based in Brum) have one of the most illustrious histories of any British club. They've won the league seven times and have even lifted the European Cup. And Stoke FC produced one of the great legends of the English game, Sir Stanley Matthews, the only footballer to have been knighted while he was still playing. (Not mid-match, you understand – waving a sword around on a muddy pitch while a bunch of blokes chased after a ball would have been dangerous – but mid-career.) Born, like Arnold Bennett, in Hanley, 'The Magician' or 'Wizard of the Dribble', as Sir Stanley was known, spent most of his career playing at outside right (up front, on the right wing) for his home town. Disciplined away from the field of action – the fact that he was a teetotaller helped him to extend his playing career until he was fifty – he was such a gentleman on the pitch that he never received a yellow card, let alone a red. And he didn't feel the need to sport an armful of tattoos or a funny haircut, either. Better still, he played at a time when footballers still wore those long shorts that almost reached down to their ankles, so you don't have to like sport to be able to enjoy clips of his career highlights on YouTube; a sense of humour about fashion will suffice to sustain your interest. He was politically courageous too: as a coach, he created an all-black team in Soweto known as 'Stan's Men' despite the apartheid laws then in force in South Africa. His ashes are interred beneath the centre circle of Stoke's current home ground, the Britannia Stadium. Argentina striker Sergio Agüero may win many medals with Manchester City but it seems unlikely that he'll ask to be buried under the turf at the Etihad.

While we're on the subject of famous people from Stoke, what do the following have in common: Gary Barlow, born in Cheshire, 1971; Howard Donald, born in Lancashire, 1968; Jason Orange, born in Manchester, 1970; Mark Owen, born in Oldham, 1972; Robbie Williams, born in Burslem, 1974? That's right – they all are, or have been (there's always some ambiguity about Robbie's status), members of boy/middle-aged-man band Take That. Now for the bigger question: what separates them, what inevitably makes them four against one (five against one, if you count the early days when the group was still managed by Mancunian music mogul Nigel Martin-Smith)? Look at the list of birthplaces again and you'll see that all bar one come from the North. The odd man out is – inevitably – Robbie Williams, the difficult one, the one who keeps quitting the group, the extremely-successful-in-his-own-right one. He's from the Midlands, and the other band members never let him forget it. In Chris Heath's excellent biographical study *Feel*, Williams himself tells the story of Martin-Smith wanting to sack him for nothing more than 'Because I was from naff Stoke-on-Trent'. Like Arnold Bennett and those Amazon-thread writers, Williams appears to have suffered from the occasional twinge of Northern Envy. Remember his improbable link-up with the Gallagher brothers at Glastonbury in 1995? No doubt he was looking to accrue a bit of rock kudos by his Oasis association, but wasn't this also an attempt at becoming – as with his time in Take That – an honorary Manc? Anyone who has studied the rivalry between the Midlands and the North could have told poor Robbie that it would never work. The fall-out from the Liam and Noel love-in was fierce.

Everything about Robbie Williams announces that he's a Midlander, not a Northerner. No wonder he's never been entirely at home in Take That. Ask a Northerner 'What does it mean to be a Northerner?' and you'll be met with a torrent of self-glorifying clichés. The North is a powerful brand, so Northerners tend to feel secure in their identity. By contrast, Williams's biggest solo hits have been described as 'melodic exercises in self-loathing'. His genius is rooted in his radical uncertainty about himself, his very inbetweenness, that endearing lack of clarity about who he is or what he stands for: rock star/light entertainer, serious artiste/ clown. Others, including Martin-Smith, have found that ambiguity to extend even to his sexual identity, a perception the no doubt thoroughly heterosexual Williams seemingly acknowledges in 'Old Before I Die' when he sings 'Am I straight or gay?' or in the title of his latest album, *Swings Both Ways*. Midlanders often suffer from a touch of identity anxiety, and Robbie Williams's career has been identity anxiety writ large. He's Stoke's decentred conurbation made flesh. This isn't a bad thing. In fact, it's what makes Robbie Robbie: mercurial, insecure, restless, a natural experimenter – in short, the interesting one, the one with charisma, the Take That Midlander. By comparison, the other members of the band (no offence, chaps) are a bit plodding, a bit meat-and-potatoes, a bit stereotypically Northern. Inevitably, it's 'Sir' Gary Barlow – the really Northern one – who's being groomed for the Establishment, but it's Midlander Robbie who's the national treasure.

* * *

Before we set off this morning, Auntie Yvonne called to say that if we were going to Stoke, we really ought to stop off on the way and see the Marmite monument – or 'Monumite' as it's been dubbed – in Burton-on-Trent. Yes, that's the kind of mental association a day out in Stoke sparks off. If you told someone statuary-minded that you were going to London, they might say: 'You really must go to look at Cleopatra's Needle on the Victoria Embankment. It's an authentic ancient Egyptian obelisk, you know.' Or any one of a thousand other things. But tell that same person you're going to Stoke and they say: 'You absolutely must make a detour to a small town off the A50 and have a look at a statue of a pot of locally produced salty spread.' You know the butterflies you get in your stomach when you're about to do something really exciting? Well, I don't have them as I drive away from Stoke and towards Burton and the 'Monumite'. As for my mother, she's nodded off again.

If Stoke is defined by pottery, neighbouring Burton is defined by brewing. Even Marmite – produced here since 1902 and originally made using yeast by-product from the local Bass brewery – is brewing-dependent. Monks were producing beer at Burton Abbey in the sixth century, but Trent-straddling Burton's booze-related reputation grew dramatically in the nineteenth century thanks to Samuel Allsopp's pale-ale experiments. Drinkers approved of Allsopp's characteristically hoppy brew with its unique sulphurous aroma, unhappily known as 'Burton Snatch'. Demand for Burton Ale grew exponentially, causing dozens of new breweries to be founded in the town. The secret of Allsopp's distinctive brew turned out to be the Trent's sulphate-rich water. Once a chemist had devised a means of replicating the local H_2O's qualities artificially – by means of a process known as 'Burtonisation' – brewers were able to achieve the same hop-accented taste elsewhere and industrial decline set in locally, though there are still half a dozen and more beer producers in the town.

Isn't it typical that the Midlands should have developed so-called 'pale' ale? If Mancunian brewers had discovered 'Manchester Snatch', they wouldn't have allowed their ale to be branded 'pale': it would have been 'strong', 'powerful', 'ale of unforgettably vivid character'. But no, this is the Midlands, so it's just 'pale' – which, my dictionary tells me, variously means 'lacking brightness or colour', 'dim or wan', and even 'feeble'. (The other name for pale ale is bitter – which is hardly any better. Language matters, you know.)

Where branding is concerned, Burton's Marmite takes the opposite, very unMidland tack. The tangy spread is the object of a classic – indeed, *the* classic – binary advertising campaign. 'You either love it or hate it,' runs the marketing line. That's North/South divide stuff. You're not allowed *not* to have a strong, polarised opinion about it. ''S'alright, s'pose' are the words no one is ever quoted as uttering after biting off a mouthful of Marmite-coated loaf. Perhaps the indifference-generating Midlands should take a leaf out of the Marmite marketing book and run an advertising campaign in which people express similarly strong opinions about the region. Imagine the following poster: 'I didn't know what living was until I moved to Coventry,' says one dazed-looking youngster standing outside that city's Transport Museum. Or how about this one: 'Leicester was too full-on for me. I couldn't sleep at night, it was that exciting,' regrets another speaker. *'That's why I had to move back to dreary Manchester.'* Boom-boom! The Midlands – you either love it or you hate it. But you're not allowed to be blandly indifferent.

When the Marmite monument was unveiled in 2010, one news source quoted a local as saying: 'Marmite fans nationwide now have a reason to come to the town to make a pilgrimage for one of our country's best-known brands.' I'm not sure how much tourism it's actually drummed up, but clearly most Burtonites are underwhelmed by the statue. When we pull over at some traffic lights to ask a sober-looking woman for directions to the 'Monumite', she starts to laugh. 'When they announced they were making one, we were expecting something quite grand,' she tells us. 'In the end it turned out to be only this high.' She indicates her knee. 'And it's nowhere near the factory and it doesn't even say "Marmite" on it,' she says. 'I wouldn't bother going to see it if I were you.'

Actually, the 'Monumite' is quite a bit bigger than our jolly informant suggests. But it is rather lacklustre – just plain stone, with no attempt to replicate the jar's famously jazzy yellow, red and black colouring. A Pop Artist with a feel for the imaginative allure of commercial design – an Andy Warhol or a Claes Oldenburg, say – could have done something really eye-catching and, in the case of Oldenburg, absolutely GIGANTIC. Check out his huge clothes-peg sculptures in the US and let your imagination run away with what he might have done in Burton. But the budget probably wouldn't stretch to that. So what the locals got instead was something boring – not at all Marmite in its effect. You can't love it; you can't hate it either. It's impossible to have strong feelings of any kind about it. The makers' most pious aspiration for their creation appears to have been that the flat top – the jar's lid – might 'provide seating for children as well as being a platform for adults at public events'. Wow. No wonder Yvonne felt we shouldn't miss the chance to see it. Opportunities like this don't come along very often.

* * *

The power is out at the house when we get back to Mansfield. My father remains lethargic and hasn't reacted very quickly to the emergency. Actually he hasn't reacted at all, which puts my mother in a grim mood.

'I've booked two tickets to Switzerland,' she tells me later, when the lights are finally back on and dinner is in the oven. It takes me a moment to twig that she's not talking about a nice tour of the Alps, but rather a one-way trip to Dignitas. 'He's taking his dose first, mind,' she says, looking over her shoulder at my father dozing peacefully in a chair. 'I'm not committing suicide and then having him back out. Oh no.'

I've finished reading *Anna of the Five Towns*, and I was right about Anna not having the gumption to secure a positive outcome for herself. (Spoiler alert: if you don't want to know how the novel finishes, look away now.) As Willie is about to set off for Australia, she jumps out at him, shoves a hundred quid into his hands and gives him a deep and meaningful look – 'I love you, I really do, but I'm too dull-witted to do anything about it,' is what her eyes tell him – and then sends him on his way. Except Willie is too devastated to emigrate to the Southern Hemisphere now that he knows Anna loves him and so decides to chuck himself down an abandoned pitshaft, where his body is left to rot undiscovered for the rest of Eternity. 'And so – the Bank of England is the richer by a hundred pounds unclaimed, and the world the poorer by a simple and meek soul stung to revolt only in its last hour,' concludes Arnold B., never one to go for the easy laugh or the facile comforts of a happy ending.

Downer.

TO CHATSWORTH

Mercia Redux, an encounter with the Green Knight,
and statelies and sexpots

What do we think of when we hear the words 'the English country-side'? The Yorkshire Dales, the Lake District, the Sussex Downs, the West Country – and let us not forget Kent, the Garden of England. But not Staffordshire, and for good reason, at least according to local boy Lemmy: 'The ugly slagheaps stretched over the landscape wherever you looked, and the air was dirty with the chimneys' smoke,' the Motörhead mainman fondly recalls in his autobiography, *White Line Fever*. I'd hazard the biggest tourist attraction in Staffordshire is Alton Towers, the UK's most popular theme park. To get there, you take a quick turn off the M1 or M6; you don't have to engage with the local landscape.

You could certainly be forgiven for driving past nondescript little Hammerwich without giving it a second look. It's not the sort of village that sets you dreaming; there's little in the way of drama in the natural surroundings either. But it was in a field here, on 5 July 2009, that Terry Herbert stood wondering what it all meant. The reason for his puzzlement? He had just found gold. Lots of it.

Herbert, a veteran metal-detecting enthusiast, had never seen the like before. He had previously trawled the site, which lies a few miles south-west of Lichfield, but had found nothing more exalted there than bits of clocks and old furniture fittings. This time, however, it yielded an unimaginable bounty. The field had recently been ploughed, which perhaps explains why on this occasion the precious hoard of gold and silver offered itself so readily for detection. It was almost as if, impatient to be rediscovered, the treasure had decided to disinter itself, rising up out of the ground to declare its long-hidden presence – as research would soon reveal, it had lain there unseen for well over a thousand years – to whoever should next happen by.

Recognising the importance of his discovery, Herbert contacted the local officer of the Portable Antiquities Scheme, and professional archaeologists quickly joined the hunt, with astonishing results. The 'Staffordshire Hoard', as the treasure has since come to be known, comprises over 1,500 individual items – most gold (5 kg), some silver (1.3 kg), many decorated with precious stones, some of them hailing from as far afield as Turkey and Sri Lanka – and almost all military in character. Weighing in at just 1.66 kg of gold, the Sutton Hoo ship burial, the greatest medieval find of the twentieth century, has nothing on it. Stylistically, most of the new find, including finely worked silver and gold sword decorations removed from weaponry, appears to date from the era of the Mercians, the Anglo-Saxon antecedents of present-day Midlanders.

In autumn 2009, Herbert's discoveries went on display, the earth still clinging to them, at the nearby Birmingham Museum and Art Gallery. The locals responded to this appeal from beyond the grave by their Mercian forebears with unwonted enthusiasm, pouring into the museum in their tens of thousands and queuing for three hours and more to get a glimpse of the enigmatic findings. To accommodate the demand, the collection had to be moved to a larger gallery and late openings laid on.

Word spread nationally. Writing in the *Guardian*, Tristram Hunt commented breathlessly, and somewhat condescendingly, that 'the region now realises it … stood at the centre of the seventh-century Anglo-Saxon world'. In truth, 'the region' had known it for some time: the period of the 'Mercian Supremacy' has long been no secret to serious historians and genned-up Midlanders. However, owing to a lack of material evidence and the fact that the most influential medieval sources are anti-Mercian in their reporting (the plot to disinherit the Midlands begins early in English history), until now it has proved extremely difficult to promulgate this message more widely.

In this respect, the Staffordshire Hoard is a game-changer. Leslie Webster, the former keeper of the Department of Prehistory and Europe at the British Museum, was among the first to grasp the wider implications of the find when she said: 'This is going to alter our perceptions of Anglo-Saxon England' – and, she might have added, of the place of Midlanders in English history more broadly.

The area of Staffordshire where the Hoard was found was part of the kingdom of Mercia, which was one of the most powerful members of what historians used to call the Heptarchy (the seven kingdoms that together comprised pre-unification England: Northumbria, Mercia, Kent, East Anglia, Essex, Sussex and Wessex). Throughout the early medieval period, the traditional narrative runs, power shifted between the larger kingdoms, with Northumbria (the precursor of the modern North) playing top dog for a while, and Wessex (the precursor of the modern South) taking the lead decisively around the end of the eighth century under King Alfred, when England is usually said to have taken shape as a nation. Mercia is usually cast in a bit-part role. The kingdom's very name, derived from the Anglo-Saxon word *Mierce*, means 'border people'; even at this early stage in history, Midlanders were identified principally by their liminality, caught between North and South, and England and Wales, their geographical inbetweenness already defining them.

But how accurate is this grand narrative? Our primary contemporary historical source for the period, the *Anglo-Saxon Chronicle*, is hardly without prejudice. After all, it was first compiled in Wessex during the reign of Alfred; perhaps unsurprisingly, as Ian M. Walker points out in his useful corrective *Mercia and the Making of England*, much of it is designed to 'highlight and, in some cases, enhance the actions of Alfred's dynasty and the West Saxons while largely ignoring or playing down the actions of others, including the Mercians'.

The standard West Saxon-centric account of the birth of England spins the line that, after the defeat of the Vikings by the cake-burning Alfred, he and his south-west-based successors moved quickly to unify the kingdom as a whole. In fact, prior to the (apparent) rise to dominance of Wessex in the ninth century, Mercian leaders were already exercising a similarly wide-reaching political authority, and they continued to play a major role in the later, much-trumpeted 'unification' process. When the Vikings were defeated at the crucial Battle of Tettenhall in 910, for instance, this famous victory was achieved in large part thanks to the presence of a vast Mercian force under King Æthelred.

The pre-Alfred Mercian Supremacy began with the reign of Æthelbald (r. 716–57), during which the Mercian leader was styled *rex Britanniae*, a title that already suggests that he was at least aspiring to rule a unified country, if not doing so in fact. Even the so-called 'father of English history' (and great Northern chauvinist) Bede, who whenever possible ignores Mercia in his *Ecclesiastical History*, admitted that all 'the southern kingdoms which reach right up to the Humber, together with their various kings, are subject to Æthelbald, king of Mercia'.

But Mercia's greatest king was Offa (r. 757–91) – 'overlord of the M5 ... friend of Charlemagne ... starting-cry of a race,' as the fine modern poet Geoffrey Hill has styled him with characteristic Midland self-deprecation. Offa exercised an even more widespread authority than Æthelbald and was referred to in contemporary documents as *rex totius Anglorum patriae* ('king of the whole of England'), although, with trademark anti-Mercian bias, the *Anglo-Saxon Chronicle* fails to accord him even the title of *Bretwalda* (a title generally applied to Anglo-Saxon rulers who achieved overlordship of at least some other kingdoms).

The *Anglo-Saxon Chronicle* may have taught us to think of Alfred 'the Great' (r. 871–99) as the first significant kingly source of learning, legal wisdom and military organisation, but many of his accomplishments were borrowed from Offa, whose prestige was recognised not only in England but on the Continent, where he maintained a regular correspondence with Charlemagne, incomparably the most important lay figure of the period. Pope Hadrian was also a pal. In a letter to Charlemagne, Hadrian even referred to a rumour that Offa had suggested having him (i.e., Hadrian) deposed. The pontiff claimed not to believe it, but it is a measure of the Mercian king's power that such tittle-tattle was considered worthy of discussion by the pope and the future Holy Roman Emperor. In sum, in the eighth century Mercia had greater achievements to its account than Wessex and Northumbria put together. It was Midlanders who sat at the top table in European affairs.

But medieval Mercian political and cultural pre-eminence was, and remains, most visibly set forth in the great earthwork that King Offa had built from the Bristol Channel to the river Dee to mark the border between Mercia and Wales. At 149 miles, 'Offa's Dyke' was actually longer than the great Northern walls constructed by the Roman emperors Hadrian and Antoninus Pius *combined*. In engineering terms, it is quite simply one of the wonders of the medieval world, providing evidence of a control of material and human resources that we rarely associate with the so-called 'Dark Ages' – the world-reconfiguring engineering genius of the eighteenth-century Lunar Society had deep medieval roots. Significantly the Dyke drew a line that left land already occupied by English settlers on the Welsh side of the border: only a ruler of great authority and prestige could have imposed such a self-denying measure on his people. Offa was Mr Big.

Wessex under Alfred has no greater proofs of power or learning to show. The big difference is that, with typical Midland insouciance, Offa failed to commission or compile a hagiography of himself and his many works along the lines of the *Anglo-Saxon Chronicle*. Consequently there was no one and nothing to crow about his importance to future generations after his passing. Big mistake: more than a thousand years of forgetting about Mercian greatness have ensued. So it's just as well that the Staffordshire Hoard took matters into its own hands recently and began to dig itself out of the earth in order to refocus historical attention.

Not that the Midlands has quite learned to sell itself properly yet. A portion of the Staffordshire Hoard was on display in Birmingham Museum and Art Gallery when I was there. Typically, it was hidden away at the top of the building while the gallery was undergoing 'improvement works'. There was a promo video that started off sounding dangerously like an ad for Marks and

Sparks – 'This isn't just treasure' – before descending into bathos – 'it's hundreds of pieces of broken treasure.' And indeed, what was on show in Birmingham didn't look like much – just bits of mangled, twisted dull gold that required serious historical imagination (and, depressingly, accompanying images from the more photogenic Sutton Hoo find) to convey their real value. As it so happens, in that day's *Birmingham Mail* there was a news item announcing that the travelling show of the Staffordshire Hoard had become the second most popular touring exhibition at the National Geographic Museum in Washington DC, behind the Chinese Terracotta Army. Presumably the best bits had been cherry-picked for the touring exhibit – diamonds to the Birmingham display's bits of old rust.

The anti-Midland bias that has its roots in Bede and the *Anglo-Saxon Chronicle* continues to this day. Take the contribution from 'WheatfromChaff' (a Southerner, presumably) that appeared on the *Guardian* website in response to Tristram Hunt's article: 'Anyway – Wessex ended up kicking Mercia's butt good and proper. If it wasn't for us, you'd all be speaking brummie :-).' Ho-ho-ho, ChafffromWheat. But as the Staffordshire Hoard and this book more generally demonstrate, in terms of both intellectual and linguistic descent, you *do* speak a derivation of Brummie. ☺

The name of Alfred the Great's ancient Anglo-Saxon kingdom was revived in the wider public consciousness when Thomas Hardy began to write his series of so-called 'Wessex' novels, starting with *Far from the Madding Crowd* (1874) and ending with *Jude the Obscure* (1895). Bram Stoker, author of *Dracula*, tried to do something similar for Mercia with his 1911 novel *The Lair of the White Worm*, but the idea didn't catch on in quite the same way and the experiment ended there. As a result of Hardy's act of ancient remembering for the south-west, the contemporary royal family includes an Earl and Countess of Wessex. Now, in the aftermath of the discovery of the Staffordshire Hoard, if/when Prince Harry marries, wouldn't it be a good idea to make him Earl of Mercia and give his wife the title Countess of Mercia?

* * *

So, as I was saying, it's not images of Staffordshire, or the West Midlands generally, that crowd into our minds when the subject of England's green and pleasant land is raised. But the land-scape around here is redolent of myth and history all the same. Just look at the writers it has inspired. The West Midlands is Tolkien Country, for one thing. Not for nothing is Birmingham the setting for the annual Middle-earth Weekend, when coachloads of Gandalfs and Hobbits descend on the city. The unevocatively named Moseley Bog in Birmingham and the walking country of Worcestershire inspired the ancient landscape of his *Lord of the Rings* saga, while the Malvern Hills were translated into the White Mountains of Gondor. His description of Hobbits in the Prologue to *The Lord of the Rings* could equally have been written about Midlanders: 'shy of the Big Folk', they have always possessed the 'art of disappearing swiftly and silently'. Nonetheless, as in the long-past time of 'Bilbo, and of Frodo his heir', Hobbits and Midlanders alike are still capable of great things. Tolkien was a Mercian at heart all right: he used Mercian terms in his description of the Kingdom of Rohan, or the Mark (which means Mercia), while a number of Rohan's kings – Fréaláf, Fréawine – share their names with historical Mercian monarchs. Basically, Middle-earth is the North-west Midlands writ mythically large and ancient.

Then there are the composers. Though he set it down in Sussex, local boy Edward Elgar associated the opening theme of his famous

Cello Concerto with the Worcester landscape. 'If ever after I'm dead you hear someone whistling this tune on the Malvern Hills,' he told a friend, 'don't be alarmed. It's only me.' I only realised Elgar was a Midlander after being hailed by a stranger as I was walking home in South London a few years ago. The man looked a bit the worse for wear and was evidently lost: he wanted to know where the nearest Pizza Express was. I pointed him in the right direction but, instead of going our separate ways immediately, we got talking and our conversation quickly turned, in the way that conversations so often do, to where we were both from. I said he sounded like a Midlander to me. The stranger nodded and drew a £20 note from his wallet, reversing it to expose the portrait of a mustachioed gent. 'I'm from the same place as him,' he said. 'Not that anyone seems to know where he's from,' he added with a sigh. The face was Elgar's. Even if, like me, they didn't know that he was a native of Lower Broadheath near Worcester, most people would instantly recognise Elgar's music. According to a 2006 survey, 'Land of Hope and Glory' would be the popular choice for a specifically English national anthem. Indeed, it is to this great Midlander that the nation almost invariably turns when it is seeking to express its passion and unity on major occasions in the annual calendar: his 'Pomp and Circumstance March No. 1' is a centrepiece of the Last Night of the Proms, while massed bands perform 'Nimrod' from the *Enigma Variations* at the Remembrance Day ceremony held every 11 November at the Cenotaph in London. Elgar's music isn't the sole preserve of high or official culture either – the Midland composer also wrote the first modern football chant, 'He Banged the Leather for Goal', inspired by Billy Malpass, striker for Elgar's beloved local club, Wolverhampton Wanderers, in 1898. But, as my interlocutor on that night pointed out, Elgar's centrality to English cultural life couldn't prevent him from getting the chop from the national currency. 'They're phasing him out in a few months, and replacing him with a Scotsman [Adam Smith is now the face on the £20 note]. Bloody New Labour.'

Actually, most of the big-name English composers of the last century were Midlanders: Gustav Holst, writer of *The Planets*, was from Gloucestershire, as was Ralph Vaughan Williams. Vaughan Williams's 'The Lark Ascending' was recently voted the most popular Desert Island Disc by Radio 4 listeners and declared the 'sound of England'. That's right: the 'sound of England' is actually the sound emanating from a Midlander's imagination, nurtured on the Midland landscape.

But the West Midland landscape was inspiring the imaginations of artists long before Tolkien, Elgar and the others trod its ancient pathways. The Malvern Hills, between Worcestershire and Herefordshire, provide the setting for the visionary fourteenth-century allegorical poem *Piers Plowman*. It was here that William Langland imagined his namesake, Will, falling asleep and undergoing his vision of a 'fair field full of folk' caught between the heavenly tower on the hill and the dungeon in the deep valley. The poem also happens to contain the earliest known reference to the Robin Hood ballads.

But how about *Staffordshire*, I hear you cry. You began the chapter talking about Staffordshire in particular, not the West Midlands generally, so now tell me something inspiring about the Staffordshire landscape. What's so exciting about it, caches of ancient coins aside?

Very well, dear reader, here goes: ancient Tamworth, capital of Offa's great Mercian kingdom, may have provided the model for Hrothgar's mead-hall Heorot, stalked by the monstrous, flesh-crunching Grendel in the thousand-plus-year-old alliterative poem *Beowulf*. The action of this famous heroic tale takes place in

Scandinavia but it's been suggested that the writer was a Mercian, who had the environs of Tamworth in mind as much as Leire on Seeland when he wrote of Beowulf, a hero with 'the strength of thirty men in the grip of his hand', doing battle with that 'notorious ranger of the borderlands', Grendel, a hellish creature descended, like all monsters and hobgoblins, from the great biblical brother-slayer Cain. As it so happens, that poem, incontestably the greatest of the Anglo-Saxon period, describes the practice of pommel stripping so evident in the Staffordshire Hoard – the find includes dozens of pommel caps (decorative sword-handle attachments). Though comparatively modest in scale and theme, *Beowulf* is the Old English equivalent of Homer's *Iliad* or Virgil's *Aeneid* but it took someone thoroughly imbued with the West Midland land-scape – one J.R.R. Tolkien, who was an Anglo-Saxon scholar when he wasn't off imagining great deeds in Middle-earth – to point out its literary merits in 1936 and make the case for this classic expression of fear of the dark as a literary masterpiece.

Today I'm heading to the Roaches, a rocky escarpment over-looking Leek that marks the point where the English lowlands give way to the English highlands. Now, everyone knows that the Lake District was an important inspiration for Wordsworth; all that stuff about hosts of golden daffodils turned the area into a major tourist destination. By comparison, few know that it was the landscape surrounding the Roaches that pricked the imagination of the so-called 'Pearl Poet', a North-west Midlander who wrote four of the greatest poems of the medieval period. His oeuvre, unlike Willie Wordsworth's, certainly didn't turn North Staffs into a haven for holiday-makers. Perhaps that has something to do with the nature of his output, particularly *Sir Gawain and the Green Knight*, the most beguiling of the quartet, an Arthurian romance written in forest-thick alliterative verse:

Siþen þe sege and þe assaut watz sesed at Troye,
Þe borȝ brittened and brent to brondeȝ and askez,
Þe tulk þat þe trammes of tresoun þer wroȝt
Watz tried for his tricherie, þe trewest on erthe.

The poem's hair-raising climactic scene, written in North-west
Midland dialect, is thought to have taken place in the Roaches,
at the site known as Lud's Church. The story runs as follows:
Gawain is one of the noblest and most valiant knights at the
court of his uncle, King Arthur. One New Year's Day the celebrations at Camelot are interrupted by a mysterious and fearsome-
looking Green Knight, who suddenly appears on a huge and no
less green horse, and proposes a gruesome and ever so slightly
preposterous challenge to his auditors: he, the Green Knight,
will allow one of Arthur's men to strike off his head if that
same knight will accept a return blow from him at a place of his
choosing in precisely a year and a day. Now, although Arthur's
followers are a bit frightened of this grimly jolly green giant –
and who can blame them: he comes swinging a huge axe, not
bearing tinned vegetables – looked at logically, it doesn't seem
too terrifying a proposition. After all, if they strike cleanly and
behead the Green Knight now, they won't have to kneel before
his axe next year, will they? Bodies separated from their heads
don't usually survive for 365-plus days. Anyway, after a bit of
embarrassing Sir Coward de Custard-style knee-quivering and
general lily-liveredness on the part of the assembled throng –
this is Camelot, remember, supposedly home to the country's
bravest knights – Gawain puts himself forward for the challenge,
strikes off the Green Knight's head … and then watches as the
verdant giant gets to his feet, picks up his severed head, mounts
his horse and rides off, pausing only to remind Gawain of their

agreement that a return blow is to be struck a twelvemonth hence at the Green Knight's home.

Understandably, this casts a bit of a pall over the remainder of Gawain's Christmas celebrations, and indeed his pleasures more generally as the seasons – winter, spring, summer and autumn – roll by across the course of the following year. But he sticks to his promise and, as Christmas approaches again, sets off north from Camelot, carefully keeping Wales to his left, slaying assorted ogres, wolves, dragons and wild men, and (largely) resisting the fleshly temptations laid before him by a friendly castellan's wife, before finally closing in on the designated meeting place, the so-called 'Green Chapel', where he must bend before the Green Knight's blade …

As I make my way along an isolated stretch of the Congleton–Buxton A54, I can't quite remember why I thought it was a good idea to come here on my own. The landscape has a cool severity about it and Gawain's tale is hardly one to warm the cockles: a chill runs up and down my back as I think of making my way to the lonely spot where Gawain was greeted by the whirring sound of the Green Knight sharpening his axe. But I steel myself and leave the main road in search of Gradbach Mill Youth Hostel, where prospective visitors are generally advised to park up if they want to follow Gawain's footsteps through an enchanted landscape of steep, sky-grazing crags, misty moors, boiling streams and wild woods. I'm determined to give myself the full Green Knight experience, so I've loaded Harrison Birtwistle's orchestral suite *Gawain's Journey* – a real primordial soup of tumbling rhythms and blaring trumpets – on my iPod. I insert my earbuds, press 'play' and set off along a muddy path that hugs the river Dane as it winds its way through Back Forest. This is wallaby country: a colony appears to have taken up residence here in the 1930s, after a London Zoo sell-off. Legend has it that nearby Cannock Chase is home to werewolves and Bigfoot too, but it's more than myth that wallabies live in these parts – though, saying that, I can't see one at the moment.

The craggy landscape is stark and there's no one else in sight, although the presence of carefully penned cows and sheep is enough to signal even to an ignorant townie like me that the area is farmed. Today the scattered buildings all appear deserted, though. I don't know why but I can't help imagining gunmen taking up positions in the trees. Is that because I have paranoid tendencies, or would the ancient starkness of this particular landscape inspire paranoia in the even most smugly complacent of human consciousnesses? Suddenly I spy two men on the hillside above me. They're not obviously armed so I call out: 'Have you got the Green Knight up there with you?' By way of answer they raise their hands in a 'don't shoot' gesture – clearly they've also been seeing snipers in the woods – and scarper in another direction. Oh well. My instinct – almost always wrong in matters geographical – tells me that Lud's Church is up the hill on the other side of the river. I'm in a hurry to get my quest over and done with and consider fording the Dane where I stand, but the river is in full spate so I decide to wait for a bridge, and sure enough five minutes later one comes along.

On the other side of the river the trees and rocks suddenly develop a hysterical green hue: this must be the right way to the Green Chapel, then. The path also grows very steep. The sense of solitude becomes almost suffocating, especially with *Gawain's Journey* blaring in my ears. I decide to remove one bud: a single ear's worth of Birtwistle's chilling suite is quite enough.

Suddenly, out of the trees above me there appears a mounted figure, not, thankfully, the Green Knight on his green steed, but a black-clad cyclist on a black mountain bike who, behind his mask of goggles and helmet, looks more like an apparition from 1940s Paris – Death's motorcycle-borne henchmen in Jean Cocteau's film *Orphée* are what come to mind. As he descends the rocky path, it looks as though he's going to ride straight through me – can't he see through those goggles? – but at the last moment he swerves away. A greeting forms on my lips but evaporates as the dark rider speeds by on his ominous, wordless way. Not very cordial, these henchmen of the Grim Reaper, I think. But of course the last thing you want is to attract the attention of the Scythe-Wielding One. I ought to be grateful to be ignored.

In typical Midland fashion, there's no fanfare – not even a modest sign – when you actually get to Lud's Church. And as with the majority of Midland treasures – the Staffordshire Hoard, for instance – you could walk right by it and not realise there's anything of particular significance to look at. Of course, in the case of Lud's Church, it was precisely its unassuming façade that made the site so popular with outlaws and religious Nonconformists seeking to evade the long arm of the law. I should explain that, despite its name, it isn't a church, or at least not one made by human hands: it's a deep, mossy chasm named (probably) for Lud, a Celtic god whose daughter Danu gave her name to the Danube as well as the local river Dane. As Gawain describes it, it's little more than a mound with an entrance at either end, overgrown with patches of grass and all hollow within: 'nobot an olde cave, / Or a crevisse of an olde cragge.' The surrounding landscape reaches for the sky, but Lud's Church, plunging fifteen metres into the ground, is the result of a landslip, pitching visitors markedly in the direction of the bowels of the earth. It's been a sacred place for millennia, and still feels like one today. Early pagans celebrated the summer solstice here, when sunlight penetrates into the deepest recesses of the mossy chasm. The Lollards, the persecuted followers of the fourteenth-century Church reformer John Wycliffe, gathered in its recesses, away from the prying eyes of the authorities, to worship. An alternative theory about the name is that it may have been derived from that of one of the Lollards, Walter de Ludank or Walter de Lud-Auk, who was captured here. Quitting their native Sherwood, Robin Hood and Friar Tuck are also supposed to have taken shelter in this secluded Staffordshire chasm.

I pass between the rocks that form the narrow entrance. After an initial descent, Lud's Church reveals a capacious natural interior – enough space for potentially hundreds to hide away in. I take a step forward and plunge into a foot and a half of mud. So this is how I'm to die, not with my head cut off by the Green Knight but drowned in black sinking sands! Despite its associations with Protestantism, I'm inclined to agree with Gawain's first impression – that it's a place fit for the Devil at midnight. There's no gift shop or café; this is Midland myth uncosified.

It's been said that when the mist rolls in here, you feel as though you're perched on the end of the world. It certainly seems fitting that this should have been the place where an Arthurian hero came face to face – or neck to blade – with a demon of the pre-Christian world, or an ancient sprite of Merrie England. Visitors regularly talk about the sensation of seeing faces peeking out at them from the rocks in the chasm. As I edge along the walls, trying not to tumble into the slime again, I can see them now: is that goodman Gawain? Or the Green Knight, preparing to deliver the death blow? And what's that sound? Someone sharpening a blade? Oh why didn't I call round all the local prisons and mental institutions to see if any homicidal lunatics had escaped with their axes this morning? I've never been particularly brave and, standing here miles from civilisation, I'm starting to feel totally spooked. Oh for a wallaby for company now! I dash back down the hill towards the car.

* * *

The Roaches stand guard at the entrance to the Peak District, craggy Staffordshire sentinels at the gateway to Derbyshire's pleasure gardens. The great limestone dome of the Peaks came into being at the same time as the Alps; 300 million years ago the area formed the bed of a great tropical ocean dense with new life forms. You can still feel the presence of Deep Time here; Erasmus Darwin, harbinger of the theory of evolution, could no doubt feel it too as he rode about the region on his horse, Doctor, taking the waters at nearby Buxton and turning it into a fashionable spa resort with his recommendations to patients. Serious climbers refine their techniques on the steepling rock formations of the fractured gritstone Edges – the Roaches in the west, Stanage to the east – that frame the area. Meanwhile, though the peaks in the Peaks proper may not be very high – the highest, Kinder Scout, is a moorland plateau that tops out at 636 metres above sea level – there's a serenity and warmth about the landscape that the more melodramatic North cannot match. Kinder Scout has its place in more recent history too: it was the site of a mass trespass in 1932 which served as a springboard for a revision of attitudes to access to the countryside. The 'right to roam' movement took shape here, ensuring the liberty of walkers nationally.

Derbyshire is lovely and so abounds in places of interest and beauty that it's hard to know where to begin: the ancient stone circles at Arbor Low and Stanton Moor, or the lovely little Saxon town of Bakewell, perhaps, with its ninth-century Christian stone crosses and nineteenth-century Bakewell pudding? Legend has it that, in 1820, the famous dessert, beloved of the sweet-toothed from Land's End to John o'Groats, was accidentally concocted by the cook at the White Horse Inn when she was instructed to make a jam tart but got her ingredients mixed up and inadvertently invented what became known as Bakewell pudding (flaked pastry and jam on the bottom, egg and almond paste on top) instead. Her employer wasn't best pleased at first but soon changed her mind when the inn's customers started asking for the recipe. *O felix culpa!*

Actually, Derbyshire is so obviously lovely that most people – my friend Elizabeth included – assume it's in the North. Indeed, because of the negative associations of that word 'Midlands', they actively *want* it to be in the North. It's not. Ask Offa; ask Derbyshire County Council. It's bang in the middle of the country (it's reckoned that half of the population of England can readily travel here in under an hour). By any definition, this is the Midlands. End of.

My wife, a woman of great judgment, didn't much fancy the trip to Stoke but has deigned to join me for this stage of my Midland odyssey. The destination today is Chatsworth, the Peak District home of the Duke and Duchess of Devonshire. Sixteen generations of Cavendishes have resided here since the arrival of Bess of Hardwick in 1549. Wily old Bess is famous for her financial acumen: she had four husbands, each successive spouse wealthier than the last, and ended up the richest woman in the country behind Queen Elizabeth I. Among other things, she used her money to erect this celebrated stately home, although the building that greets visitors today is much altered from Bess's original conception. Everyone who was anyone visited, including Mary, Queen of Scots – not that the latter was a particularly willing guest: she came as a prisoner, and was lodged in the apartment now appropriately known as the Queen of Scots Rooms.

When first you leave the Roaches and Staffordshire, the land-scape can have a yellow-and-brown lunar quality, but everything grows more verdant once you hit the dales – it's not just Yorkshire that has dales, you know; Derbyshire's are much more attractive too. As we drive along, we're listening to a local radio station when an ad comes on for a power supplier in Nottingham. It sounds to me as though it's voiced by that fine actress Olivia Colman. Aha, I think, might the Divine Olivia be a Midlander?

'I don't think actors worry about that sort of thing when they're offered voiceover work,' sounds a sceptical French voice from beside me. 'Besides, she's advertising electricity, not promoting Midland independence.'

'Could you just Google her on your phone and find out where she was born?' I urge.

'All you want to know these days is where people were born,' my wife responds coolly, but nonetheless pulling a smartphone from her handbag. 'This Midlands business is making you very reductive in your old age.'

'It isn't making me reductive at all, it's giving me *focus*,' I say with classic Midland firmness of purpose. 'So where is Olivia Colman from then?'

'What a pity, I can't get a signal,' my companion says, adopting an attitude of mock-disappointment before putting her phone determinedly back in her bag and turning up the radio to foreclose further discussion.

Really, what's the point in bringing along an assistant if she's not properly equipped to help with important research? (By the by, it turns out that Olivia Colman, great talent though she is, had the misfortune to be born outside the Midlands, in Norfolk. 'Very flat, Norfolk,' as Noël Coward wrote so pointedly.)

'Oh I love that blue,' my wife coos as she finally spies an entrance sign to the estate in the distinctive smoky hue associated with Chatsworth. 'We're here!' she cries with growing delight as the house rolls into view and we snake our way along the picturesquely conceived approach road.

It's not just my wife who likes it here, of course. Chatsworth regularly comes top of nation's-favourite-country-house polls. It's pouring with rain but the car park is still full to overflowing.

We've come to see the annual Christmas display, when the house is given a festive makeover, but we decide to start with lunch, served in the old stable block above the main house where a brass band is improbably parping out The Pogues' 'Fairytale of New York'. You can sit outside to eat if you choose, but because of the rain the courtyard is empty today, leaving the vacant plastic chairs looking particularly extravagant in all their furious purpleness. My wife remarks that the new duchess (the dowager, Deborah Devonshire, *née* Mitford, an über-*Downton Abbey* Maggie Smith, has recently moved out) likes bright colours, and adds that the rooms she decorated in the Devonshire Arms in nearby Pilsley are considered 'zingy'. How *does* she know these things?

The food is very good. Feeling unusually adventurous – my default option is fish and chips; no gastronome I – I opt for haddock scotch egg with parsley sauce and mustard mash. My wife, an enthusiastic Anglophile, can never resist an afternoon tea when it's on offer, so goes for that. For afters I plump for – what else? – the Bakewell pudding, 'hand-made by our Chatsworth bakers'. Eating the quintessence of the Midlands in the quintessential Midland ducal seat, etc, etc, truly this is the best of all possible worlds.

Except the pudding is being served with clotted cream. 'I don't know about that. Clotted cream is something you have with scones, surely?' my wife says. 'Personally I would have thought Bakewell pudding was a standalone. But what do I know, I'm French,' she laughs. 'Slap her, she's French,' she adds, quoting her favourite film title.

I have it with the clotted cream anyway – well, it's probably made with the milk of Midland cows, so how can it not be good? – but am left feeling that Frenchie is, as usual, right.

This year the theme of the decorations in the main house is 'Deck the Halls: A Visual Celebration of Carols', with different rooms decorated to illustrate different seasonal favourites. 'While Shepherds Watched Their Flocks By Night' is the theme in the west corridor, where the windows have been darkened with bits of card in which holes have been punched to suggest stars. In a witty touch there's also a washing line with socks to play on the children's variation on the lyric: 'While shepherds washed their socks by night.'

The stats are impressive: forty-four trees, fifteen thousand baubles, ten thousand fairy lights. Don't even think of trying to match that in your own home. But also, reassuringly, some of it looks a tad naff and homemade too. The barn scene in the Chapel, where Fred Astaire's sister and performing partner, Adele, tied the knot with Lord Charles Cavendish in 1932, looks a bit gaudy in such a grand setting. As is only proper at Christmas, even in the dignified setting of historic Chatsworth, children have been allowed to express themselves in the decorations.

Actually, there's a great tradition of make-do-and-mend, or down-to-earth pragmatism, here. The house used to close its doors in October but, following a foot-and-mouth outbreak that saw visitor numbers drop dramatically in 2001, someone came up with the bright idea of extending the visitor season. And so the 'Christmas at Chatsworth' idea was born: 87,000 people came that year to see the house decorated for the festive season, and the display has been repeated each year since, with variations in theme. My favourite so far was the panto-themed year: Peter Pan flying in at one window and one of the (living) attendants dressed as Captain Hook and brandishing a cutlass; Jack climbing the Beanstalk into the dome above one of the staircases; a bed with the Wolf dressed as a grandmother awaiting Little Red Riding Hood; another attendant dressed as a witch busy locking children in a cage (not in an act of random cruelty, you understand: it was a Hansel and Gretel-related scene). A visit to Chatsworth to see the decorations is a wonderful way to start Christmas.

In a side display, there's a map of the Devonshire estates in 1811, giving the annual commercial revenue from them as £5.1 million (in today's money) as against inherited debts of £21.3 million. Debt has always been a big theme in these richest of surroundings, definitively so after the introduction of death duties in 1894. After World War II, 'the spirit of the place had gone and only an incurable optimist could guess it would ever return,' later remembered the 11th Duke's wife, Deborah. It turns out that Deborah and her husband *were* incurable optimists and, having settled a huge tax bill by selling thousands of acres of land and major works of art, and transferring nearby Hardwick Hall to the National Trust, they set about infusing fresh life into the old place. It was only by embracing modernity that Chatsworth was able to survive. As if to underline the point, a notice announces that 'The 12th Duke is now on Facebook'.

There's a wishing tree in front of an expensive Lucian Freud painting, *The Skewbald Mare*, and visitors are invited to write down their wishes and tie them to the branches with ribbons. Some messages are funny, others are more poignant. I write down 'Independence for the Midlands!' as my wish, then cross it through. I'm not sure I really want complete constitutional separation, in truth. 'Greater recognition for the Midlands,' I write above the first, deleted version. My wish looks scruffy now and I – momentarily – grow self-conscious about my monomania. I put it in my pocket and shuffle on.

We look out on the beautiful mist-enshrouded grounds through the windows of the Great Dining Room, and in the Library are met with a handsome tableau of an elegant drinks party. This is the room my wife would like for herself should we ever happen to inherit the house (unlikely and, in truth, probably undesirable – the maintenance costs must be *killing*).

We turn into the ante-library. 'I would even settle for this room,' she sighs.

In the statuary gallery, I point out a statue of Napoleon's mother but my wife doesn't seem particularly interested. No sense of historical identity, these French. Not like us Midlanders.

Afterwards, there's just time for a dash through the gift shop. Though it's not run by the National Trust, the contents are largely indistinguishable from what you'd find in an NT stately shop: jams, soaps, hats and scarves, adjustable walking sticks, Keep Calm and Carry On paraphernalia, great house-branded mugs and tea towels … and a stack of Stuart Maconie's *Pies and Prejudice: In Search of the North*. Which riles me no end. Since the books on display here generally have a fairly clear connection to the house or area, I can only assume that someone in authority thinks that Chatsworth is in the North. I tell my wife I'm going to find the shop's stock buyer and give them a piece of my mind for misleading unsuspecting tourists into thinking they're in 'God's Own County' or something. This is Derbyshire, in the Midlands! I'm beginning to gesticulate just thinking about it. '*Mon dieu, non*,' my companion sighs. I desist.

On the plus side, there are just as many copies of *Pride and*

Prejudice as there are of *Pies and Prejudice*. Don't worry, I'm not about to claim that Jane Austen was secretly a Midlander. All prim bonnets and Established religion, dear Janey was a conservative Southerner through and through, and she appears to have hated Brum. ('One has no great hopes of Birmingham. I always say there is something direful in that sound,' she has one of her characters say in *Emma*.) Great writer, mind. So why is *Pride and Prejudice* stocked so prominently here? For the simple reason that Austen modelled Pemberley, Fitzwilliam Darcy's ancient family pile, on Chatsworth. The Derbyshire setting is quite explicit in the novel. That's right, ladies (and gentlemen, according to taste): Mr Darcy – the ultimate toff dish – was a Midlander. Visualise Colin Firth shirtless in that pond. Feeling a tingling sensation in your loins? Good. That's the sexy old Midlands getting you all stirred up.

Lady Chatterley was a Midlander, the Ice Age avant-garde, and the source of everything, ever

20 December. Briefly back in London before the holidays. At a swanky party (not quite sure why I was invited, and the host didn't seem too clear by the end either), a friend – a New Yorker – asks: 'Hey, how's that Middlesbrough project of yours coming along?'

'The Midlands, you mean, not Middlesbrough,' I respond coolly.

'Same difference,' she laughs.

That sets me off, I'm afraid. Amidst the champagne and canapés I decide to pursue my new favourite party strategy and quiz random strangers on their connections to the Midlands. It turns out it's a great way to keep conversations short and spiky.

I begin with a pleasant-looking woman who's momentarily been abandoned by her husband while he goes in search of drinks.

'Where are you from?' I ask, getting straight to the point.

'Oh, you know, the Home Counties,' she says airily.

'Not the Midlands then?'

'No.'

'Have you ever been to the Midlands?'

She looks round nervously but, failing to espy her husband, she steadies herself and admits to an acquaintance with Nottingham.

'Oh Nottingham! That's where I'm from, sort of,' I announce enthusiastically. 'I do think it's a lovely city, don't you?'

Alas, she doesn't. She went to university there, a choice she made, she explains, because, after a slightly sheltered schooling, she wanted to try somewhere 'rough and naff', and Nottingham – my beloved Queen of the Midlands! – seemed to fit the bill. She's retained no friends there and has never been back, she assures me, but has fond memories of the 'tacky' times she spent there.

Her husband sidles into view so I move on.

Next up is a smartly dressed businessman looking a bit lost behind his wine glass. Probably a Midlander dazzled by the bright lights of the Big City, I think. They do things differently in Mansfield, you know; suddenly pitching up in London can be disorienting.

I don't want to frighten him so I decide to start with small talk and work my way round to my main theme gradually.

As it turns out, his accent is unprovincially RP and he tells me that his business dealings carry him far and wide through the world: Saudi, LA, Delhi – and Birmingham, I finally worm out of him.

'That's in the Midlands,' I point out.

'Yes,' he agrees, slightly nonplussed. People just aren't used to this kind of straight talking when it comes to the M-word. It's the great taboo subject of our times.

Growing in confidence, I ask him where he was born. Northamptonshire, he tells me.

'So you're actually a Midlander!' I congratulate him.

'I don't know what you're talking about,' he hisses, as though I've just announced to his wife that I caught him soliciting men in the loos.

I move on again and get into conversation with a BBC type. If he's a commissioner, he might agree to me making a programme about being a Midlander, I tell myself. We chat amiably and he doesn't seem too anxious as my talk becomes increasingly explicit in matters geographical. 'Stoke' this, 'Coventry' that – I am in my element now, and he doesn't bat an eyelid. I decide to go for it. Where did he go to school?

'Rugby.'

Bull's-eye! There might be a commission in this, after all.

I clear my throat. 'Ah yes. Rugby, the great public school that did so much to define English national life in the nineteenth century – you are of course already aware of its role in the creation of the modern Olympics and rugby football. Naturally, Rugby is in the Midlands …'

Without a word, he walks away.

What have I said? Why does no one want to talk about the Midlands? I look around for fresh interlocutors but people are turning their backs on me now. Word is obviously getting round. I suddenly realise, amidst the buzz of metropolitan accents, that I am missing the Brummie burr. There's nothing lovelier than a twangy West Midland 'bab', unless of course it's a gruff North Notts 'Ey up, youth'. I yearn to return to the homeland. Feeling like the Midland Borat, I collect my coat and head out into the stupid Southern night.

21 December. Every day I strive to be a better man, and a better Midlander. I call my mother to talk about Christmas dinner arrangements. I want everything to be as nu-traditional as possible, I tell her, with the food served à la Midlands, i.e., pudding first, turkey afterwards, on either side of a single plate.

'Has somebody hit you in the head?' my mother banters with characteristic violence.

'No.'

'Perhaps they should then.'

22 December. For the journey up the M1 to Mansfield I really wanted to buy a can of spray paint so that I could stop off en route and deface all those 'The NORTH' signs and write 'Leicester – The MIDLANDS', 'Nottingham – The MIDLANDS' etc instead. But it's hard to pull over on the motorway, and we drive up in broad(ish) daylight anyway so it would be difficult to evade arrest. Is it time to mount a campaign of civil disobedience? At the very least I must write a letter of complaint to whatever authorities are responsible for the plainly discriminatory signage. 'Enough of this North/South divide stuff,' I shall write. 'I am not a slash sign! I am a Midlander and on behalf of my people I demand representation!'

Mum is in a rage when we arrive. She's been food shopping with my dad and she didn't like the way one of the young assistants addressed her in Sainsbury's.

'I've never heard anything like it,' she's saying. 'It was "duckie this" and "duckie that". Honestly, I've never heard anyone "duckie" it like that before. "Who do you think you're talking to?" I said to her. I reckon they're told to talk like that to older people. Patronising sods. And the assistant just said: "Sorry, I can't help it. Mebbe it's because I'm a Midlander."'

'Sounds like a song,' I interrupt.

My mother glares balefully at me and returns to her theme.

'But Midland people aren't *that* dreadful, are they? I'm going to look out for her next time I go to Sainsbury's.'

That young assistant would be well advised to keep a low profile for the foreseeable future.

Of late I've become a bit fixated on mobility scooters. You don't see many in central London – not enough space, I suppose – but there are fleets of them in Mansfield. I keep telling my mother that I'd like to have a go on one, so she's arranged for her old friend Joan, aka Scooter Girl, to let me ride hers.

Joan is a Midlander through and through. 'I was born in Nottingham and I consider myself a Nottingham Rose. In Nottingham they always said the women were roses,' she tells me when I get to her house.

She keeps two mobility scooters in her shed. The smaller one has the advantage of being foldable, so it can be put in a car boot, but it can only do half the speed (two rather than four m.p.h.) of the more luxurious, upholstered model, which also boasts lights and a horn.

'You don't leave your lights on too long or they run down the battery,' she warns me as she shows off the scooter's impressive functionality.

She's got her eye on an even more sumptuous ride now, the eight-m.p.h. Roadmaster Plus, but, as she explains, she doesn't have any more jewellery to sell. She only recently purchased her two-m.p.h. model. 'I've only got these earrings left but at least I've got two scooters,' she says proudly. 'When I saw this one [the foldable scooter], I thought, where can I get £150? Then I went to bed and I woke up thinking: Where's that krugerrand? It's not a full one, just a tenth of one that I bought in Africa. Where have I hid it? I thought. I found it, and there was some other jewellery with it, and I was offered £190 for the lot. And I thought: Why not? I'd forgotten I had them in the first place.'

Getting around can be a bother for Joan nowadays, but thanks to her scooters she's able to sail down the hill into town whenever she fancies it. 'You can go into the shops on it – the bigger ones at any rate: Marks and Sparks, British Home Stores, all those, and through the Four Seasons shopping centre,' she says. 'With the smaller shops you've got to use your common sense.' Here Joan stops to peer at me in a way that suggests she thinks I might not have a great deal of that particular commodity. 'If it's a small shop, I just pull up in front and peep my horn and wait for them to come out and see what I want. It's tiring to keep getting down.'

Joan is friends with the people who run the scooter boutique on Mansfield market square. They're very nice and let her park hers in the shop when she needs to. Apparently mobility scooters get nicked if they're left outside on the pavement.

It's time for my test drive. There's a dirt track behind the house that rises up to the main road. I'm to ride up and down that. There are two speed settings – 'tortoise' and 'hare' – and Joan encourages me to push the scooter to its limits.

I set off in puttering mode.

'Go on, give it some welly!' she calls after me.

So I swivel the gear lever over towards the hare symbol and the scooter begins to pick up speed. I'm accelerating now towards the road and tooting the horn madly, and suddenly I know how Toad must have felt in *The Wind in the Willows* when he first got behind the wheel of one of those newfangled motorcars. 'Poop-poop!' Oh this is the life!

Afterwards I pop into the town centre, which is gaudily dressed for the festive season. Verily, my home town is not the prettiest place on god's earth. Mansfield – ba-humbug! I think to myself. But then in the Four Seasons I overhear one man greeting another: 'Tha gets uglier every time I see thee, youth. Gie us a kiss.' It's said with such warmth and the way the men embrace is so delightful that something shifts in my soul – yes, my soul. And that's it, my Scrooge-like conversion is complete: *I love Mansfield! Ho-ho-ho! Merry Christmas, everybody!* I only exclaim these words in my head, just as I only perform the accompanying little jig in my head. You could get beaten up for making that kind of display around here. I'm not daft, you know.

23 December. A friend calls to report that he's just been driving up the M3 in Hampshire, and that the motorway signs there say to 'London' and 'The Midlands'. There's no mention of the North at all, he says. Things are looking up!

The weather isn't too bad so we drive out into Robin Hood country, to Rufford Abbey, to stretch our legs before the great digestive assault of Christmas. Did you know that, until Coca-Cola (allegedly) forced him into a figure-hugging brand-red costume in the 1930s, Santa used to wear Robin Hood green? That's right: the original Father Christmas was an avatar of the Nottinghamshire outlaw – who, in a vaguely Santa-like way, robbed from the rich to give to the poor, remember.

Actually, that's not true – I just made it up – but it's one of a series of Midland myths that I'm working on at the moment. I aim to start circulating them on the internet shortly; I reckon that, with a little help from conspiracy theorists, a few years should see most of them established as gospel truth. Whatever the Midlands currently lacks in the way of history and folklore, we can soon generate.

Anyway, back to Rufford, a large country estate built on the remains of a twelfth-century Cistercian abbey that boasts, among other attractions, a good children's playground. When we get there Hector isn't interested in the swings and roundabouts, however, and wants to play football instead. Since His Lordship's word is law, a ball is produced from the car boot, and jumpers are thrown down to serve as goalposts. Hector chooses the teams: me and him versus Grandma and Grandad.

My parents are both eighty, but looking at the energy with which they lumber about the pitch today, nursing assorted bad backs and gammy legs, you wouldn't think they were a day over seventy-nine. It makes for quite a spectacle; people stop to point and laugh.

(I'm kidding, Mum and Dad – although a crowd *did* gather and there *was* a certain amount of merriment.)

Finally Hector sends his grandmother off for a bad foul – she's more aggressive than Wayne Rooney – and it's decided that this is a good moment to retire to the abbey café for refreshments.

Not me, though. I want to wander around the grounds because some have claimed Rufford as D.H. Lawrence's model for Wragby Hall, the residence of Lady Chatterley of *Lady Chatterley's Lover* fame. Others suggest nearby Teversal Manor was the original. Either way, it was somewhere in these parts that saucy gamekeeper Mellors first told Lady Constance she had a nice tail and threaded her pubic hair with forget-me-nots.

Rufford is in the Dukeries, so called owing to the fact that in the nineteenth century the area was home to not one, not two, not three, but *four* ducal seats. The dukes of Newcastle, Kingston, Portland and Norfolk all owned vast estates carved out of the vestiges of ancient Sherwood Forest, so that North Notts was dense with the wealthy and powerful. Rufford itself wasn't occupied by a duke, although, stretching itself luxuriously over 18,500 acres, it was certainly grand enough to accommodate one.

Given these rich associations, why isn't the area better known or more widely celebrated for its natural beauty and impressive stately homes now? The answer is in Lawrence's novel. At the moment at which *Lady Chatterley's Lover* is set, the North Notts landscape was undergoing a profound change owing to a decision by the major landowners to allow the expansion of mining operations into their domains. Hence when Lawrence evokes the Chatterleys' home in the first draft of the book, the mines dominate the scene: 'Wragby Hall was a low, long old house, rather dismal, in a very fine park, in the midst of newly developed colliery districts. You could hear the chuff of winding engines, and the rattle of the sifting screens, and you could smell the sulphur of burning pit-hills when the wind blew in a certain direction over the park.' Lawrence, who hailed from nearby Eastwood, knew of the Dukeries' grand past; he notes in the novel that the area was one 'where the castles and great houses had once dominated like lions'. Now, however, 'smoke waved against steam, and patch after patch showed the new mining settlements upon the repeated slopes of the open country. One meaning blotted out another, and though the great houses still loomed, the stately homes of England, they were mostly empty, just shells ... The great landowners when they opened the collieries doomed their own ancestral halls.' Just as in Leicestershire in the years prior to the Great War, industrialisation had imposed itself on the once-Edenic landscape; Lady Constance's relationship with Mellors (or Parkin, as he was called in that first version) was designed to restore a little of that prelapsarian splendour – or at least the mythic romance of Sherwood Forest. To get to the gamekeeper's hut, Lawrence had his heroine go to 'the spring riding, the broad green way that passed by the little icy spring where Robin Hood used to drink'.

If you go there today, it's changed again. The collieries have closed down and the landscape has returned to something of its ancient glory. It's not chocolate-box stuff of the kind you find in the South – it never was – and it's too composed and self-sufficient to go in for the showy, slightly hysterical drama that Nature puts on in the North. It's determined-looking, like the people who live here; it's the kind of landscape that neither flatters nor resists, and that is a natural companion to human progress. And progress – as my travels have taught me – is what the Midlands is, and always has been, about.

Lawrence was a classic Notts outlaw, a Midland nonconformist who hated, and was in turn hated by, the Establishment. It was after he had quit England to undertake his 'savage pilgrimage' that he wrote *Lady Chatterley's*, sitting under a pine tree in the Tuscan hills. The book first appeared in an edition privately printed in Florence in 1928, when a London newspaper steamed: 'Famous Writer's Shameful Novel: A Landmark in Evil!' The book was banned.

Lawrence died two years later, from tuberculosis, but posthumously won a significant victory for free speech with his notorious book, sticking it to The Man after Penguin decided to publish it in Britain to mark the thirtieth anniversary of its author's death. As a result *Lady Chatterley's Lover* became the first novel to be prosecuted under the 1959 Obscene Publications Act and dozens of young legal eagles were delegated to underline all the naughty words in preparation for the case coming to court. In the event, the prosecution made a bit of a hash of things, causing the jury to snigger by asking them absurd questions of the following kind: 'Would you approve of your young sons, young daughters – because girls can read as well as boys – reading this book? Is it a book that you would have lying around in your own house? Is it a book that you would even wish your wife or your servants to read?' It was an objection from another age: on the whole, the members of the jury weren't of the kind to employ servants. No sooner had the jury found in the book's favour than the Swinging Sixties began. That great Midland poet Philip Larkin famously observed as much when he wrote that it was in 1963 that 'Sexual intercourse began', right after 'the end of the Chatterley ban'. You could say (it's a bit of an exaggeration but there's a flavoursome kernel of truth in it nonetheless) that, with *Lady Chatterley's Lover*, Lawrence tore down class distinctions in England and invented modern sex. Not bad for a miner's son from unfashionable Eastwood.

I meet up with the others in the car park. Hector looks as though he's just put in a shift at the colliery, but it turns out his face isn't smeared with coaldust. It's chocolate.

'Where have you been?' my mother asks accusingly.

'In search of D.H. Lawrence.'

'Did he live here?' she asks.

'No, but *Lady Chatterley's Lover* is supposed to have been set here,' I explain apprehensively.

'Ooh, I had a copy of that once. I only read the dirty bits, mind. Page 344 was *reeeally* good,' she says and mugs suggestively.

* * *

'Only an Englishman or a New Englander could have written it. It is the last word in Puritanism,' Lawrence's widow, Frieda, wrote of *Lady Chatterley's Lover*. She was being polemical, of course, but not at all ironic: the novel is born of the puritan ideals of purity and simplicity. This is hardly surprising since Lawrence grew up in an area where the puritan legacy was powerful. If, in *Lady Chatterley's Lover*, he wrote the last word in Puritanism, fellow Nottinghamshire Nonconformists three centuries earlier had written one of the first words – and one that was hardly less powerful in terms of its influence.

After our Rufford visit, the others go back to Mansfield for some last-minute Christmas shopping, but I'm heading to the very northernmost tip of the county, to Scrooby. ('Scrooby Doo? Can I come?' shouts Hector. 'It's not that exciting, sweetie,' his mother soothes him.) I should really have come here a month ago, on the fourth Thursday in November, to see whether the local pub – it's called the Pilgrim Fathers – would be serving a classic Thanksgiving dinner. Thanksgiving is a North American tradition, of course – a big one, too, bigger than Christmas – but it began here in North Notts.

Driving through, you wouldn't think you were in one of the most politically and spiritually influential spots on the face of the earth. It looks nothing like Vatican City, that's for sure; the villages are as austere and undemonstrative as the landscape. In Scrooby only the pub really proclaims the village's place in history, while in nearby Babworth the church, a handsome nine-century-old building set apart from the main settlement in a glade, houses the chalice that Richard Clyfton – a key player in this transformatory drama – used in communion services before he set off on his own savage pilgrimage. But there's no huge hoo-ha. This is the Midlands after all. There's certainly nothing to compare with what the Americans have done in Plymouth, Massachusetts, to commemorate the same set of events. There, the 1888 National Monument to the Forefathers rises to a height of 81 feet (that is, it's as tall as the *Mayflower* – the ship on which the Pilgrims travelled from England to America – was long). On the sculpture's central pedestal stands the heroic figure of Faith, while at his feet sit four further emblems of the principles on which the Pilgrims founded their original commonwealth, and which were adopted more widely as the pillars of the United States of America a century and a half later: Freedom, Morality, Law and Education. The rear panel features a quotation from Governor William Bradford's famous history of the colonists' early experiences in America, *Of Plymouth Plantation*: 'Thus out of small beginnings greater things have been produced by His hand that made all things of nothing and gives being to all things that are; and as one small candle may light a thousand, so the light here kindled hath shone unto many, yea in some sort to our whole nation; let the glorious name of Jehovah have all praise.'

Those 'small beginnings' can be traced to Scrooby, a handsome village that four centuries ago was regularly called upon to offer hospitality to Elizabeth I as she made her progress up the Great North Road. A few years after the queen's death in 1603, it began to play host to a no less significant if rather less grand group when William Brewster, the spiritually dissatisfied but well-connected occupant of Scrooby Manor, extended his protection to the aforementioned Richard Clyfton, a radical preacher who had just been stripped of his position in Babworth. Clyfton was a Separatist: that is, he wanted nothing to do with the Church of England, which, in the view of many dissenting puritans, was little better than Catholicism without the pope. When Clyfton and his fellow Scrooby Separatists decided to go abroad to escape persecution, their first port of call was liberal Holland, then known as the United Provinces. But following a military coup in 1618, flight to the untamed expanses of North America, already regarded as the land of opportunity, became increasingly tempting. And so it was that the Separatists applied to the Virginia Company for a grant of land and boarded the *Mayflower* in search of freedom.

The Pilgrims established their colony in 1620 and the rest is history, though not in the dead, the-past-is-another-country sense of that word. The Notts-led Pilgrim Fathers, a central theme in United States history, have bequeathed several important and vibrant legacies to the modern nation, beginning with the 'Mayflower Compact', a civil covenant created by the colonists that effectively established the first democratically elective government in the New World. As President John Quincy Adams would later claim, the Compact was the foundation stone of the 1787 US Constitution, perhaps the most influential document ever enacted in the name of 'the people'. You could say that those first persecution-fleeing Midlanders invented the concept of the Land of the Free. Jefferson's America was built on Midland ideals; progressive contemporary America continues to be nurtured by those same ideals.

Another of their legacies is Thanksgiving, which began with the celebrations held by the Pilgrim Fathers in 1621 in gratitude for their first successful harvest in the New World. It was then adopted as a national holiday in the US in 1863, and has been observed at the end of November ever since, with the turkey – introduced to the colonists at the beginning of their adventure by friendly Native Americans – serving as a centrepiece of the festivities.

So you might say that it was East Midlanders who gave birth to modern America. From the Pilgrim Fathers to the miners' strike 'scabs' of the 1980s, democracy and liberty of conscience have been crucial principles in Nottinghamshire life. Can the glorious North match that? While you're thinking about your answer (which is 'no', by the way), try this for a bit of genealogy: one of the Scrooby leaders, William Brewster, counts among his descendants President Zachary Taylor, the poet Henry Wadsworth Longfellow, General Ulysses S. Grant and John Howard Payne, writer of 'Home, Sweet Home'. The future independent state of the Midlands (capital: Mansfield) should adopt 'Home, Sweet Home' as its national anthem.

Really, without the radicalism and utopianism of North Notts, where would the USA be today? How about that for a Midland foundation myth – a founding foundation myth, as it were: we invented modern America, the Land of the Free.

11pm. Have been looking through *England and the English* (1955) by the linguist and travel writer Charles Duff again. Duff isn't exactly a Midland enthusiast, but he has some interesting things to say about the character of the people here, particularly in relation to the Pilgrim Fathers. Mulling over the latter's great transatlantic legacy, he reflects: 'I could not help thinking how easily one can be led to misjudge the people ... who did that great piece of pioneering. I should say that the people there [i.e., in the East Midlands] to-day do not differ greatly from their upright ancestors and, until one knows them fairly well, their quiet, unostentatious demeanour, their matter-of-fact and one might say their almost humdrum way of life, gives a first impression of good and reliable but rather uninteresting people.' Fortunately, Duff got beyond first impressions: 'One may be somewhat misled by their reserved manners, but all their apparently rather unexuberant façade is quickly thrown aside when something has to be done which demands initiative, energy and courage.'

I think that about sums it up. Don't be fooled by that unexuberant façade. Midlanders are doers.

And so to bed.

24 December. Agitated dreams last night. That founding foundation myth stuff is good, but is it enough? Is Hector going to be persuaded by it? After all, this isn't the late 1980s when the Berlin Wall was tumbling and the Cold War was giving way to what (very briefly) felt like the End of History and the eternal triumph of the American Way. Back then, it would have been churlish not to cheer the Midlands' role in shaping Uncle Sam's liberty-loving land, but in the wake of Dubya, Abu Ghraib, Extraordinary Rendition, etc, people are more sceptical about the moral pre-eminence of the USA. We're in China's century now, and all evidence at the moment points to the Midlands having had very little influence on the thinking of Confucius.

But, as I said at the beginning of my journey, surprising new evidence of all sorts keeps turning up when it comes to 'deep' history. Take Creswell Crags, an unassuming-looking limestone gorge just off the A60 on the Nottinghamshire–Derbyshire border. It was here, a decade ago, that a team of archaeologists discovered what has since come to be known as 'the Sistine Chapel of the Ice Age'.

Until Drs Paul Pettitt, Paul Bahn and Sergio Ripoll entered Church Hole Cave at Creswell Crags and found 'the world's most elaborately carved ceiling', it had generally been assumed that Britain had produced no Palaeolithic cave art. While plenty of evidence has been uncovered to demonstrate that hunter-gatherer artists were busy beautifying their homes in neighbouring France, Spain and Italy (the British Isles were joined to the European continental landmass at the time), cave-dwelling British philistines had apparently failed to raise a finger to decorate their rocky residences. But now the Church Hole discovery has definitively given the lie to that idea. A bit more than that, actually: it turns out that the supposedly history-less North Midlands contains the most extensive cache of prehistoric bas-reliefs *anywhere in the world*.

The subject matter of the engraved images – created by modifying the natural limestone topography of the caves – includes animals (bison, birds) as well as what appear to be the earliest human nudes in the history of British art. 'We found these boomerang shapes which represented women bent-kneed, thrusting out their bottoms,' said Pettitt. 'I interpret at least two of those long-necked birds as women – possibly some ritual dance undertaken by females, and possibly in the cave itself.' It's good to know that there's cultural continuity across the ages. In pubs and clubs around the market squares on a Friday night, Nottingham and Mansfield gals are still doing that dance in the twenty-first century AD.

It appears that the archaeological team weren't actually the first to spot the carvings. When they made their historic discovery, Bahn and co found one wall in Church Hole decorated with modern graffiti – a more recent cave artist had added a beard and the initials 'PM' to a 13,000-year-old image of a deer. 'We don't know when it was done, but someone had discovered the first ever cave art in Britain and instead of publishing it, they vandalised it,' commented Bahn. It's not that surprising, really: as I've said before, Midlanders aren't easily impressed. 'So what if we invented BritArt,' we sniff. 'Tell us something I didn't already know, youth, and hand me that pen so I can deface it while you're about it.'

'Where are you going?' asks Hector, blocking the door as his mother and I try to make our way unobserved out of the kitchen.

'To do a final piece of research into our Midland origins, my boy.'

'Oh. Will Scooby be there?'

'No, that was yesterday. And it was Scrooby.' I roll the 'r' in that special way he hates so much.

'Why is Mummy going with you? She's not a Miglander,' he probes.

'Because she's a sucker for punishment,' the Parisian sighs. She loves the Midlands really.

We drive out through Mansfield Woodhouse, Church Warsop and Spion Kop. The landscape is flat and bland, the architecture is utilitarian and modern. But then, just before Cuckney, we go over a ridge and our surroundings begin to change. There's a sudden infusion of colour and gravitas, and you can feel a more ancient spirit rising up despite that huge white-grey industrial chimney looming in the distance. A road sign points the way to Creswell Crags and we turn off the main road.

'Inspiring visitors for 50,000 years,' announces the sign at the entrance to the site.

In the tearoom they're playing 'Do They Know It's Christmas?'. Santa has been holding one of his annual meet-and-greets here – presumably he was wearing reindeer skins – but, since this is Christmas Eve, he's now gone back to the North Pole to prepare for his Big Night. The visitor centre has a permanent exhibition and also offers tours. We're just in time for a guided visit of Robin Hood Cave.

We wait downstairs by a stuffed hyena, which, in an eerie seasonal touch, has a garland of tinsel wrapped around its throat. Presently our guide, a small, squirrelly woman with a bright smile and pleasant self-effacing manner, comes to collect us. The first thing she does is hand out hard hats with little lights on them for us to put on – which reminds me of my mining heritage – and then we're ready to venture out into the prehistoric Midland wilds.

We head into the limestone gorge. An Arctic wind is blowing today so it's not hard to imagine how it might have felt here in the Ice Age. Cliffs tower on either side, while the basin in the middle is half taken up with a lake. This was created in the 1860s by the Duke of Portland (one of the Dukeries' dukes), who indulged in a spot of artificial damming in order to prevent the railways from being allowed to develop the land. 'He did us a bit of a favour really,' comments the guide. And himself, of course: His Lordship enjoyed boating in the gorge. One of the caves – Boat House Cave – has been named in memory of his recreational tastes. 'By all accounts the Duke was quite an eccentric man,' our guide says, smiling.

'Creswell is the most northerly point in Europe where evidence has been found of Ice Age people's activities,' she continues. 'From Yorkshire and up into Scotland the land was covered in about a mile of snow, but from what we've found here, for short periods of time in summer months enough ice and snow must have melted away to allow some vegetation to grow through.'

'You mean,' I interrupt, a note of triumph in my voice, 'there was nothing going on in the North? It was a complete wasteland? No signs of life at all?'

She nods.

Yes! I cheer inwardly. Incoming score from the 'Contributions to Mankind's Prehistoric Development' Cup Final: The Midlands 1, The North 0.

Unperturbed, our guide continues: 'The landscape here has changed quite dramatically over time. Going back about 120,000 years this was actually a tropical area and we've found evidence of hippopotamuses, who would have wallowed in the river there.' The story she tells in her lovely, melodious way is highly dramatic but she's not straining to sell it to us. 'In the Ice Age it would have been very barren, similar to the way the Siberian tundra looks today,' she says. There would have been small shrubs but no trees as such, just enough to encourage migrating animals to come here: woolly mammoth, woolly rhinoceros, packs of wolves and hyenas, cave bears and lions. Consequently it was quite a dangerous place for Ice Age people to come, but also a good place to catch yourself a meal or two.

Small tribes of Ice Agers would have followed migrating animals into the gorge. They may have come originally from Spain or France, across Doggerland, the landmass that once connected

Britain to mainland Europe. Animals were tempted into the gorge by its vegetation. This made it an excellent site for hunting. Various techniques may have been employed to catch roving woolly mammoth and the like: trapping them in caves, or even chasing them off the edge of the surrounding cliffs. The meat from a woolly mammoth would have kept the hunters going for a month and more.

The Notts/Derbyshire county border runs straight down the lake in the gorge, which creates a convenient division between the caves ranged on either side of the water. The warmer, south-facing side lies in Nottinghamshire; this is where the Ice Agers had their domestic dwellings. The cooler half is in Derbyshire, which is where various ceremonial or ritualistic activities took place. Church Hole Cave, the main site of those recent discoveries, is on this side.

We're staying on the Notts side of the border today. We tramp down past Mother Grundy's Cave (home to a local witch, according to legend) and come to Robin Hood Cave, so named by the Victorians, who liked to think that the local hero had a hiding place here. You certainly can't imagine the Sheriff of Nottingham's nesh followers pursuing 'Oodie into the Crags.

The artworks have only recently come to light but the Ice Age settlements themselves were rediscovered in the nineteenth century, after local farmers who used the caves for their cattle found bones in them and became suspicious. Investigations were carried out, which led to large amounts of dynamite being deployed to blast away the flowstone – calcite that had formed owing to the passage of water over cave walls and floors – that was obscuring the prehistoric surfaces; a lot of precious objects and stalactites were destroyed in this 'clearing' process. If the Victorians had known what we know today about responsible archaeological practices, they wouldn't have used explosives. But if the Victorians had known what we know today, they wouldn't have been the Victorians, would they? They'd have been us. The past is always so useful when we feel the need to point a finger of blame.

It's time to go into the cave and take a journey back in time tens of thousands of years. We mount wooden steps and then pause while the guide unlocks the grille that keeps unwanted visitors out. Before stepping in, we put our helmets on.

At first it doesn't look like very much at all – how quintessentially Midland that first nothing-to-see-here impression is. It's dark and the walls and ceiling seem to lack texture, in no small part thanks to the interventions of those dynamite-happy Victorians. But as you delve further, its riches become more evident – how very Midland that is too.

The caves weren't only used in the Ice Age; earlier nomads also made temporary homes here. Our guide has replica tools for us to handle reflecting three separate layers or periods of occupation, beginning with all-purpose flint hand-axes used by the caves' first detected inhabitants, the Neanderthals, who set up home here some 50,000 years ago. The tools become more advanced and more specific with the second wave of inhabitants, Cro-Magnon this time, who were here 30,000 years ago. The guide asks us to guess what the various examples were used for: I'm clueless at this game – because I'm stupid, basically – whereas my wife is very good at it. Assorted flint knives and flint scrapers are passed between us. There are some particularly delicate-looking leaf-shaped spear tips, too, which were once tied to wooden spears with animal intestine or sinew. Then we're shown the tools from the final, Ice Age phase of occupation, 13,000 years ago: a hammer made from reindeer antler, with a hole in it so that it could be tied to the user's clothing; a reindeer rib-bone needle used to sew animal skins together to make clothing and bags; what looks like a training spear designed to be used by children learning to hunt. It's sophisticated stuff, but then you'd expect nothing less from Britain's first generation of visual artists. These are the lot who created the 'Sistine Chapel of the Ice Age' just across the way, don't forget.

We squeeze through a very low passageway into another space. It's cold and extremely dark, so humans are unlikely to have come down here very often. Animals, on the other hand, favoured it – not least hyenas, who digest the bones of other animals. That's a gross practice, obviously, but it means their fossilised faeces are a great source of information about other species and their bones. We're given a plastercast replica of the shin bone of a baby woolly mammoth to handle. A complete bear skeleton was recovered here; bats still like to nest down here too.

In a niche near the entrance the corpses of two rats lie stretched out on an upside-down shopping basket. Our guide explains that these were first brought here as part of a student experiment in the 1980s, when dead rats were placed throughout the caves; all of them decomposed except the pair staring blindly back at us today, who became mummified owing to the very low relative humidity in that particular part of the cave – the lesson being that dwellers could have stored meat here. 'The rats are a little bit squishy to the touch still,' our guide smiles. Thankfully she doesn't suggest we actually give them a poke.

As I said, most of the recently uncovered art is in Church Hole Cave, but there is one example our guide can show us *chez* Robin Hood. 'It's abstract,' she says. Is there a note of embarrassment in her voice? Instructing us to turn the lights on our helmets off, she places her torch at an angle of about forty degrees to the wall to illuminate three lines incised into the stone. 'That,' she begins, 'has been identified as a piece of Ice Age art. It's quite a common motif, an upside-down triangle.' There's an awkward silence. 'Has it got something to do with fertility?' interposes my wife. She's French, so she's not afraid to talk about this sort of thing. 'That's right,' smiles our guide. 'It represents the vulva of a woman. They only lived to about the age of thirty-five so that sort of thing was important!'

So there you have it: from the Ice Age to D.H. Lawrence, Midlanders have been putting coition at the centre of their art. We invented sex in both ancient *and* modern times.

Like the USA, the Midlands has been said to have no deep history: no medieval forebear to rival those great Southern and Northern figureheads, King Alfred and the Venerable Bede, never mind anything more ancient. To quote that twentieth-century source on the subject again: 'England's prehistoric antiquities are mostly to be found south of a line drawn from Worcester to Ipswich; and north of a line drawn from Blackpool to Hull' – lines that almost completely exclude the Midlands. But this traditional picture has begun to be radically redrawn in the first years of the new millennium. The recently recovered 'Staffordshire Hoard' has underlined the political and economic dynamism of the Midlands in the Middle Ages, while the discovery at Creswell Crags of 'the Sistine Chapel of the Ice Age' shows Midland dynamism stretching back into prehistory. In other words, whether you go back 1,300 or 13,000 years, the Midlands is where it was at. It all started here.

* * *

Hector's bedtime. The stage has been set for Santa's visit tonight. A sign has been placed in the garden, a tray bearing a glass of cheap sherry and a supermarket mince pie has been carefully placed by the Christmas tree. By way of return Hector is expecting plentiful supplies of Lego and Playmobil.

Before he retires for the night, however, I want to set out some of my Midlands-related findings for him. He is just finishing brushing his teeth as I approach.

'Now, my boy,' I begin, displaying my trademark easy and unfussy paternal manner. 'Have a good gargle, that's it, and attend to what your papa has to tell you. You know that you're half-French?'

'Yes.'

'Well, you're also half-Midlander too. And you should be proud of that. We Midlanders have done great things. In the Ice Age we were responsible for the first British art. In the Middle Ages we shaped England as we know it today. But that wasn't enough for us – oh no – so we went overseas and created the Land of the Free. We produced World Literature's Greatest Genius™. We gave birth to the Industrial Revolution. Then a Midlander named Lawrence reinvented … er, s – e – x.'

'What's that?'

'Never you mind, and don't interrupt. We've produced all the best politicians and scientists and thinkers and musicians. All the greatest inventions are ours. Cars, carriages, bicycles, aeroplanes: they all took life here. The Olympics – that's ours. We invented both gravity and evolution – that's the Midland spirit in a nutshell: feet on the ground, advancing at high speed. We've even won the European Cup – or whatever they call it now – three times (Forest twice, Villa once), which is more than any Southern club has ever managed. We eat desserts before mains and use only a single plate to do so. As that example shows, we also have the best sense of humour in the world. We're much funnier than Northerners, that's for sure. And, to top it all, unlike Northerners, we're not boasters. What do you think of that as a cultural legacy? Not bad, eh? I promised your mother something staggering, and I do believe that

I've fulfilled that promise in the course of my travels. You might have been taught that the Midlands is a dreary no-man's-land, that it's beyond the pale, as Jilly Cooper put it when discussing where the grander sort of folk choose to live. But in fact the Midlands has been Bang in the Middle of everything, ever ...'

'Dad?' Hector interrupts me, his eyes filling with tears.

'Yes?'

'I don't know what you're talking about. I'm only five.'

Pause.

'Fair point, son. Already you speak with the wisdom of a Midlander. Don't cry now. Remind me to talk to you about this Midlands business again when you're seven or eight. And in the meantime – Happy Christmas.'

ACKNOWLEDGEMENTS

This book is based on a tour of the Midlands that I began in autumn 2011. Most of the details of the places I describe remain current, although I know, for instance, that there have been attempts to reopen Grantham Museum since I visited the town, and that the World Conker Championships have a new venue (though still in Northamptonshire). In the course of my travels, I spoke to and in various ways consulted a large number of people, all of whom I would like to thank here. My rather large extended family made a particularly big contribution to the project: some conducted me on guided tours, others provided anecdotes and ideas, and all added to my sense of the Midlands. Without them I couldn't have written this book, so I would like to dedicate *Bang in the Middle* to them. I would also like to thank the following for their contributions, some more sustained than others but all equally gratefully received: Emma Benson, Jules Clarke, the late Joseph Cripwell, Matthew Downing, Philip Garwood, Annabel Hobley, Katie Jennings, Sonia Johnson,

Peter Longhurst, Andrzej Lukowski, Justin Needle, Suzanne Nicholas, Kieron Quirke, Joan Radford, John Raine, Nicole Sandells, the late Alan Sillitoe, Colin Speed, Sophie Spiers, Brian Tatler, Elizabeth Winter, Muriel Zagha. This list is far from exhaustive: I spoke to many people on my travels without discovering their names. I would like to thank these anonymous contributors too. Thanks also to Malcolm Croft, my copyeditor, Rachel Faulkner, my editor, and, of course, to Scott Pack, my publisher, and to James Wills, my agent.

FIFTY GREAT THINGS TO COME OUT OF THE MIDLANDS

Prove sceptics wrong with this list of fifty surprising but brilliant things to come out of the Midlands.

In order of ascending stupendousness ...

50) Watchmen

49) Gravity

48) The Sistine Chapel

47) Mercians

46) Christmas

45) Jonathan Agnew

44) A Sense of Centredness

43) Walkers Crisps

42) America

41) Spaghetti Junction

40) Roundabouts

39) The Great Reform Act

38) Arthur Seaton

37) Gary Lineker

36) Rebecca Adlington

35) Proper Dialect

34) The Major Oak

33) The Olympics

32) Rugby

31) Bob Dylan

30) The Sally Army

29) Motörhead

28) Conkers

27) Stilton

26) The Industrial Revolution

25) The Phrase 'Painting the Town Red'

24) Marmite

23) Lampy the Gnome

22) Mass Tourism

21) Jet Propulsion

20) Diana, Princess of Wales

19) Philip Larkin

18) Canals

17) Hamlet

16) Evolution

15) Land of Hope and Glory

14) Dr Samuel Johnson

13) Sexual Intercourse

12) The Archers

11) Paul Smith

10) The Enlightenment

9) Robbie Williams

8) The Battle of Britain

7) Lady Godiva

6) 2 Tone

5) Brian Clough

4) Balti

3) Tony Hancock

2) Hobbits

1) Mr Darcy

For more information about these Midland wonders and why they're so great, download the free ebook: Fifty Great Things to Come Out of the Midlands.

Feel free to agree, disagree or debate with me online by tweeting me @Robert_M_Shore